Lecture Notes of the Institute for Computer Sciences, Social Informatics and Telecommunications Engineering

523

The LNICST series publishes ICST's conferences, symposia and workshops.
LNICST reports state-of-the-art results in areas related to the scope of the Institute.
The type of material published includes

- Proceedings (published in time for the respective event)
- Other edited monographs (such as project reports or invited volumes)

LNICST topics span the following areas:

- General Computer Science
- E-Economy
- E-Medicine
- Knowledge Management
- Multimedia
- Operations, Management and Policy
- Social Informatics
- Systems

Jianghua Liu · Lei Xu · Xinyi Huang

Editors

Tools for Design, Implementation and Verification of Emerging Information Technologies

18th EAI International Conference, TRIDENTCOM 2023
Nanjing, China, November 11–13, 2023
Proceedings

Editors
Jianghua Liu
Nanjing University of Science
and Technology
Nanjing, China

Lei Xu
Nanjing University of Science
and Technology
Nanjing, China

Xinyi Huang
Hong Kong University of Science
and Technology
Hong Kong, China

ISSN 1867-8211   ISSN 1867-822X (electronic)
Lecture Notes of the Institute for Computer Sciences, Social Informatics
and Telecommunications Engineering
ISBN 978-3-031-51398-5   ISBN 978-3-031-51399-2 (eBook)
https://doi.org/10.1007/978-3-031-51399-2

This Springer imprint is published by the registered company Springer Nature Switzerland AG
The registered company address is: Gewerbestrasse 11, 6330 Cham, Switzerland

Paper in this product is recyclable.

Preface

We are delighted to introduce the proceedings of the 18th EAI International Conference on Tools for Design, Implementation and Verification of Emerging Information Technologies (EAI TRIDENTCOM 2023). This conference has brought together researchers, developers and practitioners around the world who are leveraging and developing new technologies for network and information security. The theme of EAI TRIDENTCOM 2023 was current and emerging aspects of technologies in network and information security.

The technical program of TRIDENTCOM 2023 received 30 submissions, and finally accepted 9 full papers after double-blind reviews from 3 reviewers for each paper. The conference included two tracks: Main Track and Late Track. Each of the high-quality technical accepted paper was presented by the authors.

Coordination with the steering chair and the senior conference manager was essential for the success of the conference. We sincerely appreciate their constant support and guidance. It was also a great pleasure to work with such an excellent organizing committee team for their hard work in organizing and supporting the conference. In particular, the Technical Program Committee, led by our General Chair Xingyi Huang and TPC chair Lei Xu, who have completed the peer-review process of technical papers and made a high-quality technical program. We are also grateful to the Conference Manager, Ivana Bujdakova, her support and to all the authors who submitted their papers to the TRIDENTCOM 2023 conference.

We strongly believe that TRIDENTCOM provides a good forum for all researchers, developers and practitioners to discuss all science and technology aspects that are relevant to network and information security. We also expect that future TRIDENTCOM conferences will be as successful and stimulating as indicated by the contributions presented in this volume.

December 2023

Jianghua Liu
Lei Xu
Xinyi Huang

Organization

Steering Committee

Victor C. M. Leung   University of British Columbia, Canada

Organizing Committee

General Chair

Xinyi Huang   Hong Kong University of Science and
Technology (Guangzhou), China

General Co-chairs

XingLiang Yuan   Monash University, Australia
Meng Li   Hefei University of Technology, China

TPC Chair and Co-chairs

Jianghua Liu   Nanjing University of Science and Technology,
China
Lei Xu   Nanjing University of Science and Technology,
China
Chungen Xu   Nanjing University of Science and Technology,
China

Local Chair

Siyu Liu   Nanjing University of Science and Technology,
China

Workshops Chair

Yifeng Zheng   Harbin Institute of Technology (Shenzhen), China

Publicity and Social Media Chair

Cong Zuo   Beijing Institute of Technology, China

Publications Chair

Chao Lin   Fujian Normal University, China

Web Chair

Lichuan Ma   Xidian University, China

Technical Program Committee

Borui Cai	Deakin University, Australia
Xiaoning Liu	RMIT University, Australia
Taotao Cai	Macquarie University, Australia
Longxia Huang	Jiangsu University, China
Tao Jiang	Xidian University, China
Jinhui Liu	Northwest Polytechnical University, China
Yannan Li	University of Wollongong, Australia
Jianting Ning	Fujian Normal University, China
Cong Peng	Wuhan University, China
KaiTai Liang	Delft University of Technology, The Netherlands
Shigang Liu	Swinburne University of Technology, Australia
Yanbin Li	Nanjing Agricultural University, China
Fucai Luo	Zhejiang Gongshang University, China
Hui Ma	Chinese Academy of Sciences, China
Shifeng Sun	Shanghai Jiao Tong University, China
Yunling Wang	Xi'an University of Posts and Telecommunications, China
Tianbo Wang	Beihang University, China
Jianghong Wei	State Key Laboratory of Mathematical Engineering and Advanced Computing, China
Xiaoyu Xia	RMIT University, Australia
Ning Xi	Xidian University, China
Changsong Yang	Guilin University of Electronic Technology, China
Jianfeng Wang	Xidian University, China
Yi Zhao	Chang'an University, China
Chuan Zhao	University of Jinan, China
Xiaoling Yu	Taiyuan University of Technology, China

Chao Chen	RMIT University, Australia
Xiaoshuang Shi	University of Electronic Science and Technology of China, China
Xiao Chen	Monash University, Australia
Ning Lu	Northeastern University at Qinhuangdao, China
Yulong Fu	Xidian University, China
Chunpeng Ge	Shandong University, China
Xiaoqiang Sun	Shenzhen Institute of Information Technology, China
Leo Zhang	Griffith University, Australia
Zhiyuan Sui	Central University of Finance and Economics, China
Yong Xie	Qinghai University, China
Depeng Chen	Anhui University, China
Pengfei Wu	National University of Singapore, Singapore
Mingfu Xue	Nanjing University of Aeronautics and Astronautics, China
Chen Wang	Zhejiang Sci-Tech University, China
Xin Yao	Central South University, China
Guixin Ye	Northwest University, China
Shangqi Lai	Monash University, Australia
Yingjie Xue	Hong Kong Polytechnic University (Guangzhou), China
Jie Li	Yunnan Normal University, China

Contents

Blockchain and Its Applications

A Novel Cross-Chain Relay Method Based on Node Trust Evaluation

Yafeng Li[1], Wantao Tuo[2], Qiaozu Hu[2], and Lichuan Ma[2(✉)]

[1] China CETC Key Laboratory of Technology on Data Link, Xi'an, China
xxddxdd@yeah.net
[2] Xidian University and Shaanxi Key Laboratory of Blockchain and Secure Computing, Xi'an, China
23151214211@stu.xidian.edu.cn, lcma@xidian.edu.cn

Abstract. With the increasing complexity of blockchain network business requirements, there is a growing demand for interconnection mechanisms among different blockchains, leading to the emergence of cross-chain technology. This article discusses three mainstream cross-chain technologies: the notary mechanism, hash time lock, and side chain/relay mode, and highlights their limitations. In order to address issues such as low efficiency in relay chain reorganization and instability in cross-chain systems within the relay mode involving node turnover, this paper proposes a node trust-based cross-chain relay scheme. The scheme includes the construction of a trust model for blockchain nodes, the design of a weighted random election algorithm for relay nodes, and the development of a complete cross-chain transaction process. Simulation experiments are conducted to demonstrate the performance of the proposed scheme.

Keywords: blockchain · cross-chain relay · node trust evaluation

1 Introduction

Although blockchain technology has made significant advancements in recent years and some blockchain projects have gained traction, the overall development of current blockchain technology reveals that each blockchain remains a closed and independent system. This characteristic makes individual blockchains susceptible to forming value islands [1]. With the increasing application of blockchain technology across various fields, the business requirements of blockchain networks in different scenarios have become more complex. This complexity has driven a growing need for interconnection mechanisms between diverse blockchains, thereby promoting the emergence of cross-chain technology.

Vitalik Buterin, the founder of Ethereum, has provided a significant summary of cross-chain technology [2]. He also analyzed the development of cross-chain solutions and proposed that mainstream cross-chain technology can be primarily categorized into three types based on implementation principles: notary mechanism, hash time lock, and side chain/relay mode. However, upon examining

J. Liu et al. (Eds.): TridentCom 2023, LNICST 523, pp. 3–20, 2024.
https://doi.org/10.1007/978-3-031-51399-2_1

the current research landscape, it becomes evident that these three technologies each have their inherent limitations.

Aiming to address the issues of low efficiency in relay chain reorganization and the instability of cross-chain systems stemming from node turnover and reorganization, this paper proposes a node trust-based periodic turnover relay cross-chain scheme. The scheme establishes a blockchain node trust model to calculate the trust value of each node in the cross-chain system. This trust value is utilized to design the election algorithm for the relay chain, ensuring the security and efficiency of the algorithm within the cross-chain system. Utilizing the relay model, this scheme attains cross-chain functionality and encompasses various design aspects. The main contributions of this paper can be summarized as follows:

1. The trust model of blockchain nodes in the cross-chain system is constructed, and the trustworthiness of the nodes is derived through quantitative analysis of their various behaviors. Based on this model, a classification standard for node types is formulated. The trust model assists in completing the formation and governance cycle of the relay chain, effectively constraining the relay nodes, and significantly improving the stability of the cross-chain system.
2. Based on the trust model, a weighted random election algorithm for relay nodes has been designed. The algorithm incorporates cryptographic techniques, including encryption, signature, zero-knowledge proof, etc. It utilizes the trust value of the nodes as the basis for the election process. By integrating verifiable random functions, nodes with higher trust values have an increased probability of being randomly selected. This algorithm ensures both randomness and protection against various attacks.
3. A comprehensive cross-chain transaction process has been developed, which encompasses a shared cross-chain message transmission protocol, a cross-chain transaction processing flow, and a mechanism for handling exceptions. The integrity and atomicity of cross-chain transactions are ensured through the careful design of the transmission protocol and the implementation of process controls.
4. Extensive experiments are undertaken to validate the effectiveness and efficiency of the proposed method.

The rest of this paper is organized as follows. Related work is summarized in Sect. 2. The system model is presented in Sect. 3. In Sect. 4, the novel cross-chain relay method based on node trust evaluation is derived. Experimental results are provided in Sect. 5 to show the superior performance of the proposed method and Sect. 6 concludes the paper.

2   Related Works

So far, various schemes have been proposed to support interactions among different blockchains. In [3], the Tendermint team proposed Cosmos Network to achieve was proposed to transferring assets between different blockchains, with cross-chain consensus powered by the Byzantine Consensus [4]. The blockchains in the Cosmos Network communicate with each other using the Inter-Blockchain Communication Protocol (IBC), which is a set of rules and standards that allow for the transfer of value and data between these separate blockchains. The IBC also ensures security during the transfer of assets. Cosmos serves as a relay chain to facilitate interactions between blockchains by exchanging information, and its emergence has inspired many developers, leading to the design of cross-chain platforms

After the emergence of Cosmos Network, the Polkado whitepaper was released in [5] at the end of 2016. Unlike Cosmos, Polkadot is suitable for cross-chain operations in a broader range of scenarios. Polkadot acts as a relay chain to facilitate transaction transfer and consensus among parallel chains. Polkadot's governance is based on the Proof of Stake protocol, with the main goal of ensuring that a majority of the stakes can always control the network [6].

In [7], sidechain technology and hash-locking are combined to build a new blockchain as a third-party transaction platform. This platform can be a public or private chain used to record transaction credentials, and the scheme ensures the transfer of trust between different blockchains. The authors of [8] propose a new protocol for atomic cross-chain exchanges. This protocol extends previous results in cross-chain interaction to support atomic exchanges to blockchains without hash time-locking functionality, enabling asset transactions between blockchains with only multi-signature functionality. In [9], a cross-chain transaction model based on the combination of notary and hash locking is proposed to address security issues in traditional hash locking. This scheme can prevent malicious participants from creating large traffic that blocks the channel based on the key of the unlocking condition. Additionally, a notary multi-signature scheme is designed to solve the problem of trust in the traditional model.

The authors of [10] design an addressable storage model based on the relay model, reducing the operational cost of existing relay solutions and outlining how relays can be utilized to achieve blockchain interoperability. In [11], a message relay scheme for heterogeneous blockchains is put forward via the periodic turnover of cross-chain nodes. This scheme helps in delivering messages between different blockchains by periodically forming a cross-chain relay chain committee. Recently, a relay system for cross-chain energy trading has been designed in [12]. This system addresses the trading problem of the power system and enables the trading of the same kind of energy within the chain and heterogeneous energies across different chains. a cross-blockchain asset transfer protocol is designed in [13] to support the transfer of arbitrary assets while adhering to the global consistency requirement and improving flexibility in asset transfer. In [14], the authors put forward EOVPC, a cross-chain transaction processing algorithm. This algorithm achieves the atomicity of cross-chain transactions with an optimistic cross-chain consensus method. A comprehensive cross-chain interaction system is proposed in [15] to allow assets on different chains to be mapped to corresponding assets on proxy chains for cross-chain asset transactions. After this work, a decentralized cross-chain data integrity verification scheme is designed by the authors of [16] to achieve secure and accurate cross-chain data sharing between different blockchains. The focus of this scheme is to address the data integrity verification problem in cross-chain interaction.

3   System Model

In this section, the underlying system architecture is first given where multiple blockchains coexist and interactions frequently occur among them. Given this architecture, useful parameters and definitions are then offered.

3.1   System Architecture

The overall architecture is shown in Fig. 1. Here, there exist multiple blockchains that are maintained via different nodes. These blockchains interact with each other via the newly introduced component Relay Chain.

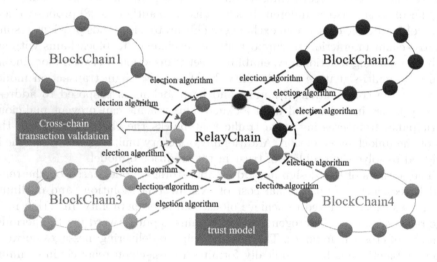

Fig. 1. The system architecture

The whole system works as follows. For each complete node of these different blockchains, a trust value for it is obtained based on its behavior. This value helps to construct the relay chain. After node trust values are obtained, a relay node election algorithm is designed to choose the proper nodes that maintain the relay chain. Once the construction of the relay chain is completed, the rule for cross-chain transactions is put forward to support interoperability and interaction among different blockchains.

3.2 Parameters

In the proposed architecture, we use N^* to denote the set of all nodes in a blockchain denoted as $*$. Each node within the blockchain $*$ is represented as n_i^*, where i refers to the node's position in the blockchain sequence. For example, the set of nodes $\{n_1^*, n_2^*, n_3^*, \ldots\}$ is connected through P2P communication, forming a blockchain network that jointly maintains the same blockchain ledger. The notation $N^* = \{n_1^*, n_2^*, n_3^*, \ldots\}$ is used to express this relationship. Within the blockchain N^*, multiple transaction information exists. These transactions are defined as $Tx^*(i, j)$ in this paper, representing the j-th transaction data of the i-th block generated by the blockchain denoted as $*$. The cross-chain scheme proposed in this paper not only requires the establishment of a cross-chain blockchain collection, but also involves the division of trust values among all blockchain nodes. Based on their respective trust values, these nodes are assigned to different trust domains. Hence, we assume a collection of trust domains with varying levels of trust, denoted as $\{T_1, T_2, T_3, \cdots\}$. Each blockchain node is assigned to its corresponding trust domain based on its own trust value. Within the cross-chain system, nodes belonging to different trust domains possess different privileges.

Meanwhile, in the cross-chain system, there exist multiple collections of blockchains. In order to facilitate cross-chain transactions between different blockchains, a relay chain is required to verify such transactions. In this paper, the relay chain is denoted as R. According to the cross-chain model proposed in this paper, the relay chain is generated by the nodes within each blockchain utilizing an election algorithm. Therefore, this paper defines the equation as follows (3-1):

$$N^1 \ominus N^2 \ominus N^3 \ominus \cdots = R \qquad (3\text{-}1)$$

where $\ominus$ represents the selection of nodes for the relay chain, and Eq. (3-1) denotes the set of nodes that are jointly elected among the participating blockchains in the cross-chain process to produce the relay blockchain R. Additionally, the relay chain R needs to run its own cross-chain consensus in order to facilitate the verification of cross-chain transactions.

Using the above parameters, the interaction between any two nodes from the same blockchain or different blockchains can be denoted in a more strict manner. Suppose that nodes n_1^1 and n_2^2 belong to different blockchains, i.e., $n_1^1 \in N_1$, $n_2^2 \in N_2$. If n_1^1 can interact with n_2^2 via R to modify the ledger data of n_2^2 and generate transaction $Tx^2(2, j)$, then $n_1^1 \rightarrow n_2^2$ is used to indicate the interaction. Similarly, if n_2^2 can interact with n_1^1 via R to modify the ledger data of n_1^1 and generate transaction $Tx^1(1, j)$, then $n_2^2 \rightarrow n_1^1$ is used to indicate the interaction. Therefore, blockchain cross-chain interactions are denoted as $n_1^1 \leftrightarrow n_2^2$, and the relay reward is allocated after the completion of the cross-chain transaction, thus completing the entire cross-chain operation. Hence, the blockchain cross-chain interaction is represented as $\Psi(i)$, and the system incentive is allocated accordingly once the cross-chain transaction is finalized, thereby completing the entire cross-chain operation.

4   The Proposed Cross-Chain Relay Method

In this section, the details of the proposed cross-chain relay method are presented. This method is composed of three main components: cross-chain node trust model, weighted randomized relay node election, and cross-chain transaction construction. At first, the trust values of enrolling relay nodes are evaluated via the trust model, where the factors of communication reliability, service time degree, transaction credibility, and historical trust values are considered. After the relay node trust values are computed, a weighted randomized relay node election algorithm is put forward to balance randomness, fairness, security, and efficiency. Subsequently, how cross-chain transactions are completed is illustrated. Moreover, some special cases, like system initialization, transaction exception, and blockchain joining and exiting, are taken into consideration.

4.1   Cross-Chain Node Trust Model

At a high level, the node trust model is composed of four factors, namely communication reliability, service time, transaction credibility, and historical trust values.

(1) Communication reliability

Ideally, the system aims for the nodes to maintain a continuous state of normal communication. To quantify the communication reliability mathematically, Eq. (4-1) is designed:

$$T_{com} = \frac{t_{normal}}{t_{total}} \qquad (4\text{-}1)$$

where T_{com} represents the quantitative result of a node's communication reliability, t_{normal} denotes the time when the node is able to communicate normally with other nodes in the cross-chain system throughout the entire cycle, and t_{total} represents the total cycle time.

However, node communication is affected by multiple factors, such as fluctuations in the transmission channel during communication and potential interference from noise or other uncontrollable situations. In this manuscript, we aim to enhance the fault tolerance of nodes by implementing threshold control on communication reliability. Specifically, we set the upper limit of the node communication threshold as θ_1 and the lower limit as θ_2. If the communication reliability of a node exceeds θ_1, it indicates that the node's communication is problem-free. Conversely, if it falls below θ_2, it suggests that the node's communication cannot be stable and thus this node is not reliable when fulfilling cross-chain relay tasks. Equation (4-2) provides a detailed description of this concept.

$$T_{com} = \begin{cases} 1 & \frac{t_{normal}}{t_{total}} \geq \theta_1 \\ \frac{t_{normal}}{t_{total}} & \theta_2 < \frac{t_{normal}}{t_{total}} < \theta_1 \\ 0 & \frac{t_{normal}}{t_{total}} \leq \theta_2 \end{cases} \qquad (4\text{-}2)$$

(2) Service time degree

The second factor that affects the trust value of a relay node is the service time that undertaking relay tasks. Let T_{time} denote the influence of this factor. It can be computed via Eq. (4-3):

$$T_{time} = e^{-\frac{a}{t}} \tag{4-3}$$

Here, t represents the time experienced by the node after joining the cross-chain system. The parameter $a(a > 0)$ is the time regulation factor, which can regulate the growth rate of T_{time} by adjusting the value of a. The larger the value of a, the slower T_{time} grows. Overall, the value of T_{time} increases with the value of a and tends to be 1. This means that as more nodes join the cross-chain system, their service time degree gradually approaches 1, in line with the design expectations.

(3) Transaction credibility

In a blockchain system, the transactions of a node serve as an important indicator of the integrity of the node's behavior. All the data within the blockchain is generated through a series of transactions after consensus is reached. Hence, the performance of each node in the transaction process plays a crucial role. This paper introduces the concept of transaction credibility for nodes and provides a mathematical quantification. The transaction credibility is defined as shown in Eq. (4-4):

$$T_{trans} = \rho \cdot b \cdot \left(\frac{tx}{tx_{total}} + \frac{con}{con_{total}} \right) \tag{4-4}$$

where T_{trans} is the quantitative result of node transaction credibility. b is the correlation coefficient and is set to 0.5 to ensure that the value of transaction credibility is in the range of 0 to 1. tx is the number of packaged transactions of the node after joining the system, and tx_{total} is the total number of transactions determined by the whole system. con is the number of times nodes participate in the consensus verification, while con_{total} is the number of times that the system as a whole has been verified by the consensus. ρ is the control factor ($0 \le \rho \le 1$). When nodes participate in transactions to reach a certain number, ρ can become 1. The growth rate of T_{trans} can be controlled by regulating ρ. From Eq. (4-4), it can be seen that nodes actively participating in transaction packaging and consensus will have higher transaction credibility. There is a control factor ρ to ensure that its value does not grow rapidly when the nodes only participate in a small number of transactions after joining the cross-chain system.

(4) Historical trust values

When there is a lack of prior knowledge, establishing a trust relationship requires gradual accumulation over time. Therefore, the trust model should include the influence of historical trust values to better reflect the evolution of trust. To achieve this, this manuscript introduces the following design: it records the list of trust values of the node as $\{h_1, h_2, h_3, \cdots\}$, representing the results of trust value calculations by the node using the trust model in previous instances. To better capture trustworthiness fluctuations, this paper defines D as the trust fluctuation value, with specific calculations shown in Eq. (4-5):

$$D = \sqrt{\frac{\sum_{1}^{n}(\bar{h} - h_i)^2}{n}} \tag{4-5}$$

In this formula, n represents the number of recorded node trust values, $\bar{h}$ represents the average value of n trust values and h_i represents the i-th trust value of the node. The formula reflects the fluctuation of the node's trust value, where a larger value of D indicates more drastic changes in the node's trust value.

The trust value may fluctuate greatly during the process of change, either due to malicious nodes or node downtime. However, the proposed method aims to maintain the historical trust value of the node within a certain fluctuation range to ensure node stability and reliability. Consequently, this paper introduces a parameter ξ as a threshold to constrain D. Building upon this, the historical trustworthiness is defined as shown in Eq. (4-6):

$$T_{history} = \begin{cases} \bar{h} & D \leq \xi \\ 0 & D < \xi \end{cases} \tag{4-6}$$

As a result, the current trust value of a node is defined as $T_{current}$, which represents the combined trustworthiness of the node across multiple dimensions. The specific calculation method is illustrated in Eq. (4-7).

$$T_{current} = \eta(t) \times (w_1 T_{com} + w_2 T_{time} + w_3 T_{trans} + w_4 T_{history}) \tag{4-7}$$

Here, w_i represents the weights assigned to each factor, where the trustworthiness of each dimension should be assigned different weights based on the specific requirements. ξ is the control factor of $T_{current}$. By regulating $\xi(t)$, the growth rate of $T_{current}$ can be controlled, ensuring that the trust value of nodes does not increase too quickly and thereby threatens the security of the entire system. The system calculates the trust value of each node by monitoring every node and disseminates it to all member nodes of the chain through consensus uplinking, after which it is regularly updated and maintained.

Subsequently, we introduce an update cycle denoted as C. When each time a cycle C is completed, the trust value of a node is updated based on its historical trust value and the model computation. This update aims to facilitate the subsequent update of the relay chain nodes. Additionally, since the trust value is utilized for the relay node election process, it is updated accordingly before the turnover of the relay chain cycle. In cases where a node exhibits malicious behavior within the system, its trust value is instantly reset to zero during the next trust value update, and it will not be incremented thereafter.

The trust value of a node, calculated by the trust model presented in this paper, ranges between 0 and 1. To enhance node categorization, this paper

Table 1. Node Trust Domain Distribution Table

Node Trust Domain	Distribution of confidence values
High-trust nodes	$0.8 \leq T_{current} \leq 1$
common node	$0.6 \leq T_{current} < 0.8$
low-trust node	$0 < T_{current} < 0.6$
evil nexus	$T_{current} = 0$

divides the nodes into various trust domains based on their trust values. Please refer to Table 1 for further details.

Nodes are assigned to different trust domains based on their trust values, which are categorized as high-trust nodes, ordinary nodes, low-trust nodes, and evil nodes. These trust values directly influence the subsequent election of relay chain nodes. To ensure the overall system security, this paper imposes restrictions on the privileges of nodes within different trust domains. Evil nodes are prohibited from participating in the election process of the relay chain and are only allowed to exist in the source blockchain. Low-trust nodes have a low probability of being elected as relay chain nodes, and even if elected, they can only serve as observer nodes within the relay chain. They are not allowed to participate in the voting session of cross-chain consensus and cannot be elected as master nodes of cross-chain consensus. Both ordinary nodes and high-trust nodes have the ability to participate in the cross-chain consensus within the relay chain. Therefore, all nodes are expected to maintain positive behaviors and strive to improve their trust values.

4.2   Weighted Randomized Relay Node Election Algorithm

Here, we propose a new election concept: the probability of a node becoming a relay node is directly proportional to its trust value. Building upon this concept, we outline the following objectives for the election algorithm to ensure its effectiveness:

1. Randomness: the outcome of a single election cannot be predicted;
2. Fairness: in the long run, the probability of a node being selected should be consistent with the proportion of trust value it has. The higher the trust value, the higher the probability of being selected;
   The above are the hard metrics that need to be met, and here are the performance metrics:
3. Security: Security means that the system can operate normally in the presence of malicious nodes and withstand external attacks;
4. Efficiency: Efficiency means that the algorithm calculates the final result quickly. In other words, the algorithm can swiftly select the relay chain nodes without wasting computational power.

Then, the system determines a threshold value τ, which determines the total number of nodes expected to be elected by the algorithm in this round.

A network-wide recognized random number s is generated and broadcasted throughout the cross-chain network. The node generates the VRF function proof based on the broadcasted random number s and its own private key sk as shown in Eq. (4-8), which is implemented by performing the signature operation on the combined number generated by s and sk through the ECDSA algorithm:

$$proof = VRF\_Proof(sk, s) \tag{4-8}$$

The node will generate the proof of the VRF function through the hash function for mapping calculation, the output has a random nature represented by the value $random$, as shown in Eq. (4-9). Specifically, in this paper, the hash function SHA256 is used for implementation:

$$random = Hash(proof) \tag{4-9}$$

The node normalizes the generated random number $random$ to generate a random number n in the range of 0 to 1 as shown in Eq. (4-10):

$$n = \frac{random}{\alpha} \tag{4-10}$$

where α is 2^{256}, which is also the maximum value of the hash map.

The node calculates the probability of not being selected in this round based on the trust value as shown in Eq. (4-11):

$$p = B(k, T, \omega) = C_T^k \cdot \omega^k \cdot (1 - \omega)^{T-k} \tag{4-11}$$

Here, $B(\cdot)$ is the binomial distribution formula, C_T^k is the combination coefficient, T represents the node trust value (rounded to facilitate calculation, after uniformly expanding it by 100), ω denotes the weight, given by $\omega = \tau/T_1$, where τ is the threshold value determined by the system in step 1, and T_1 is the sum of trust values of all nodes. Since the calculation assesses the probability of not being selected, k is set to 0. In the formula, as the node's trust value increases, the value of p decreases, resulting in a higher probability of being selected.

Each node compares the random numbers above to determine whether it can be elected as a relay node for the next round, as shown in Eq. (4-12):

$$\begin{cases} n \in [p, 1] & election success \\ n \in [0, p) & election failure \end{cases} \tag{4-12}$$

Finally, the node that determines that its election is successful broadcasts the result of the computation across the network, containing $proof$, $random$, and n. The other nodes validate the received message to verify whether the random number generated by the successfully elected node is legitimate or not, in order to determine whether the node is selected or not. This process is depicted in Eqs. (4-13) and (4-14):

$$result\_verify = VRF\_P2H(proof) \tag{4-13}$$

$$verify = VRF\_Verify(proof, random, n, pk) \tag{4-14}$$

The above description presents a single election process. However, based on the previous analysis, it can be inferred that if the nodes of the relay chain remain fixed, it is challenging to eliminate both the dormant nodes and the malicious nodes. Additionally, restraining the power of the relay chain nodes becomes difficult. Consequently, if this state persists for an extended period, the entire cross-chain system will encounter significant security issues. To address this, the relay chain in this paper will undergo a re-election process based on specific rules to eliminate abnormal nodes from the relay chain.

The re-election of the relay chain can guarantee the security of the chain. However, if re-elections occur too frequently, it can create substantial overhead, even with an efficient election algorithm. Therefore, it is necessary to specify the rules for re-election. This paper defines the specific rules for the reorganization of the relay chain:

1. The system sets the time period λ and reorganizes the cycle every time λ passes;
2. Whenever a new blockchain is added to the cross-chain system, reorganize;
3. Reorganize whenever the cross-chain system suffers a serious security incident.

4.3 Cross-Chain Transactions

After the relay chain is formed during the election, it can execute cross-chain operations. To ensure the smooth functioning of transactions, it is essential to

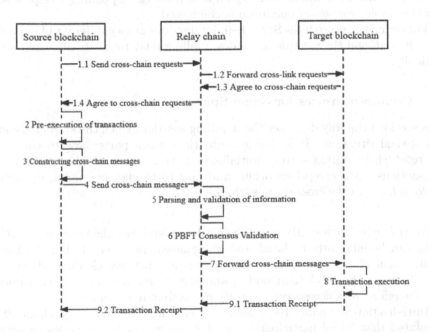

Fig. 2. Cross-chain transaction process

specify the transaction process in detail. The cross-chain transaction process in this program is as follows, Fig. 2:

Step 1: The source blockchain initiates a cross-chain request, and the relay and target blockchains respond to the request;

Step 2: The source blockchain pre-executes the cross-chain transaction and generates the corresponding transaction block;

Step 3: The source blockchain generates the corresponding transmission message according to the cross-chain information transmission protocol and signs the message using the request node in the source blockchain;

Step 4: The source blockchain sends the signed transmission message to the transaction pool of the relay chain and waits for the relay chain to perform the relevant verification process;

Step 5: The relay chain takes the message from the source blockchain out of its own transaction pool, parses it accordingly, and verifies the signature;

Step 6: The relay chain takes out the content of the parsed transaction, performs the PBFT consensus of the relay chain on it, and verifies the existence of the transaction through SPV technology;

Step 7: If the validation passes, it indicates that the transaction in the source blockchain has indeed been executed, then the transmission message is submitted to the target blockchain with the signature of the relay node;

Step 8: After receiving the message from the relay chain, the target blockchain parses and checks the message, and completes the corresponding transaction through its own internal consensus;

Step 9: After the transaction is completed, the corresponding receipt is sent and the whole cross-chain operation is completed.

Following the procedures **Step 1–9**, interactions among different blockchains are achieved, and the rewards for nodes fulfilling relay tasks are allocated automatically.

4.4   Countermeasures for Some Special Cases

This section primarily discusses the handling solutions when the system encounters special situations. It is divided into three main parts: how to construct the relay chain during system initialization, how to ensure the atomicity of transactions when exceptions occur, and how to handle the joining or exiting of blockchains in the cross-chain system.

System Initialization. By using the election algorithm, the nodes of the relay chain can be efficiently replaced and reorganized. However, during the initial construction of the relay chain, the system has not yet established connections between the blockchain nodes, and the system has not started running yet. Therefore, it is necessary to specify the system initialization.

Initialization is mainly responsible for creating the first relay chain. It is stipulated that initial participating blockchains each select n nodes to jointly form the initial relay chain. The value of n can be determined based on the number of participating blockchains and the required number of relay nodes. After the initial relay chain is constructed, connections are established between the blockchains, and the various modules of the system can run. Subsequently, the relay chain is periodically reorganized and replaced according to the relay node election algorithm.

After completing the creation of the first relay chain, the relay chain nodes will synchronously collect block header data from the participating blockchains, facilitating subsequent relay chains to verify cross-chain transactions through SPV technology. The main purpose of the first relay chain is to establish the initial connection between the blockchains and does not engage in cross-chain consensus. After this, the periodic construction of the relay chain begins, and the system operates normally.

Handling Transaction Exceptions. Transaction exceptions can be categorized into transactions not executed on the source chain and transactions not executed on the target chain.

The relay chain can verify the existence of transactions on the source blockchain through PBFT consensus, the Proof field in cross-chain messages, and SPV verification. If the verification fails, it means that the source blockchain did not execute its own transactions. In this case, the relay chain will reject the request from the source blockchain, and the entire cross-chain transaction is terminated. If the source blockchain wishes to continue the transaction, it needs to initiate a new cross-chain transaction and send the new cross-chain transaction information to the relay chain for verification based on the cross-chain message transmission protocol.

If the relay chain verifies the transactions on the source blockchain and the target blockchain does not execute the final cross-chain transaction within a certain period, the relay chain will notify the source blockchain to cancel the cross-chain transaction. The source blockchain will roll back the pre-executed transactions and execute the transactions in reverse order to ensure the atomicity of the cross-chain transaction. As a result, the entire cross-chain transaction is terminated.

Blockchain Joining and Exiting. When a blockchain wants to join the cross-chain system, it needs to submit a cross-chain joining request. Then, it must undergo consensus among the current relay chain, and only when consensus is reached, it will be eligible to join the cross-chain system. After the joining process is completed, a new round of relay chain election will commence for the entire cross-chain system.

Similarly, as the cross-chain system operates, some blockchains may no longer have the need for cross-chain transactions and want to exit the cross-chain system. In that case, they can submit an exit request to the relay chain. After consensus among the relay chain, the blockchain will be excluded in the next relay chain reorganization. However, if a blockchain encounters significant security issues, such as generating denial of service or malicious behavior, the relay chain will immediately perform a reorganization and exclude the blockchain from the entire cross-chain system to ensure system security.

5   Experiments

This experiment evaluates the performance of the scheme by creating multiple processes, each simulating a node of the blockchain. Experimental settings are listed in the following table (Table 2).

Table 2. Experimental Settings

Setting	Parameters
System	Windows 10 and Ubuntu 16.04
CPU	Intel Core i7-10750H
GPU	GTX 1650
RAM	16 GB
Tool	IntelliJ IDEA(2020.2.3)
Language	Java (JDK 8)

5.1   Trust Model Testing

In order to facilitate a more accurate comparison, the trust value changes of three types of nodes are tested: normal nodes, downtime nodes, and evil nodes. Normal nodes actively participate in cross-chain related operations upon joining the cross-chain system. They remain connected to other nodes and do not engage in any malicious behavior. Downtime nodes, on the other hand, exhibit periods of inactivity after joining the cross-chain system, ceasing their interactions with the cross-chain system. Evil nodes, after a certain period of time within the cross-chain system, deliberately send incorrect information and engage in malicious behavior. The variation of trust values for these three types of nodes is depicted in Fig. 3.

As observed in the figure, the trust value of a normal node steadily increases upon joining the cross-chain system through active participation in normal cross-chain behavior. Over time, it transforms into a high-trust node. Conversely, when a downtime node occurs, its trust value gradually declines and does not recover within a given period. Eventually, it becomes a low-trust node. As for the evil node, its trust value drops to 0 following the engagement of malicious behavior, and it remains stagnant without any further increase in trust value.

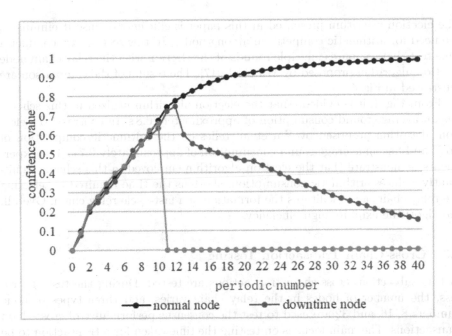

Fig. 3. Node trust value changes

5.2 Algorithm Testing

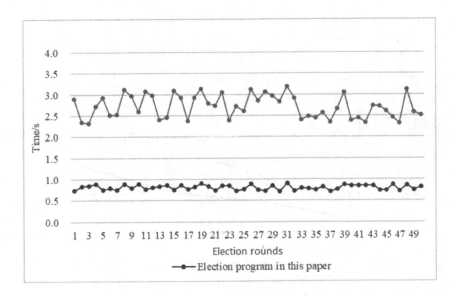

Fig. 4. Algorithm comparison

The election algorithm presented in this paper is efficient because it eliminates the need for arithmetic competition among nodes. In this section, we conduct a time test that compares multiple rounds of the election with the relay chain node election algorithm proposed by Wu et al. [17]. The results of the comparison are illustrated in Fig. 4.

From Fig. 4, it is evident that the election algorithm utilized in this scheme has an average round consumption of approximately 0.8 s. In contrast, the election algorithm proposed by Wu et al. relies on the arithmetic competition of PoW and has an average round consumption of approximately 2.7 s. The experiments demonstrate that the election algorithm employed in this scheme significantly reduces arithmetic consumption, shortens the time required for electing the relay chain, and facilitates the formation of a fast-cycle relay chain. Overall, the algorithm exhibits high efficiency.

5.3 Cross-Chain Transaction Testing

In this subsection, cross-chain transactions are tested. During the testing process, the number of nodes in the relay chain varies, and three types of node numbers 8, 16, and 32 are used to test the consensus performance of cross-chain transactions. The main focus is on testing the time taken for a transaction to be successfully submitted to the relay chain and then verified by cross-chain consensus. The experimental results are shown in Fig. 5. From Fig. 5, it can be observed that the time delay increases as the number of relay chain nodes increases. This is a normal phenomenon due to message broadcasting between the PBFT con-

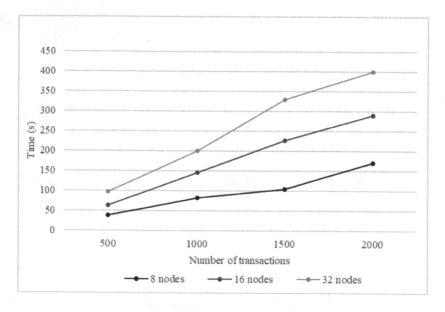

Fig. 5. Cross-chain transaction testing

sensus nodes. Additionally, when the number of nodes is fixed, the transaction processing time increases with a higher number of cross-chain transactions.

6 Conclusion

In this paper, a node trust-based cycle turnover relay cross-chain scheme is proposed to support cross-chain interaction between different blockchains. The trust model of blockchain nodes in the cross-chain system is first constructed, and the trust value of each node is calculated by evaluating multiple dimensions. Based on this evaluation, nodes are categorized into evil nodes, low-trust nodes, ordinary nodes, and high-trust nodes. This categorization effectively constrains node behaviors in the system and improves the stability of the cross-chain system. Furthermore, to tackle the challenging problem of relay chain formation, the paper introduces a weighted random election algorithm based on node trust. This algorithm, which incorporates VRF technology, enables safe and efficient turnover and reorganization of the relay chain. It ensures randomness while also offering resistance against various attacks. Additionally, the paper specifies the process of cross-chain transactions and guarantees the atomicity of such transactions through SPV verification technology. Finally, the proposed scheme is extensively evaluated through numerous simulation experiments, and the experimental results demonstrate the good performance of the various modules in the scheme.

Acknowledgement. This work is supported by the Key Research and Development Programs of Shaanxi under Grants 2021ZDLGY06-03 and the National Natural Science Foundation of China under Grant 62132013 and 61902292.

References

1. Zhang, J., Liu, Y., Zhang, Z.: Research on cross-chain technology architecture system based on blockchain. In: Liang, Q., Wang, W., Liu, X., Na, Z., Jia, M., Zhang, B. (eds.) CSPS 2019. LNEE, vol. 571, pp. 2609–2617. Springer, Singapore (2020). https://doi.org/10.1007/978-981-13-9409-6_318
2. Buterin, V.: Chain interoperability. R3 Res. Pap. **9**, 1–25 (2016)
3. Kwon, J., Buchman, E.: Cosmos whitepaper. http://cosmos.network/resources/whitepaper (2019)
4. Assiri, B., Khan, W.: Enhanced and lock-free tendermint blockchain protocol. In: IEEE International Conference on Smart Internet of Things, pp. 220–226 (2019)
5. Polkadot, W.G.: Vision for a heterogeneous multi-chain framework. White Pap. (2016)
6. Abbas, H., Caprolu, M., Di Pietro, R.: Analysis of polkadot: architecture, internals, and contradictions. IEEE Int. Conf. Blockchain **2022**, 61–70 (2022)
7. Deng, L., Chen, H., Zeng, J., Zhang, L.-J.: Research on cross-chain technology based on sidechain and hash-locking. In: Liu, S., Tekinerdogan, B., Aoyama, M., Zhang, L.-J. (eds.) EDGE 2018. LNCS, vol. 10973, pp. 144–151. Springer, Cham (2018). https://doi.org/10.1007/978-3-319-94340-4_12

8. Zie, J.-Y., Deneuville, J.-C., Briffaut, J., Nguyen, B.: Extending atomic cross-chain swaps. In: Pérez-Solà, C., Navarro-Arribas, G., Biryukov, A., Garcia-Alfaro, J. (eds.) DPM/CBT -2019. LNCS, vol. 11737, pp. 219–229. Springer, Cham (2019). https://doi.org/10.1007/978-3-030-31500-9_14

9. Dai, B., Jiang, S., Zhu, M., et al.: Research and implementation of cross-chain transaction model based on improved hash-locking. In: International Conference on Blockchain and Trustworthy Systems, pp. 218–230 (2020)

10. Frauenthaler, P., Sigwart, M., Spanring, C., et al.: Leveraging blockchain relays for cross-chain token transfers. Gas **300**, 600 (2020)

11. Wu, Z., Xiao, Y., Zhou, E., et al.: A solution to data accessibility across heterogeneous blockchains. In: 2020 IEEE 26th International Conference on Parallel and Distributed Systems (ICPADS), Hong Kong, pp. 414–421 (2020)

12. Shaomin, Z., Cong, H.: Model of decentralized cross-chain energy trading for power systems. Global Energy Interconnection **4**(3), 324–334 (2021)

13. Sigwart, M., Frauenthaler, P., Spanring, C., Sober, M., Schulte, S.: Decentralized cross-blockchain asset transfers. In: 2021 Third International Conference on Blockchain Computing and Applications (BCCA), Tartu, Estonia, pp. 34–41 (2021)

14. Wang, W., Zhang, Z., Wang, G., Yuan, Y.: Efficient cross-chain transaction processing on blockchains. Appl. Sci. **12**(9), 4434 (2022)

15. Yiming, H., Dawei, L., Chi, Z., et al.: Practical agentchain: a compatible cross-chain exchange system. Future Gener. Comput. Syst. **130**, 207–218 (2022)

16. Jiang, J., Zhang, Y., Zhu, Y., et al.: DCIV: decentralized cross-chain data integrity verification with blockchain. J. King Saud Univ.-Comput. Inf. Sci. **34**(10), 7988–7999 (2022)

17. Wu, Z, Xiao, Y., Zhou, E., et al.: A solution to data accessibility across heterogeneous blockchains. In: 2020 IEEE 26th International Conference on Parallel and Distributed Systems (ICPADS), Hong Kong, pp. 414–421 (2020)

Collateral-Efficient Instant Contingent Payments: The Promise of a Hardware-Driven Off-Chain Payment System

Anxin Zhou, Yuefeng Du, and Xiaohua Jia[✉]

City University of Hong Kong, Hong Kong, People's Republic of China
anxin.zhou@my.cityu.edu.hk, {yf.du,csjia}@cityu.edu.hk

Abstract. As the cryptocurrency universe continues to expand at an unprecedented pace, efficient and routine transactions have become a critical necessity. Yet, the current transaction processing capabilities of many blockchains fail to meet the burgeoning demands of retail payments. While off-chain scaling solutions present promising alternatives to augment blockchain throughput and uphold compatibility with established blockchains, they often impose impractical burdens on users or experience significant payment latency. This study introduces a hardware-driven off-chain payment system designed to accommodate contingent payments. Merchants can accept payments instantly without waiting for transaction confirmation. Our assessment reveals that this system can achieve a peak throughput of approximately 10000 payments per second, representing an 84-fold improvement over traditional Ethereum transactions. This hardware-driven solution holds significant promise for instant and collateral-efficient transactions, effectively unlocking the untapped potential of instant payments with high throughput.

Keywords: Off-chain transaction · Contingent payment · Trusted hardware

1 Introduction

With the cryptocurrency market witnessing unprecedented growth, the interest in utilizing cryptocurrencies for everyday transactions is steadily increasing. It's estimated that nearly 18% of the adult population in the US [7], approximately 46 million consumers, are considering making retail purchases with cryptocurrencies. Furthermore, both large retailers (85% of 202 surveyed) [11] and small businesses (32% of owners and top-level executives surveyed) [1] have begun accepting cryptocurrencies as a method of payment. Major payment providers like PayPal [12], Visa [15], and leading crypto exchanges such as Binance [3] and Coinbase [6] have also broadened their financial services to accommodate cryptocurrency payments.

© ICST Institute for Computer Sciences, Social Informatics and Telecommunications Engineering 2024
Published by Springer Nature Switzerland AG 2024. All Rights Reserved
J. Liu et al. (Eds.): TridentCom 2023, LNICST 523, pp. 21–37, 2024.
https://doi.org/10.1007/978-3-031-51399-2_2

Despite the original vision of a decentralized payment network [4], retail cryptocurrency payments remain predominantly controlled by companies. For example, payments made through PayPal [12] or Binance [3] occur between accounts managed by these companies. Consumers of Visa [15] and Starbucks [13] must first convert their cryptocurrencies into fiat currencies or gift cards. However, cryptocurrency markets may not be well regulated, leading to potential misrepresentation of financial positions [8] and insufficient client protection in the event of company bankruptcy [14]. Moreover, companies may unilaterally ban clients from certain regions due to political considerations [10].

Direct cryptocurrency use for retail payments could eliminate centralized control over consumers' funds. Yet, the transaction processing capabilities of popular blockchains, such as Bitcoin and Ethereum, which together constitute 60% of the global crypto market, are inadequate for handling the demands of retail payments. Their blockchains can only process around 7 and 15 transactions per second, respectively, with confirmation times reaching up to an hour and 15 min. This stands in stark contrast to Visa, which handles an average of 1700 transactions per second with minimal confirmation latency. Therefore, it is crucial to devise solutions that provide comparable throughput and latency for cryptocurrency payments.

Off-chain scaling [20,23,28,34,39] seeks to enhance blockchain throughput while preserving compatibility with existing blockchains. This approach transitions the processing of transactions from the blockchain to off-chain components, typically relying on the inherent security mechanisms of the blockchain to protect these off-chain processes. However, existing solutions such as payment channels [39] and commit-chains [32] suffer from usability issues for retail payments, as they necessitate periodic online activity from customers. Sidechains [28] are believed to lack security, as evidenced by real-world incidents when using a small number of nodes for performance. Rollups [20] have high latency as transaction data must be stored back on-chain for transactions to be committed.

Our Contribution. In this work, we introduce a hardware-driven off-chain payment system designed for practical throughput and low latency without requiring continuous online involvement from customers. An untrusted server processes payments off-chain, similar to rollups, and is required to periodically commit processed payments on-chain. This allows users to retrieve off-chain funds even in the event of server misbehavior. We innovatively enable merchants to accept unconfirmed payments without waiting for on-chain commitment, facilitating prompt goods or services delivery.

Our unique approach allows unconfirmed payments to be re-executed on the blockchain if the server fails to commit payments on-chain promptly. To ensure successful re-execution, we leverage the integrity protection offered by trusted execution environments (TEEs)-secure hardware that has found widespread application and support from leading cloud service providers. The untrusted server is required to operate off-chain funds within a TEE and thus cannot revert a payment that has been re-executed.

We implement a prototype and evaluate our system on Ethereum. The average gas cost for a payment is around 250 (compared to 21000 for a standard

Ethereum transfer). Based on this, we estimate the maximum throughput and transaction fee of a payment. Using the current block gas limit (30M) and block interval (12.11 s) as well as the gas price (14.3 gwei) and ETH price (1919.55 USD), we find the average transaction fee of a payment to be approximately $6.78 * 10^3$. The maximum payment throughput stands at about 10000 payments per second, an 84-fold improvement over Ethereum transfers. Payment can be immediately accepted once processed by the server, with an average processing time of 0.21 ms.

In summary, our contributions in this paper are threefold:

1. We design an off-chain payment system that offers low latency and practical throughput.
2. We propose a hardware-driven solution that allows merchants to safely accept unconfirmed payments without using collateral.
3. We implement and evaluate a system prototype. The experiment shows promising performance and low transaction fees.

2   Preliminaries

Distributed Ledger. A distributed ledger, also known as a blockchain system, involves transactions that typically encompass simple transfers or calls to on-chain smart contracts. Clients initiate transactions by broadcasting them to peer nodes within the blockchain network. These nodes leverage a consensus protocol, for instance, proof of work, to agree on the sequence for transaction execution. To optimize efficiency, nodes batch multiple transactions into a single block, forming a chain of these blocks as a blockchain. Depending on the consensus protocol, a block is either deterministically finalized [33] when added to the blockchain, or considered irreversible with overwhelming probability [27].

Trusted Execution Environment. We instantiate TEE with Intel Software Guard Extensions (SGX), which are a set of security-related instruction codes integrated into certain modern Intel CPUs. These instructions enable developers to create protected enclaves within the processor that safeguard sensitive data and code from unauthorized access or modification, even by the operating system or hypervisor. A key feature of Intel SGX is remote attestation, which lets a remote entity confirm the integrity and authenticity of an enclave operating on a different system. Remote attestation is a procedure that allows a trusted remote entity to verify the identity and secure environment of an enclave on a remote system. The process usually involves the following steps: 1) the remote enclave generates a key pair and securely stores the private key within the enclave; 2) the enclave creates a report containing its identity, measurement, and the newly generated public key; 3) the report is signed with the private key and transmitted to the remote party; 4) the remote party verifies the report using the public key, and checks the signature, ensuring that a genuine SGX enclave created it.

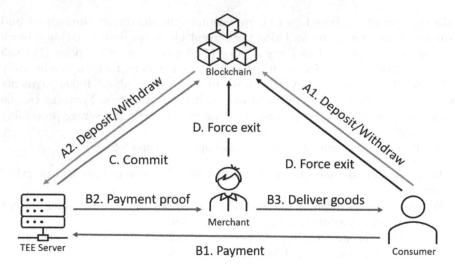

Fig. 1. System overview.

3   Problem Statement

3.1   System Model

Our system is made up of four roles. The server runs an off-chain payment service designed to expedite and economize cryptocurrency transactions. In real-world applications, the server might be a major payment processor or an online retail platform, both intent on attracting consumers and merchants eager to transact using cryptocurrencies.

Consumers and merchants are users of our system. They have the capability to deposit cryptocurrencies on the blockchain, thereby accumulating funds in their off-chain accounts. These funds can be transferred back to the blockchain when needed. Our primary objective is to enable instantaneous payments for merchants who typically ship goods after payment has been received. By reducing this delay, we can make crypto payments more competitive compared to traditional methods. However, our system does not take into account merchants who accept payments but fail to deliver goods.

Our infrastructure employs a public blockchain that supports smart contracts. In our design, we utilize a smart contract to ensure that users can withdraw funds when the server acts improperly, such as in the event of denial of service. We integrate a TEE that offers integrity protection and attested execution functions. The server, through a TEE, administers off-chain funds, ensuring that balance tampering is not possible and that other roles can verify the server's operations. While we use the Ethereum blockchain and SGX enclaves in this work as examples, it's worth noting that other blockchains or TEEs with similar capabilities could also be used.

Threat Model. While maintaining the off-chain payment service, the server is inherently restricted in its potential for malfeasance due to the employment of a Trusted Execution Environment (TEE). Thanks to the integrity protection offered by the TEE, we can assure that the off-chain balance updates correctly and exclusively by predefined program code. Falsely reporting a related message to other roles in the system is ineffective, as the authenticity of the message can be verified through the TEE's attested execution. However, it should be noted that the server retains control over the TEE's network stack. This means the server can potentially block, delay, or tamper with messages sent to or from the TEE. In this context, we dismiss the likelihood of tampering as it can be easily detected through an authentication mechanism [38].

Given that the TEE already mitigates many forms of misbehavior, we mainly focus on two threats in this work. Firstly, we consider the scenario where a malicious consumer colludes with the server to double-spend. For instance, if a merchant accepts an unconfirmed payment and proceeds with delivery, the server could then refuse to confirm the payment. Secondly, we consider the possibility of the server censoring a user's request, resulting in the user's inability to transfer funds back to the blockchain. It's worth noting that we consider it beyond the scope of our work to address situations where merchants fail to deliver goods or services post-payment. Our primary objective is to enable cryptocurrency payments in a retail setting without the need for trusted custodians, not to ensure the secure exchange between merchants and customers.

3.2 Design Goals

We aim to design an off-chain payment system where customers can transfer cryptos to their off-chain accounts for efficient payment, merchants can safely accept instant (unconfirmed) payments, and both customers and merchants can transfer their funds back to the blockchain on demand. The system should also meet the following properties:

- *Correctness.* On-chain and off-chain funds should be updated according to transactions confirmed on the blockchain.
- *Censorship resistance.* A user eventually can withdraw off-chain funds.
- *Finality.* A confirmed transaction cannot be reverted.
- *Secure instant payment.* An instant payment accepted by an honest merchant should eventually be confirmed.

The first two properties jointly secure users' funds. The last two properties ensure double spending is not possible.

4 Design

Figure 1 highlights the main interaction between the roles. In the normal case when the server behaves honestly, there are three kinds of operations. A walk-through of payment is shown as step B1-B3. After receiving a consumer's payment, the server processes the payment and notifies the merchant, which then delivers goods (or services) to the consumer. Deposit or withdraw (step1 A1-A2) allows a user to transfer on-chain funds to its off-chain account or vice versa. The user first submits the request on-chain. The blockchain and the server in turn update the corresponding on-chain and off-chain accounts.

Periodically, the server submits transaction data to the blockchain (step C) so that the blockchain can serve as the last resort for a user to withdraw its off-chain funds even when the server rejecting processing the user's withdrawal request. As the blockchain is transparent and public available, a user can accumulate the transaction data and re-construct the off-chain states. In this way, a user can prove its off-chain balance to the blockchain and withdraw the funds during the exit phase (step D). In this phase, the merchants can also submit unconfirmed payments to the blockchain which confirm the transactions by re-excuting them.

In the following, we present our system design. The functionalities of blockchain and TEE are shown in Fig. 2 and 3 respectively. For simplicity, we assume the roles by default can verify the authenticity and integrity of the messages from each other. However, this does not include the interaction between the TEE server and the blockchain because the malicious server, as the TEE host, can feed fake blockchain data to the TEE. Unfortunately, exist solutions are only applicable to proof-of-work blockchains [19,31] since the solutions rely on the consensus's computational difficulty. As recent blockchains are using more energy-efficient consensus, our system uses a general approach which relies on the related roles to verify if the server is using fake blockchain data.

4.1 Normal-Case Operation

In the normal case, the server will honestly collect and process the deposit, withdrawal and payment requests from users. In each epoch (the interval is up to configuration), the server submits a commitment commt including the transaction data, to the blockchain. When the commitment is finalized on-chain, the included transactions are also committed. The commitment later can also be used for the users to retrieve off-chain funds when the server misbehaves.

Initialize. Initially, the server generates a key pair $(\mathsf{pk}_{tee}, \mathsf{sk}_{tee})$. The private key sk_{tee} is stored inside the TEE while the public key pk_{tee} is submitted to the blockchain. A user verifies that the public key pk_{tee} is indeed generated by the TEE via remote attestation before using the system.

Deposit. A deposit transaction aims to transfer a consumer $\mathcal{C}$'s on-chain funds to its off-chain account. A consumer first submits on-chain a request depReq, including the on-chain account onBal and amount amnt. On receiving the Deposit message, the blockchain debits the account first to ensure that the request can be finished. Then the blockchain marks the request's status as pending. The status will be turned into finished when the transaction is later committed on-chain.

Next on receiving the Deposit message from the blockchain, the server credits the customer's off-chain account offBal. However, the new funds cannot be used for payment until the deposit transaction is committed on-chain. Otherwise, in the *exit* phase, a consumer may not be able to re-execute a payment depending on the deposit. Thus, the server will treat the new funds as pending by recording

---

Initialize(pk$_{tee}$):

  set pk$_{tee}$ as the TEE's public key and stopBlockHeight := exitBlockHeight := ∞

On receive ("Deposit", depReq) **from** $\mathcal{C}$

  assert not SysStopped(), parse depReq as $(\mathcal{C}, \text{amnt})$

  set $\mathcal{C}$.onBal $-=$ amnt and depReq.status := pending

On receive ("Withdraw", wdReq) **from** $\mathcal{U}$

  assert not SysStopped()

  set wdReq.status := pending and wdReq.expiry := blockHeight $+ \delta$

On receive ("Commit", commt, σ_{tee}) **from** $\mathcal{S}$

  assert not SysStopped() and Σ_{tee}.Verify(pk$_{tee}$, σ_{tee}, commt)

  assert commt.Epoch $=$ epoch, set epoch $+= 1$

  for all depReq in commt.depReqs **do**

    assert depReq is the first pending deposit, set depReq.status := finished

  for all wdReq in commt.wdReqs **do**

    assert wdReq is the first pending withdrawal, parse wdReq as $(\mathcal{U}, \text{amnt})$

    set $\mathcal{U}$.onBal $+=$ amnt and wdReq.status := finished

On receive ("StopSys") **from** $\mathcal{U}$

  assert not SysStopped(), let wdReq be the earliest pending withdrawal

  assert curBlockHeight $>=$ wdReq.expiry

  set stopBlockHeight $=$ curBlockHeight and exitBlockHeight $=$ stopBlockHeight $+ \epsilon$

On receive ("CancelDep", depReq) **from** $\mathcal{C}$

  assert SysStopped() and depReq.status $=$ pending

  parse depReq as $(\mathcal{C}, \text{amnt})$, set $\mathcal{C}$.onBal $+=$ amnt and depReq.status $=$ aborted

On receive ("ComLeftPay", payReq, payProof) **from** $\mathcal{M}$

  assert payReq.status! $=$ finished, parse payProof as $(\sigma_{tee}, \text{epoch}, \text{comEpoch})$

  assert SysStopped() and not ExitStarted() and comEpoch $\leq$ epoch $\leq$ payProof.epoch

  assert Σ_{tee}.Verify(pk$_{tee}$, σ_{tee}, payReq, payProof.epoch, comEpoch)

  parse payReq as $(\mathcal{C}, \mathcal{M}, \text{amnt})$, set $\mathcal{C}$.onBal $-=$ amnt

  set $\mathcal{M}$.onBal $+=$ amnt and payReq.status := finished

On receive ("Exit", bal, merklePath) **from** $\mathcal{U}$

  assert SysStopped() and ExitStarted()

  let commt be the recent commitment and merkleRoot := commt.merkleRoot

  assert MerkleVerify(merkleRoot, $(\mathcal{U}, \text{bal})$, merklePath), set $\mathcal{U}$.onBal $+=$ bal

Function SysStopped()

  Return curBlockHeight $>=$ stopBlockHeight

Function ExitStarted()

  Return curBlockHeight $>=$ exitBlockHeight

Fig. 2. Blockchain functionalities.

it in the variable balToConfirm, which keep a record of pending funds in each epoch. Those pending funds will be set as confirmed when the corresponding epoch is committed on-chain. Finally, the server adds the deposit request depReq to the commitment commt as the preparation to commit the transaction.

Withdraw. A withdrawal transaction aims to transfer a user's off-chain funds to its on-chain account. Similarly, a user first submits on-chain a request wdReq.

```
Initialize:
    pk_tee, sk_tee = TEE.GenKey(), output pk_tee
On receive ("Deposit", depReq) from B
    parse depReq as (C, amnt), set C.offBal += amnt
    add (C, amnt) to balToConfirm[epoch] and depReq to commt.depReqs
On receive ("Withdraw", wdReq) from B
    parse wdReq as (U, amnt)
    if U = C  then Set U.comOffBal -= amnt and U.offBal -= amnt
    else if U = M then set M.offBal -= amnt
    add wdReq to commt.wdReqs
On receive ("Payment", payReq) from C
    parse payReq as (C, M, amnt), set C.comOffBal -= amnt, C.offBal -= amnt
    set M.offBal += amnt and σ_tee := TEE.Sign(payReq, epoch, comEpoch)
    add payReq to commit.payReqs, output (σ_tee, epoch, comEpoch) to C
Function Commit()
    set commit.merkleRoot := merkleTree.root and σ_tee := TEE.Sign(commit)
    set oldCommit := commit, reset commit, set epoch += 1
    set commit.epoch := epoch, return (oldCommit, σ_tee)
Function ConfirmEpoch()
1: Set comEpoch += 1
2: for all (C, amnt) in balToConfirm[comEpoch] do set C.comOffBal += amnt
```

Fig. 3. TEE server functionalities.

On receive the Withdraw message, the blockchain then marks the request's status as pending and specially sets the request's expiry time to blockHeight + δ, which is the current block height plus a hyper-parameter. This timeout ensures that a user can retrieve its off-chain funds given an untrusted server.

Next on receiving the Withdraw message from the blockchain, the server starts to debut the user's off-chain balance. If the user is a merchant M, the server debits the merchant's off-chain account offBal. If the user is a consumer C, the server debits the account comOffBal, in which the funds received are from confirmed deposits. This ensures that the consumer only use funds from confirmed deposits for withdrawal. Meanwhile, the server deducts the equivalent amount from offBal, which records the consumer's total off-chain balance, including the funds from unconfirmed deposits. Finally the server adds the request wdReq to the commitment commt to commit the transaction later.

Payment. A payment transaction aims to transfer a consumer's off-chain funds to a merchant. A consumer C first submits a request payReq to the server. On receiving the Payment message, the server debits the consumer's account comOffBal and offBal to ensure that the consumer only uses funds from confirmed deposits for payment. Then the server credits the merchant's account offBal accordingly. Next the server adds the request to the commit to commit the transaction later. Finally, the server uses the TEE's private key sk_tee (unknown to the server host for the TEE's privacy ensurance) to sign the request together with the current epoch and the confirmed epoch comEpoch in the TEE. The generated σ_{tee} and the signed epoch variables can serve as a payment proof payProof that a consumer later can use to re-execute unconfirmed payments in the *exit* phase.

Next the server notifies the merchant with the payment proof payProof attached. First, the merchant verifies the signature σ_{tee} to ensure that the payment proof is indeed generated by the TEE. Besides, the merchant has to verify that the epoch comEpoch has been committed on-chain. The reason, as we stated before is that the TEE's network stack is controlled by the untrusted server host, and there is no authenticated channel between the TEE and the blockchain. So, the TEE may not know when an epoch's commitment would be finalized on-chain. Our design is to let the server itself decides when to confirm an epoch in the TEE while let the merchant itself verify the genuinity. With an accurate comEpoch, the TEE guarantees that the consumer only used the funds from confirmed deposits for payment. After verifying the payment proof, the merchant can deliver goods or services immediately to the consumer without waiting for the payment transaction to be committed.

Commit. At the start of each epoch, the server commits the executed transactions on the blockchain. The server first executes the function Commit which adds the current merkleRoot to the commitment commt and uses the TEE's private key to sign the commitment.

Next the server submits the function outputs, including the commitment commt and the TEE's signature σ_{tee}, to the blockchain. On receiving the Commit message, the blockchain first verifies the signature and checks that the commitment's epoch matches the expected epoch. Then the blockchain retrieves pending deposits and withdrawals to check they match the requests included in the commitment in order. For each withdrawal, the blockchain also credits the corresponding account. Afterwards, the requests' statuses are marked as finished, indicating that the transactions cannot be reverted once the commitment is finalized on the blockchain.

Finally, after observing that the commitment commt has been finalized on-chain, the server invokes the function Confirm to proceed the epoch in the TEE. The function releases the pending funds accumulated dring the earliest unconfirmed epoch to each corresponding consumer's account comOffBal. A consumer thereafter can use the funds for instant payment.

4.2   Force Exit

When the server misbehaves, a user can submit a withdrawal request to the blockchain to withdraw off-chain funds. If the server honestly responds to the request before the timeout, users can get back the funds; this will also help a merchant confirm unconfirmed payments since a commitment will finalize all the previously executed transactions in the TEE. Otherwise, as in rollups and commit-chains, any user can stop the system on the blockchain. After that, the server and blockchain no longer accept new requests. Specifically, the merchants should submit unconfirmed payments before consumers can withdraw off-chain funds. This ensures that the consumers have enough funds to cover the payments.

Stop System. Once a user notice that the earliest pending withdrawal request wdReq times out, i.e. the current block height surpasses wdReq.expiry, the user sends the StopSys message to the blockchain. After verifying that the request indeed has timed out, the blockchain halts the system by setting stopBlockHeight to the current block height. The exit time exitBlockHeight is set to the stop time plus the hyper-parameter epsilon so that merchants have enough time to submit unconfirmed payments before users withdraw their off-chain funds. The blockchain will no longer accept deposits, withdrawals and commitments after the system is stopped. Thereafter, a consumer can first cancel an unfinished deposit by sending the CancelDep message to the blockchain, which credits the on-chain account onBal and sets the deposit's status to aborted. As introduced below, a consumer also and withdraw its off-chain account after merchants confirming unfinished payments.

Confirm Unfinished Payments. A merchant has time to submit unconfirmed payments before the exit block height is reached. For each payment, the merchant submits the request payReq together with the payment proof payProof on-chain. On receiving the ComLeftPay message, the blockchain first verifies the payment proof as the merchant has done, i.e., checking the TEE's signature and verifying that the epoch comEpoch attached to the payment proof has been confirmed. Besides, the blockchain verifies that the epoch attached to the proof is less or equal than the current on-chain epoch. This makes ensure that the merchant only submit unconfirmed payments. Finally, the blockchain executes the payment according to the request. It's acceptable if the consumer's account onBal has a balance below zero since it is compensated by the consumer's off-chain funds.

Withdraw Off-chain Funds. A user can withdraw all its off-chain funds after the block height surpasses exitBlockHeight. Since all transaction data have been posted on-chain along with the commitments, a user can re-construct the Merkle tree that records everyone's balance. To withdraw the funds, the user submits the balance bal and the corresponding Merkle tree path merklePath to the blockchain. On receiving the Exit message, the blockchain uses the tree path and the Merkle root in the recent commitment to verify that the balance is indeed a part of the tree leaf node. Finally, the balance is credited to the user's account onBal.

4.3   Analysis

Without instant payments, our design has the same security property as zkRollups since we majorly replace zero knowledge proofs with the a TEE on the server side. We next show our system is still secure after bringing in instant payments.

It is easy to verify that instant payments can correctly update the funds in the system and cannot be reverted once finalized on the blockchain. We mainly argue that an honest merchant can finally confirm an instant payment once receiving the valid payment proof. In the first case when the server submits the next commitment on the blockchain in time, the instant payment will be confirmed once the commitment is finalized on-chain. Due to the TEE's integrity, the instant payment should have been stored in that commitment or a commitment before. In the other case when the server fails to submit a commitment in time, the honest merchant or other users can stop the system by invoking stopSys function. After that, the merchant can make the instant payment confirmed by submitting and re-executing it on the blockchain.

Note that an honest merchant should not accept an instant payment before receiving a valid payment proof. In this case, the payment is treated as non-instant payment and will be confirmed later when the server submits the next commitment on-chain. Besides, an honest user should not accept an instant payment after the system has stopped but the time for submitting instant payments has passed. Otherwise, the user cannot submit and confirm the payment on-chain.

5 Evaluation

Our experiments aim to answer the following questions: *1) What is the maximum throughput of the transactions that users may frequently make? 2) What are the transaction fees of the transactions involving interaction with the blockchain?*

A transaction's maximum throughput in our system may depend on several factors. If an transaction is solely on-chain, then its throughput depends on the transaction's gas cost, which decides the largest number of transactions that can be included in a block. If an transaction also needs the server's assistance, then its throughput also depends on the server's capacity. Besides throughput, another aspect impacts user experience is transaction fees. We mainly focus on on-chain transaction fees since these fees cannot be easily avoided in practice. A transaction's fee also can be computed from the transaction's gas cost.

In summary, our measurement includes two parts. First, we measure the gas cost of the transactions involving the interaction with the blockchain. Based on that, we estimate the frequently-used operations' maximum on-chain throughput. Here, we use the term *maximum* because we assume the ideal case when blocks in the blockchain can be fully used by the transactions in our system. Finally, we measure the frequently-used operations off-chain throughput.

Setup. We use Ethereum as the underlying blockchain. The blockchain functionalities are implemented with a smart contract using Solidity 0.8.18. The TEE functions are implemented with SGX SDK using C++. The server and users use the Ethereum's native signature scheme ECDSA to sign messages. We assume users sign their transactions before the transactions are sent to the server.The Merkle tree that stores users' off-chain funds uses the Ethereum's native hash function keccak256. To fully test the system's capacity, we use a static Merkle tree pre-filled with the maximum user numbers. We will test the impact of different numbers on the system performance.

5.1 Off-Chain Throughput

Deposits, withdrawals and payments are the operations that the server may need to execute most of the time. Figure 4(a) shows the execution time of the operations on the server side. It can be seen that the time grows linearly with the number of transactions. In one second, the server can process around 4845 payments, 9307 deposits and 9395 withdrawals. The performance gap between payments and deposits/withdrawals comes from the fact that an payment operation needs to generate a payment proof. Otherwise, the operations have similar performance. Another factor that may impact performance is the number of users, which decides the depth of the Merkle tree. The three kinds of operations also need to update the Merkle tree when updating off-chain balance. But as suggested by Fig. 4(b), the number of users have little impact. The performance is majorly capped by verifying user signatures on transactions. We expect that the performance can be further improved by parallelizing the signature verification.

5.2 On-Chain Throughput and Transaction Fee

To estimate the throughput and transaction fee, we need to first measure the gas cost. Table 1 shows the gas cost of the smart contract functions that users or the server needs to invoke multiple times. Payments do not incur gas cost until being committed on the blockchain. Figure 5(a) shows the gas cost of committing payments when there are no deposits or withdrawals to be committed at the same time. It can be seen that the gas cost grows linearly with the payment numbers. On average, one payment only incurs 250 gas. In contrast, one transfer incurs around 21000 gas in Ethereum. One reason that off-chain payment is more efficient is that off-chain payment can be expressed in a concise form. As in rollups, an account can be expressed as 4-bytes integer instead of 20-bytes address in Ethereum, and similarly an payment amount can be expressed as 4-bytes float instead of 32bytes unsigned integer. Another reason is that payments only need to be submitted as transaction payload and do not have to be executed.

Deposits and withdrawals first need to start the operation on the blockchain. As shown in Table 1, the two corresponding smart contract functions incurs 124.4k and 146.39k gas respectively. Then the two kinds of operations need to be committed on the blockchain. As suggested by Fig. 6(a), the cost of the two operations grow linearly with the number of transactions. The average gas cost of committing a deposit or a withdrawal is around 34.33k. Overall, deposits or withdrawals are not faster than plain transfers in Ethereum since both operations need to operate on-chain balance. The extensive use of the two operations will slow down payments since a commitment comitts payments as well. Figure 5(b) shows the impact on payments. For a commitment that consumes 3M gas, the number of max payments drops linearly from 12000 to 0 when the number of deposits and withdrawals grows from 0 to 90. (Here, we assume there are equal number of deposits and withdrawals). Thus, users are expected to use deposits and withdrawals minimally.

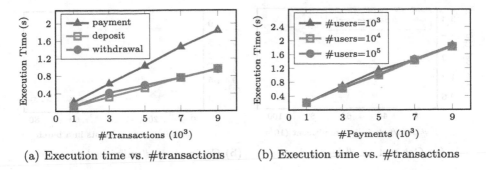

(a) Execution time vs. #transactions   (b) Execution time vs. #transactions

Fig. 4. (a): execution time of payment/deposit/withdrawal transactions. **(b)::** payment execution time under different number of users

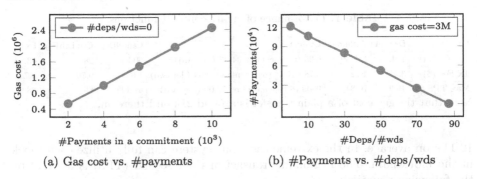

(a) Gas cost vs. #payments   (b) #Payments vs. #deps/wds

Fig. 5. (a): #payments and #deposits/withdrawals in a commitment that consumes 3M gas. **(b):** gas cost of a commitment without deposits and withdrawals.

When the server misbehaves, users need to confirm unfinished instant payments and retrieve their off-chain funds. The gas cost of committing one single instant payment is k. This cost can be further reduced by batching the payments to be confirmed. In the normal case, instead of returning a payment proof proving the current payment, the TEE server returns the proof proving the payments in an epoch. Figure 6(b) shows the impact of such optimization. The gas cost is reduced from 94.07k to 28.85k when number of payments in a batch grows from 1 to 80. This optimization basically saves the cost of verifying the payment proof for every payment. Besides, users need to retrieve their off-chain funds with the exit function, which verifies a Merkle proof proving the balance. The number of users decides the depth of the Merkle tree, thus impacting the gas cost of the exit function. Fortunately, the impact is minor. The gas cost of one call only increases from 63.44k to 74.7k as the number of users increases from 100 to 10k. Finally, users need to invoke the function CancelDep to revert pending deposits. One function call incurs the gas cost of 63.44k.

Maximum On-chain Throughput. Based on the gas costs, we can estimate the throughput of each function on the blockchain. As per May 7, the maximum gas of a block in Ethereum has been increased to 30M, the block time is

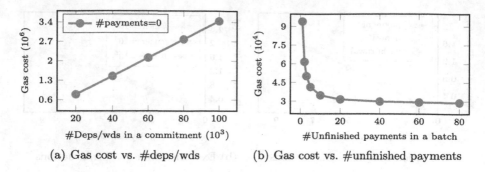

(a) Gas cost vs. #deps/wds   (b) Gas cost vs. #unfinished payments

Fig. 6. (a): gas cost of a commitment without payments. **(b):** gas cost per unfinished payment under batching.

Table 1. Performance of smart contract functions.

Function	Deposit	Withdraw	Commit		CancelDep	ComLeftPay	Exit
Gas Cost (k)	124.4	146.39	0.25 (payment) or 34.33 (dep/wd)		60.24	28.85	63.44
Tx Fee ($)	3.41	4.02	$6.78 * 10^{-3}$ (payment) or 0.94 (dep/wd)		1.65	0.79	1.74
Max TPS	19.9	16.84	9909.16 (payment) or 72.09 (dep/wd)		41.123	85.8	38.98

Note that the gas cost of a plain transfer is around 21k on Ethereum.

12.11 s on average. In the extreme case, our system can fully utilize each block in the blockchain. The maximum transactions per second (TPS) is decided by the following equation:

$$\text{TPS} = \frac{\text{Block Gas Limit}}{\text{Transaction Gas Cost * Block Time}} \quad (1)$$

As shown in Table 1, all the operations but payments have similar slow throughput to Ethereum, while the max throughput of payments are quite appealing, which is as high as 9909 TPS. The throughput is comparable to the reported statistics from some rollups in industry. But we also have addressed the latency issue. So far, the off-chain throughput of deposits (9307 TPS) and withdrawals (9395 TPS) is already fast enough. Although that of payments (4845 TPS) is around half of the maximum on-chain throughput, we consider it acceptable as our system cannot fully use every block in the blockchain, while we stress that the off-chain throughput still have much room for improvement.

Transaction Fees. We also can estimate the transactions fees given the gas costs. As per May 7 2023, we use the standard gas price 14.3 gwei and use the ETH price 1919.55$, as suggested by [9]. The transaction fees are shown as in Table 1. Since all the operations except payments are expected to be used infrequently, we consider their transaction fees acceptable. For payments, the transaction fees are relatively cheap when the server commit multiple payments at the same time. The average fee is $6.78*10^{-3}$ for 10000 payments and $7.32*10^{-3}$ for 2000 payments, far more cheaper than the transfer cost 0.58$ in Ethereum.

6   Related Work

On-chain Scaling. On-chain scaling methods aim to boost performance by reimagining the blockchain protocol. These strategies include replacing the proof of work mechanism with more efficient consensus protocols [25,29,33] and leveraging parallelism by proposing multiple blocks at the same time [17,35,41]. However, these on-chain scaling solutions often face compatibility issues with pre-existing blockchains. Furthermore, they typically exhibit high latency and limited throughput, or their real-world performance hasn't been fully evaluated and verified. Nonetheless, if a high-performance blockchain were to exist, it would be beneficial to off-chain protocols, which typically rely on the underlying blockchain for security. Off-chain protocols also prove beneficial in distributing the workload of the blockchain.

Off-chain Scaling. Off-chain scaling instead processes transactions outside the blockchain. Existing works are trustless (e.g., [20–22,24,30,32] or trust-based(e.g., [16,18,26,28,34,36,40]). The trust-based solutions need to totally trust the off-chain components, usually a committee, for processing transactions. The committee may be compromised as evidenced by real-world incidents [2,5]. Trustless solutions on the other hand use the blockchain as a trust anchor to verify off-chain operations. However, payment channels [22] and commit chains [24,32] require users to be periodically online to secure their funds and also have high collateral requirement as analyzed in [37]. Rollups [20,24,32] and Ekiden [21] have high transaction latency for committing transactions on the blockchain. While snappy [37] allows fast transaction confirmation by compensating potential loss with collateral, their design does not improve the transaction throughput and the collateral amount scales with the system's transaction volume.

7   Conclusion

We introduce an off-chain payment system characterized by low latency and practical throughput. Uniquely, our system incorporates a hardware-driven solution that permits merchants to securely accept unconfirmed payments without requiring collateral. However, a limitation of our current design is the lack of privacy assurance, as transaction data posted to the blockchain remains in plaintext. Looking forward, we plan to integrate TEE and cryptography to simultaneously achieve off-chain efficiency and on-chain privacy.

Ackowledgement. This work was fully supported by the Research Grants Council of Hong Kong under GRF Grant CityU 11213920, and RIF Grant R1012-21.

References

1. Accepting bitcoin payments. https://www.skynova.com/blog/accepting-bitcoin, Accessed 27 Aug 2022
2. Are blockchain bridges safe? why bridges are targets of hacks. https://www.coindesk.com/learn/are-blockchain-bridges-safe-why-bridges-are-targets-of-hacks/, Accessed 27 Aug 2022
3. Binance. https://pay.binance.com/en, Accessed 27 Aug 2022
4. Bitcoin: a peer-to-peer electronic cash system. https://www.ussc.gov/sites/default/files/pdf/training/annual-national-training-seminar/2018/Emerging_Tech_Bitcoin_Crypto.pdf, Accessed 27 Aug 2022
5. Bitcoin SV suffers a new 51% attack. https://forkast.news/headlines/bitcoin-sv-bsv-suffers-new-51-attack/, Accessed 27 Aug 2022
6. Coinbase. https://commerce.coinbase.com/, Accessed 27 Aug 2022
7. Cryptocurrency payments report: how consumers want to use it to shop and pay. https://www.pymnts.com/wp-content/uploads/2021/05/PYMNTS-Cryptocurrency-Payments-Report-May-2021.pdf, Accessed 27 Aug 2022
8. Cryptocurrency tether is fined $41 million for lying about reserves. https://fortune.com/2021/10/15/tether-crypto-stablecoin-fined-reserves/, Accessed 27 Aug 2022
9. Eth gas station. https://ethgasstation.info, Accessed 27 Aug 2022
10. Mastercard, visa, Paypal suspend Russian operations - no love for Russia? https://bitcoinist.com/mastercard-visa-paypal-suspend-russian-operations/, Accessed 27 Aug 2022
11. Paying with cryptocurrency: What consumers and merchants expect from digital currencies. https://www.pymnts.com/study/paying-with-cryptocurrency-shopping-consumer-finance-digital-wallets/, Accessed 27 Aug 2022
12. Paypal. https://www.paypal.com/us/digital-wallet/manage-money/crypto, Accessed 27 Aug 2022
13. Starbucks now accepts bitcoin as payment (kind of...). https://www.foodandwine.com/news/starbucks-bitcoin-frequent-flyer-miles-payment-gift-cards, Accessed 27 Aug 2022
14. Tech embattled crypto lender celsius files for bankruptcy protection. https://www.cnbc.com/2022/07/19/what-happens-to-my-funds-if-a-crypto-exchange-goes-bankrupt.html, accessed 27 Aug 2022
15. Visa. https://www.visa.com.hk/content/VISA/usa/englishlanguagemaster/en_US/home/solutions/crypto.html, Accessed 27 Aug 2022
16. Avarikioti, Z., Kokoris-Kogias, E., Wattenhofer, R., Zindros, D.: Brick: asynchronous incentive-compatible payment channels. In: Proceedings of FC (2021)
17. Bagaria, V.K., Kannan, S., Tse, D., Fanti, G.C., Viswanath, P.: Prism: deconstructing the blockchain to approach physical limits. In: Proceedings of ACM CCS (2019)
18. Baudet, M., Danezis, G., Sonnino, A.: Fastpay: high-performance byzantine fault tolerant settlement. In: Proceedings of ACM AFT (2020)
19. Bentov, I., Ji, Y., Zhang, F., Breidenbach, L., Daian, P., Juels, A.: Tesseract: real-time cryptocurrency exchange using trusted hardware. In: Proceedings of ACM CCS (2019)
20. Buterin, V.: On-chain scaling to potentially 500 tx/sec through mass tx validation. https://ethresear.ch/t/on-chain-scalingto-potentially-500-tx-sec-through-mass-tx-validation/3477, Accessed 27 Aug 2022

21. Cheng, R., et al.: Ekiden: a platform for confidentiality-preserving, trustworthy, and performant smart contracts. In: Proceedings of EuroS&P (2019)
22. Decker, C., Wattenhofer, R.: A fast and scalable payment network with bitcoin duplex micropayment channels. In: Proceedings of SSS (2015)
23. Dziembowski, S., Fabiański, G., Faust, S., Riahi, S.: Lower bounds for off-chain protocols: exploring the limits of plasma. In: Proceedings of ITCS (2021)
24. Erwig, A., Faust, S., Riahi, S., Stöckert, T.: Commitee: an efficient and secure commit-chain protocol using tees. Cryptology ePrint Archive (2020)
25. Eyal, I., Gencer, A.E., Sirer, E.G., van Renesse, R.: Bitcoin-ng: a scalable blockchain protocol. In: Proceedings of NSDI (2016)
26. Gai, F., Niu, J., Tabatabaee, S.A., Feng, C., Jalalzai, M.: Cumulus: a secure BFT-based sidechain for off-chain scaling. In: Proceedings of IWQoS (2021)
27. Garay, J., Kiayias, A., Leonardos, N.: The bitcoin backbone protocol: analysis and applications. In: Proceedings of Eurocrypt (2015)
28. Gaži, P., Kiayias, A., Zindros, D.: Proof-of-stake sidechains. In: Proceedings of S&P (2019)
29. Gilad, Y., Hemo, R., Micali, S., Vlachos, G., Zeldovich, N.: Algorand: scaling byzantine agreements for cryptocurrencies. In: Proceedings of SOSP (2017)
30. Kalodner, H., Goldfeder, S., Chen, X., Weinberg, S.M., Felten, E.W.: Arbitrum: scalable, private smart contracts. In: Proceedings of USENIX Security (2018)
31. Kaptchuk, G., Green, M., Miers, I.: Giving state to the stateless: augmenting trustworthy computation with ledgers. In: Proceedings of NDSS (2019)
32. Khalil, R., Zamyatin, A., Felley, G., Moreno-Sanchez, P., Gervais, A.: Commit-chains: secure, scalable off-chain payments. Cryptology ePrint Archive (2018)
33. Kiayias, A., Russell, A., David, B., Oliynykov, R.: Ouroboros: a provably secure proof-of-stake blockchain protocol. In: Proceedings of CRYPTO (2017)
34. Kiayias, A., Zindros, D.: Proof-of-work sidechains. In: Proceedings of FC (2019)
35. Li, C., et al.: A decentralized blockchain with high throughput and fast confirmation. In: Proceedings of ATC (2020)
36. Lind, J., Naor, O., Eyal, I., Kelbert, F., Sirer, E.G., Pietzuch, P.: Teechain: a secure payment network with asynchronous blockchain access. In: Proceedings of SOSP (2019)
37. Mavroudis, V., Wüst, K., Dhar, A., Kostiainen, K., Capkun, S.: Snappy: fast on-chain payments with practical collaterals. In: Proceedings of NDSS (2020)
38. Pass, R., Shi, E., Tramer, F.: Formal abstractions for attested execution secure processors. In: Proceedings of Eurocrypt (2017)
39. Poon, J., Dryja, T.: The bitcoin lightning network: scalable off-chain instant payments (2016). https://lightning.network/lightning-network-paper.pdf
40. Wüst, K., Matetic, S., Egli, S., Kostiainen, K., Capkun, S.: Ace: asynchronous and concurrent execution of complex smart contracts. In: Proceedings of CCS (2020)
41. Zamani, M., Movahedi, M., Raykova, M.: Rapidchain: scaling blockchain via full sharding. In: Proceedings of CCS (2018)

Emerging Applications

A Survey on Edge Intelligence for Music Composition: Principles, Applications, and Privacy Implications

Qinyuan Wang[1], Youyang Qu[2,3](✉), Siyu Nan[4], Wantong Jiang[5], Bruce Gu[2,3], and Shujun Gu[1,2,3,4](✉)

[1] Sydney Conservatorium of Music, University of Sydney, Camperdown, Australia
[2] Key Laboratory of Computing Power Network and Information Security, Ministry of Education, Shandong Computer Science Center, Qilu University of Technology (Shandong Academy of Sciences), Jinan, China
{quyy,gusj}@sdas.org
[3] Shandong Provincial Key Laboratory of Computer Networks, Shandong Fundamental Research Center for Computer Science, Jinan, China
[4] Central Conservatory of Music, Beijing, China
[5] Chinese Conservatory of Music, Beijing, China

Abstract. The field of music composition has seen significant advancements with the introduction of artificial intelligence (AI) techniques. However, traditional cloud-based approaches suffer from limitations such as latency and network dependency. This survey paper explores the emerging concept of edge intelligence and its application in music composition. Edge intelligence leverages local computational resources to enable real-time and on-device music generation, enhancing the creative process and expanding accessibility. By examining various aspects of music composition, including melody creation, harmonization, rhythm generation, arrangement and orchestration, and lyric writing, this paper showcases the potential benefits of incorporating edge intelligence. It also discusses the challenges and limitations associated with this paradigm, such as limited computational resources and privacy concerns. Through a review of existing AI-based music composition tools and platforms, examples of edge intelligence in action are highlighted. The survey paper concludes by emphasizing the transformative potential of edge intelligence in revolutionizing the field of music composition and identifies future research opportunities to further advance this promising domain.

Keywords: Edge Intelligence · Music Composition · Artificial Intelligence · Large Machine Learning Models

1 Introduction

Music composition is a creative process that has evolved over centuries, but recent advancements in technology, particularly in the field of artificial intel-

J. Liu et al. (Eds.): TridentCom 2023, LNICST 523, pp. 41–74, 2024.
https://doi.org/10.1007/978-3-031-51399-2_3

ligence (AI), have opened up new possibilities for composers [21,22,51]. AI-based approaches have demonstrated their ability to generate melodies, harmonies, rhythms, and even lyrics, transforming the landscape of music composition [11,16]. However, traditional cloud-based approaches that rely on centralized computing infrastructures suffer from limitations such as latency, network dependency, and privacy concerns.

In response to these limitations, a new paradigm known as edge intelligence has emerged. Edge intelligence leverages local computational resources, such as smartphones, tablets, and Internet of Things (IoT) devices, to perform data processing and analysis at the network edge [54,55]. This shift from cloud-based processing to on-device computation offers several advantages for music composition [43]. By harnessing the power of edge intelligence, real-time and on-device music generation becomes possible, enabling composers to have immediate access to creative tools and eliminating the need for constant network connectivity [20].

This survey paper aims to explore the concept of edge intelligence in the context of music composition. By leveraging edge computing resources, composers can experience enhanced creative capabilities, personalized music composition experiences, and reduced latency. This paper will examine the potential applications of edge intelligence in various aspects of music composition, including melody creation, harmonization, rhythm generation, arrangement and orchestration, and lyric writing. Furthermore, it will address the challenges and limitations associated with incorporating edge intelligence in music composition systems, such as limited computational resources and privacy concerns.

Through a review of existing AI-based music composition tools and platforms, this survey paper will showcase examples that utilize edge intelligence in their design and implementation. By highlighting the features, capabilities, and user experiences of these tools, we aim to provide insights into the transformative potential of edge intelligence for composers and the music industry as a whole.

The main contributions of this paper are as follows.

- This survey paper sets out to present an overview of edge intelligence for music composition, emphasizing the advantages it brings to the creative process.
- By harnessing the power of edge computing, composers can unlock new opportunities for real-time music generation, personalized composition experiences, and reduced reliance on cloud-based infrastructure.
- In addition, this paper delves into specific applications, challenges, and future research directions in the field of edge intelligence for music composition.

To provide a comprehensive exploration of edge intelligence for music composition, this survey paper is organized as follows. The background and related work section will provide an overview of traditional music composition techniques, the emergence of AI in music composition, and a review of existing literature on AI-based music composition. This will set the foundation for understanding the significance of edge intelligence in the field. The subsequent section will delve into the concept of edge intelligence in music composition, discussing its advantages, capabilities, and potential for real-time and on-device music generation. Following that, the paper will explore various applications of edge intelligence in music composition, focusing on melody creation, harmonization, rhythm generation, arrangement and orchestration, and lyric writing. The challenges and limitations section will address the potential hurdles, such as limited computational resources and privacy concerns, associated with incorporating edge intelligence. The paper will then review existing AI-based music composition tools and platforms that utilize edge intelligence, highlighting their features, capabilities, and user experiences. Finally, the paper will conclude by summarizing the key findings, emphasizing the transformative potential of edge intelligence in music composition, and identifying future research opportunities in this promising domain.

2   Background and Related Work

In this section, we present background and related work considering the development of advanced technologies, including AI, for music composition.

2.1   Traditional Music Composition Techniques and Challenges

Traditional music composition has long relied on the expertise and creativity of human composers. Throughout history, composers have used various techniques to craft melodies, harmonies, rhythms, and arrangements, drawing inspiration from musical theory, cultural influences, and personal expression [17]. The process typically involves manual composition using musical instruments, notation systems, and extensive knowledge of music theory [26]. While traditional composition techniques have yielded remarkable musical works, they are time-consuming and require significant expertise [17]. As technology has advanced, there has been a growing interest in leveraging artificial intelligence (AI) to augment and automate aspects of the composition process, leading to the emergence of AI-based music composition [13,15,19].

Early AI-based music composition systems focused on rule-based approaches, where predefined sets of rules and heuristics were used to generate musical sequences [15]. However, these systems often struggled to capture the intricacies and nuances of human compositions [7]. The introduction of machine learning techniques, particularly deep learning models such as recurrent neural networks (RNNs) [13,27,29] and generative adversarial networks (GANs) [9,38,52], revolutionized the field of AI-based music composition. These models have shown promise in generating realistic and expressive musical sequences by learning patterns from vast amounts of musical data [21]. With the help of AI, composers gained access to powerful tools that could aid in the creative process and inspire new musical ideas.

The use of AI in music composition has seen rapid progress in recent years, with researchers and developers exploring various approaches and methodologies. Some focus on generating melodies, while others aim to harmonize melodies [16], generate rhythms [35], or create complex arrangements [10]. These AI-based composition systems can serve as valuable tools for composers, providing inspiration, generating alternative musical ideas, and augmenting their creative capabilities [12]. However, the reliance on cloud-based infrastructure for computation and data storage has introduced certain limitations, such as latency and privacy concerns [42]. To overcome these limitations, the concept of edge intelligence has gained attention in the field of music composition, opening up new possibilities for real-time, on-device composition experiences.

2.2 Discuss the Emergence of Artificial Intelligence (AI) in Music Composition

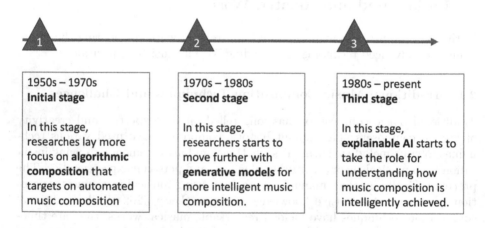

Fig. 1. History of AI for Music Composition

The emergence of artificial intelligence (AI) has brought significant advancements to the field of music composition. AI techniques, such as machine learning and deep learning, have opened up new possibilities for generating musical compositions that exhibit creativity [36], stylistic coherence [32], and emotional expressiveness [31] (Fig. 1).

One of the early breakthroughs in AI-based music composition was the development of rule-based systems. These systems utilized predefined sets of musical rules and heuristics to generate compositions [18]. While these approaches showed promise, they often lacked the ability to capture the complexities and subtleties of human musical expression.

With the rise of machine learning, specifically deep learning models, AI-based music composition took a significant leap forward. Recurrent Neural Networks (RNNs) and Long Short-Term Memory (LSTM) networks revolutionized the field by enabling the modeling of long-term dependencies and capturing the temporal structure of music [19]. These models have proven adept at learning patterns and styles from large datasets of existing music, allowing them to generate original compositions that align with specific genres, artists, or musical eras.

In addition to RNNs and LSTM networks, Generative Adversarial Networks (GANs) have also made their mark in AI-based music composition. GANs involve the training of two neural networks: a generator network that produces music and a discriminator network that evaluates the quality of the generated music [47]. Through an iterative process, GANs can generate music that exhibits realistic musical characteristics by learning from the interplay between the generator and discriminator networks.

AI-based music composition techniques have not only focused on generating melodies but have also expanded to harmonization, rhythm generation, and arrangement. By incorporating AI models into these aspects of music composition, composers have gained access to powerful tools that can inspire new musical ideas, provide alternative harmonizations, generate diverse rhythmic patterns, and suggest orchestration choices.

The emergence of AI in music composition has fueled creative exploration and pushed the boundaries of musical expression. Composers, musicians, and researchers alike continue to delve into the possibilities offered by AI, harnessing its capabilities to augment the creative process and generate music that captivates audiences. However, to further enhance the potential of AI in music composition, the limitations of cloud-based approaches, such as latency and privacy concerns [33], have led to the exploration of edge intelligence as an alternative paradigm (Fig. 2).

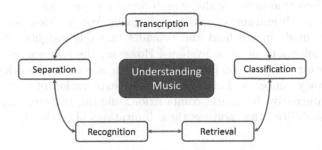

Fig. 2. The Way How AI Understands Music

2.3 Review Existing Literature on AI-Based Music Composition Techniques

The exploration of AI-based music composition has garnered significant attention from researchers, musicians, and technology enthusiasts. A wealth of literature exists that examines the application of AI techniques in various aspects of music composition. These studies encompass a wide range of methodologies and approaches, showcasing the versatility of AI in the creative domain.

Some researchers have focused on melody generation, utilizing neural networks and probabilistic models to generate melodic sequences that exhibit musical coherence and stylistic fidelity. These models have shown the ability to capture melodic patterns from large datasets and generate melodies that align with specific genres or composers' styles [53]. Additionally, researchers have explored the use of reinforcement learning algorithms to improve the quality of generated melodies by iteratively learning from human feedback.

Harmonization, the process of creating accompanying harmonies for a given melody, has also been a subject of interest. AI-based harmonization systems leverage techniques such as chord progression modeling, harmonic analysis, and machine learning algorithms to generate harmonies that complement the melodic line [28]. These systems provide composers with alternative harmonizations, enabling them to explore different musical possibilities and experiment with various chord progressions.

Rhythm generation is another area where AI has shown promise. By training models on vast collections of rhythmic patterns, researchers have developed algorithms that can generate diverse and compelling rhythmic sequences [53]. These models can capture the complexities of rhythm, including syncopation, accents, and variations, and produce rhythmically rich compositions that align with specific musical styles or preferences.

Furthermore, AI-based approaches have been applied to arrangement and orchestration, where the goal is to transform a basic musical sketch into a fully orchestrated composition [57]. By learning from existing musical scores and orchestration techniques, AI models can suggest instrumentations, dynamics, and articulations that enhance the overall musical experience.

The existing literature on AI-based music composition showcases the advancements made in the field and provides valuable insights into the capabilities and limitations of these systems. However, the reliance on cloud-based infrastructure for computation introduces challenges such as network latency and potential privacy concerns. This motivates the exploration of edge intelligence as a viable alternative for music composition, offering real-time and on-device processing capabilities that address these limitations [34] (Fig. 3).

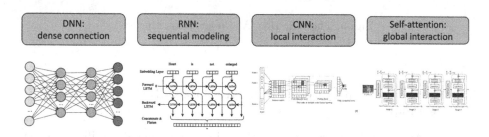

Fig. 3. Example of AI Composition

2.4   Highlight the Limitations of Cloud-Based Approaches and the Need for Edge Intelligence

While cloud-based approaches have played a significant role in the advancement of AI-based music composition, they are not without limitations. The reliance on centralized cloud servers for computation and data storage introduces challenges that can impact the overall music composition experience [57].

One of the primary limitations is latency, which refers to the delay in communication between the user's device and the cloud server [24]. Real-time music generation often requires immediate feedback and interaction, which can be hindered by the inherent latency associated with cloud-based approaches. The delay introduced by network transmission can disrupt the creative flow and responsiveness of the composition process, leading to a less intuitive and dynamic user experience.

Moreover, cloud-based approaches heavily depend on continuous network connectivity [23]. This dependency poses challenges in scenarios where internet connectivity is unstable or unavailable. Composers may find themselves limited in their ability to access the composition tools and resources, hindering their creative process and autonomy.

Another concern relates to privacy and data security [48]. Cloud-based approaches involve uploading and processing music data on remote servers, which may raise privacy concerns for composers. The storage and handling of sensitive musical compositions and personal information on external servers can be a barrier for those who prioritize data privacy and security.

Recognizing these limitations, there is a growing need for edge intelligence in the field of music composition. Edge intelligence leverages local computational resources on devices such as smartphones, tablets, or IoT devices to perform data processing and analysis at the network edge [6,40,49]. By shifting the computation closer to the user, edge intelligence can address the latency issue, providing real-time and on-device music generation capabilities that align with the immediate needs and preferences of composers.

Furthermore, edge intelligence can enhance privacy and data security by enabling composers to retain control over their music compositions. Since the data processing occurs locally on the composer's device, sensitive musical data can be kept within their immediate control, reducing the reliance on external servers and mitigating privacy concerns.

In summary, the limitations of cloud-based approaches, such as latency, network dependency, and privacy concerns, have highlighted the need for edge intelligence in the context of music composition [49]. The utilization of local computational resources can provide real-time, on-device processing, ensuring a more responsive, seamless, and private music composition experience for composers.

3   Edge Intelligence in Music Composition

The field of music composition has experienced a transformation with the emergence of edge intelligence. Edge intelligence refers to the utilization of local computational resources, such as smartphones, tablets, and Internet of Things (IoT) devices, to perform data processing and analysis at the network edge [30]. This paradigm shift from relying solely on centralized cloud servers to leveraging on-device computation opens up new possibilities for real-time and on-device music generation, enhancing the creative process and expanding accessibility for composers [40].

Traditional cloud-based approaches for music composition often introduce latency due to the communication delay between the user's device and the remote server [37]. This latency can disrupt the real-time interaction and responsiveness required in music composition, impacting the composer's ability to explore ideas and make instantaneous adjustments. Additionally, cloud-based systems are dependent on continuous network connectivity, limiting the accessibility of music composition tools and resources in environments with limited or unstable internet access [45].

By contrast, edge intelligence enables composers to perform music composition tasks locally on their devices, reducing the latency associated with cloud-based approaches. Real-time feedback and on-device processing empower composers to experiment and iterate with musical ideas without the delays introduced by network transmission. The local computational resources also provide more autonomy and flexibility in the music composition process, ensuring that composers can work seamlessly even in environments with limited or intermittent internet connectivity.

Furthermore, edge intelligence offers potential benefits in terms of privacy and data security [56]. With cloud-based approaches, composers often need to upload and process their musical compositions on external servers, raising concerns about data privacy and control. By leveraging edge intelligence, composers can keep sensitive musical data on their own devices, retaining greater control over their compositions and alleviating privacy concerns associated with cloud-based systems.

In summary, the shift from cloud-based approaches to edge intelligence in music composition addresses the limitations of latency, network dependency, and privacy concerns. By leveraging local computational resources, edge intelligence enables real-time and on-device music generation, empowers composers with greater autonomy, and enhances the privacy and security of their musical compositions. The subsequent sections will delve into the specific applications, challenges, and potential future developments in the field of edge intelligence for music composition (Fig. 4).

3.1 Define the Concept of Edge Intelligence in the Context of Music Composition

Edge intelligence, in the context of music composition, refers to the utilization of local computational resources on devices such as smartphones, tablets, or IoT devices to perform data processing and analysis at the network edge. Unlike traditional cloud-based approaches that rely on centralized servers, edge intelli-

AI based Music Composition	
Area	**Subareas**
Soft computing based music composition methods	• Heuristic Composition Methods • Deep Learning Composition • Stochastic Composition Methods
Symbolic AI based music composition methods	• Agent Composition Methods • Declarative Programming Composition Methods • Grammar Composition Methods

Fig. 4. Classification of AI for Music Composition

gence brings the computation closer to the user, enabling real-time and on-device music generation.

In edge intelligence for music composition, the devices used by composers become active participants in the creative process [50]. Compositional algorithms and models are deployed directly on the devices, leveraging their processing power and storage capabilities. This allows composers to generate music, experiment with different compositional elements, and receive immediate feedback without the need for constant network connectivity.

The core principle of edge intelligence is to overcome the limitations of cloud-based approaches, such as latency and network dependency, by reducing the distance between the composer and the computational resources. By processing data locally on the devices, edge intelligence ensures a more responsive and interactive music composition experience, fostering creativity, exploration, and improvisation in real-time.

Moreover, edge intelligence offers the potential for personalized music composition experiences. Composers can have greater control over their creative process by customizing the algorithms and models running on their devices, tailoring the music generation to their specific preferences, styles, or project requirements. This personalization aspect enables composers to develop unique and distinctive musical compositions that align with their artistic vision.

In summary, edge intelligence in the context of music composition brings computation and data processing closer to the composer, leveraging local computational resources on devices. It enables real-time and on-device music generation, reduces latency and network dependency, fosters creativity and improvisation, and allows for personalized composition experiences. By harnessing the power of edge intelligence, composers can have more control and flexibility in their music composition process, leading to enhanced creativity and the potential for groundbreaking musical expressions.

3.2   Explain the Advantages and Capabilities of Edge Computing for Music Composition

Edge computing offers several advantages and capabilities that are highly beneficial in the field of music composition. By leveraging local computational resources on devices, edge computing enables real-time and on-device music generation, fostering a more seamless and responsive creative process.

One key advantage of edge computing is reduced latency. With edge intelligence, composers can generate music and receive immediate feedback without the delay introduced by network transmission to remote servers. The near-instantaneous response allows for more dynamic and interactive composition experiences, empowering composers to explore ideas, experiment with different musical elements, and make spontaneous adjustments in real time.

Another capability of edge computing is the ability to operate in environments with limited or intermittent internet connectivity. Cloud-based approaches often require continuous network connectivity for data processing and retrieval, which can be problematic in situations where internet access is unreliable or unavailable. Edge computing overcomes this limitation by leveraging on-device resources, enabling composers to continue working on their compositions even in offline or low-connectivity scenarios.

Edge computing also enhances the privacy and security of music compositions [39]. Cloud-based approaches often involve uploading and processing sensitive musical data on remote servers, which raises concerns about data privacy and control. With edge intelligence, the musical data stays within the composer's device, reducing the exposure to external servers and providing composers with greater control over their compositions.

Additionally, edge computing allows for personalized music composition experiences [46]. Composers can customize the algorithms, models, and parameters running on their devices to align with their artistic preferences, styles, or project requirements. This personalization aspect enables composers to develop unique musical compositions that reflect their individuality and creative vision.

Furthermore, the on-device processing capabilities of edge computing enable composers to work independently of cloud-based infrastructure, providing a level of autonomy and flexibility. Composers can generate music on the go, without the need for constant network connectivity or reliance on external servers. This freedom allows for spontaneous creativity, capturing musical ideas in the moment, and embracing the unique inspirations that arise from different environments.

In summary, edge computing offers advantages and capabilities that greatly enhance the music composition process. Real-time and on-device music generation, reduced latency, offline capabilities, enhanced privacy and security, personalized composition experiences, and increased autonomy are some of the key benefits that edge computing brings to music composition. By leveraging these capabilities, composers can have more seamless, responsive, and personalized experiences in their creative endeavors.

3.3   Discuss the Potential of Real-Time and On-Device Music Generation Using Edge Intelligence

Real-time and on-device music generation is one of the significant potentials unlocked by edge intelligence in music composition. By leveraging local computational resources on devices, composers can experience immediate and interactive music generation without relying on cloud-based infrastructure.

Real-time music generation using edge intelligence enables composers to explore musical ideas and receive instantaneous feedback. The reduced latency allows for a more dynamic and responsive creative process, fostering a sense of flow and exploration. Composers can iterate and experiment with different musical elements, such as melodies, harmonies, rhythms, and arrangements, in real time, making immediate adjustments to achieve the desired musical expression.

Furthermore, on-device music generation eliminates the dependency on continuous network connectivity. Composers can generate music even in environments with limited or intermittent internet access, such as during travel or in remote locations. This opens up opportunities for creative expression in various settings and empowers composers to work independently, free from the constraints of network availability.

The potential of real-time and on-device music generation extends beyond individual composers. It also enables collaborative music composition experiences. Composers can gather in the same physical space, each equipped with their own edge intelligence-enabled devices, and engage in real-time composition sessions. This fosters a dynamic and interactive creative environment, allowing for instant sharing of musical ideas, improvisation, and collective decision-making.

Additionally, real-time and on-device music generation using edge intelligence can enhance live performances and improvisation. Composers and musicians can use edge intelligence-enabled devices to generate musical elements in real time, creating unique compositions during live concerts or jam sessions. This adds a layer of spontaneity and innovation to performances, enabling new forms of musical expression and interaction with audiences.

In summary, real-time and on-device music generation using edge intelligence presents a wealth of opportunities for composers and musicians. It enables immediate feedback, interactive exploration of musical ideas, and real-time adjustments. The independence from continuous network connectivity expands creative possibilities in various environments, while fostering collaboration and enhancing live performances. By leveraging edge intelligence, composers can experience a new level of dynamism, creativity, and responsiveness in their music composition endeavors.

3.4   Explore the Possibilities of Enhancing the Creative Process and Expanding Accessibility

Edge intelligence in music composition holds immense potential for enhancing the creative process and expanding accessibility, revolutionizing the way composers engage with their craft and enabling new avenues of musical expression [8].

One of the primary possibilities is the augmentation of the creative capabilities of composers. Edge intelligence provides composers with powerful tools for generating musical ideas, exploring different compositional elements, and experimenting with various styles and genres. By leveraging on-device computation, composers can have immediate access to real-time music generation, enabling them to capture inspiration as it strikes and nurturing a continuous flow of creativity. This augmentation of the creative process can lead to the development of innovative musical compositions that push the boundaries of traditional practices.

Furthermore, edge intelligence enhances accessibility by reducing barriers to entry in music composition. Cloud-based approaches often require continuous network connectivity and specialized software, limiting access for those with limited resources or internet access. With edge intelligence, the processing and generation of music compositions occur directly on the composer's device, eliminating the need for constant internet connectivity and reducing the reliance on expensive software licenses. This empowers a wider range of individuals, regardless of their geographic location or economic circumstances, to engage in music composition and pursue their artistic aspirations.

The potential for personalization is another aspect that edge intelligence brings to the forefront. Composers can tailor the algorithms, models, and parameters running on their devices to match their unique preferences, styles, and project requirements. This personalization allows composers to create music that aligns with their artistic vision, enabling the development of distinct musical identities and fostering individuality in composition. The ability to customize the composition tools to suit individual needs expands the range of possibilities and encourages diverse forms of musical expression.

Additionally, edge intelligence has the potential to foster collaboration and collective creativity. Composers can leverage edge intelligence-enabled devices to facilitate real-time composition sessions, enabling multiple composers to work together synchronously. This opens up avenues for collaborative composition, where ideas can be shared, merged, and expanded upon in real time, fostering collective innovation and the creation of unique compositions that blend the perspectives of multiple artists.

In summary, edge intelligence in music composition has the potential to enhance the creative process and expand accessibility. It empowers composers with augmented creative capabilities, reduces barriers to entry, encourages personalization, and fosters collaborative and collective creativity. By embracing edge intelligence, composers can unlock new possibilities, push the boundaries of musical expression, and create compositions that resonate with their artistic vision and the wider audience.

4   Applications of Edge Intelligence in Music Composition

The applications of edge intelligence in music composition are diverse and transformative, opening up new avenues for composers to explore and innovate. By leveraging local computational resources on devices, edge intelligence enables real-time and on-device music generation, enhancing the creative process and expanding the possibilities of musical expression (Table 1).

Table 1. Applications of Edge Intelligence in Music Composition

Application	Description
Melody Creation	Real-time and on-device generation of melodic sequences
Harmonization	Automated chord progression and harmonization suggestions
Rhythm Generation	Real-time generation of rhythmic patterns and variations
Arrangement	Assistance in orchestrating and arranging musical compositions
Lyric Writing	On-device generation of lyrics based on themes and moods

Traditionally, music composition involves various aspects such as melody creation, harmonization, rhythm generation, arrangement and orchestration, and lyric writing [44]. Each of these aspects plays a crucial role in crafting a compelling musical composition. With the advent of edge intelligence, these areas of music composition can be augmented and enriched, offering composers new tools and capabilities to enhance their creative output.

The application of edge intelligence in melody creation enables composers to generate melodic sequences in real time, providing a constant stream of musical ideas that can be shaped and refined. By leveraging local computational resources, edge intelligence models can capture stylistic patterns and generate melodies that align with specific genres or composers' styles, expanding the possibilities for melodic exploration.

Harmonization, the process of creating accompanying harmonies for a given melody, is another area that can benefit from edge intelligence. Composers can leverage on-device processing to generate harmonies that complement the melodic line, exploring different chord progressions and harmonic possibilities in real time. This opens up new avenues for composers to experiment with harmonizations that enhance the overall musical expression and emotional impact of their compositions.

Rhythm generation is yet another area where edge intelligence can provide valuable assistance. By leveraging local computational resources, composers can generate diverse and dynamic rhythmic patterns in real time. This capability enables composers to experiment with different rhythmic styles, syncopations, and variations, enhancing the rhythmic complexity and richness of their compositions.

Arrangement and orchestration, the processes of transforming a basic musical sketch into a fully orchestrated composition, can also benefit from edge intelligence. Composers can leverage on-device processing to explore different instrumentations, dynamics, and articulations, receiving immediate feedback on how these choices affect the overall composition. This allows composers to make informed decisions and create intricate, expressive, and well-balanced orchestrations.

Furthermore, edge intelligence can be utilized in the context of lyric writing. Composers can leverage on-device language processing capabilities to generate or suggest lyrics that align with the mood, theme, or style of the musical composition. This provides valuable assistance and inspiration for composers, helping them to craft meaningful and evocative lyrics that resonate with the musical context.

In summary, the applications of edge intelligence in music composition encompass various aspects such as melody creation, harmonization, rhythm generation, arrangement and orchestration, and lyric writing. By leveraging local computational resources, composers can experience real-time and on-device processing, enabling them to explore, refine, and shape different musical elements with immediate feedback. The subsequent sections will delve into each of these application areas, exploring the potential and implications of edge intelligence in enhancing the creative process of music composition.

4.1   Explore Various Aspects of Music Composition that Can Benefit from Edge Intelligence

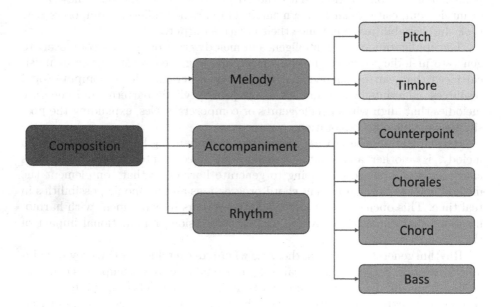

Fig. 5. Music Composition Workflow

Edge intelligence brings a wealth of opportunities to various aspects of music composition, revolutionizing the creative process and empowering composers with new tools and capabilities. By leveraging local computational resources on devices, edge intelligence enhances real-time and on-device music generation, transforming the following aspects of music composition [57] (Fig. 5).

a. Melody Creation: Melodies serve as the foundation of musical compositions, and edge intelligence can greatly assist in their generation. Composers can leverage on-device processing to explore different melodic patterns, variations, and transformations in real time. Edge intelligence models can learn from vast musical datasets to generate melodies that align with specific genres, styles, or composers' preferences, providing a constant stream of melodic ideas for composers to shape and refine.

b. Harmonization: Harmonization is the process of creating accompanying harmonies for a given melody. Edge intelligence offers valuable assistance in exploring harmonization possibilities in real time. Composers can leverage on-device computation to generate harmonies that complement the melodic line, experiment with chord progressions, and instantly assess the harmonic impact on the overall composition. This capability enables composers to create harmonizations that enhance the emotional impact and musical expression of their compositions.

c. Rhythm Generation: Rhythmic patterns play a vital role in music composition, and edge intelligence can enhance the rhythmic exploration process. By leveraging local computational resources, composers can generate diverse and dynamic rhythmic patterns in real time. Edge intelligence models can capture rhythmic intricacies and variations from extensive music databases, allowing composers to experiment with different rhythmic styles, syncopations, and accents. This opens up new creative possibilities and adds depth and complexity to compositions.

d. Arrangement and Orchestration: The process of transforming a musical sketch into a fully orchestrated composition can be enriched by edge intelligence. Composers can leverage on-device processing to explore different instrumentations, dynamics, and articulations, receiving immediate feedback on the impact of these choices. Edge intelligence assists composers in making informed decisions regarding the placement of musical elements, resulting in intricate, expressive, and well-balanced orchestrations that enhance the overall musical experience.

e. Lyric Writing: Edge intelligence can also play a role in the realm of lyric writing. By harnessing on-device language processing capabilities, composers can generate or receive suggestions for lyrics that align with the musical composition's theme, style, or mood. This assistance provides composers with valuable inspiration and guidance, helping them to craft meaningful and evocative lyrics that resonate with the musical context.

In summary, edge intelligence brings transformative possibilities to various aspects of music composition. By leveraging local computational resources, composers can experience real-time and on-device processing, enabling exploration, refinement, and shaping of melodies, harmonies, rhythms, arrangements, orchestration choices, and lyric writing. The utilization of edge intelligence expands creative horizons, fostering innovation and pushing the boundaries of musical expression in the composition process.

4.2 Discuss the Potential of Edge Intelligence in Melody Creation, Harmonization, Rhythm Generation, Arrangement and Orchestration, and Lyric Writing

Edge intelligence presents immense potential in transforming various aspects of music composition, revolutionizing the creative process, and providing composers with new tools and capabilities. Let's explore the potential of edge intelligence in melody creation, harmonization, rhythm generation, arrangement and orchestration, and lyric writing.

a. Melody Creation: Edge intelligence can greatly assist in melody creation by providing composers with real-time and on-device music generation capabilities. By leveraging local computational resources, composers can explore a multitude of melodic patterns, variations, and transformations in real time. Edge intelligence models can learn from vast musical datasets, allowing composers to generate melodies that align with specific genres, styles, or composers' preferences. This empowers composers with a continuous stream of melodic ideas that can be shaped and refined to create unique and expressive musical compositions.

b. Harmonization: Harmonization is an essential aspect of music composition, and edge intelligence can greatly enhance this process. Composers can leverage on-device processing to explore various harmonization possibilities in real time. Edge intelligence assists in generating harmonies that complement the melodic line, allowing composers to experiment with chord progressions and instantly assess their harmonic impact. By providing immediate feedback and alternatives, edge intelligence enables composers to create harmonizations that enhance the overall musical expression and emotional depth of their compositions.

c. Rhythm Generation: Edge intelligence brings exciting possibilities to rhythm generation, allowing composers to explore diverse and dynamic rhythmic patterns. By leveraging local computational resources, composers can generate intricate and compelling rhythms in real time. Edge intelligence models can capture rhythmic complexities and variations from vast music databases, enabling composers to experiment with different rhythmic styles, syncopations, and accents. This empowers composers to create rhythmically rich compositions that captivate listeners and add depth and texture to their musical creations.

d. Arrangement and Orchestration: Edge intelligence offers significant potential in the realm of arrangement and orchestration, enabling composers to transform their musical sketches into fully orchestrated compositions. Composers can leverage on-device processing to explore different instrumentations, dynamics, and articulations, receiving immediate feedback on their choices. Edge intelligence assists composers in making informed decisions about the placement of musical elements, leading to intricate, expressive, and well-balanced orchestrations. This capability empowers composers to create compositions that evoke specific emotions and create captivating musical experiences.

e. Lyric Writing: Edge intelligence can also play a role in enhancing the process of lyric writing. By harnessing on-device language processing capabilities, composers can generate or receive suggestions for lyrics that align with the theme, style, or mood of the musical composition. Edge intelligence provides valuable assistance and inspiration, helping composers craft meaningful and evocative lyrics that resonate with the musical context. This capability enables composers to create compositions where the lyrics harmoniously complement the melodic and harmonic elements, enhancing the overall impact of the musical piece.

In summary, edge intelligence holds tremendous potential in melody creation, harmonization, rhythm generation, arrangement and orchestration, and lyric writing. By leveraging local computational resources, composers can experience real-time and on-device processing, leading to innovative and expressive musical compositions. The utilization of edge intelligence in these areas of music composition expands creative horizons, enables experimentation, and provides composers with valuable tools to shape their musical ideas into unique and captivating compositions.

4.3   Provide Examples and Case Studies Showcasing the Application of Edge Intelligence in These Areas

The application of edge intelligence in music composition has already begun to yield exciting results, showcasing its potential in melody creation, harmonization, rhythm generation, arrangement and orchestration, and lyric writing. Here are some examples and case studies that highlight the practical application of edge intelligence in these areas:

a. Melody Creation: - Composer's Assistant [25]: An edge intelligence-powered composition tool that provides real-time melodic suggestions based on the composer's input. It leverages on-device processing to generate melodies that align with specific styles or genres, helping composers overcome creative blocks and explore new melodic possibilities.
b. Harmonization: - Harmony Composer [41]: An edge intelligence-based system that assists composers in harmonization by generating accompanying chord progressions in real time. Composers can input their melodies, and the system generates harmonies that complement the melodic line, offering alternative harmonization choices for composers to experiment with.
c. Rhythm Generation: - Rhythm Innovator: An edge intelligence-driven tool that generates intricate and dynamic rhythmic patterns in real time. Composers can interact with the system, exploring different rhythmic styles, syncopations, and variations to create engaging and rhythmically rich compositions.
d. Arrangement and Orchestration: - Orchestral Maestro [14]: An edge intelligence-powered software that assists composers in orchestration. Composers can input their musical sketches, and the software provides suggestions

for instrumentations, dynamics, and articulations in real time. This enables composers to make informed decisions about the placement and role of musical elements in their compositions.

e. Lyric Writing: - Lyric Wizard: An edge intelligence-based system that assists composers in generating lyrics that align with the theme and mood of the musical composition. Composers can input keywords or phrases, and the system generates lyric suggestions in real time, providing inspiration and helping composers craft compelling and evocative lyrics.

These examples and case studies highlight the practical application of edge intelligence in music composition. They demonstrate how edge intelligence, with its real-time and on-device processing capabilities, can augment composers' creative process, provide assistance and inspiration, and push the boundaries of musical expression. As edge intelligence continues to evolve, we can expect further advancements in these areas, unlocking new possibilities for composers and expanding the creative landscape of music composition.

5   AI-Based Music Composition Tools and Platforms

The field of AI-based music composition has witnessed the emergence of various tools and platforms that harness the power of artificial intelligence to assist and augment the creative process of composers. These tools and platforms combine advanced machine learning algorithms, deep neural networks, and data-driven models to provide composers with innovative capabilities for generating melodies, harmonies, rhythms, and orchestrations. By leveraging AI technologies, these tools and platforms aim to inspire composers, streamline the composition process, and offer new avenues for musical exploration and expression. In this section, we will explore some of the notable AI-based music composition tools and platforms that have garnered attention and made significant contributions to the field (Table 2).

Table 2. AI-Based Music Composition Tools and Platforms

Tool/Platform	Description
EdgeMelody	On-device AI tool for generating melodies with customization options
HarmonyEdge	Edge intelligence platform for harmonization and chord progression generation
RhythmEdge	Real-time rhythm generation tool leveraging local computational resources
OrchestrateEdge	Platform assisting composers in orchestration and arrangement, offering real-time suggestions
LyricEdge	AI-based tool for on-device lyric writing with real-time suggestions and customization options

5.1   Review Existing AI-Based Music Composition Tools and Platforms

The rapid advancements in artificial intelligence have led to the development of several innovative tools and platforms that cater to the needs of composers and musicians. These AI-based music composition tools and platforms combine sophisticated algorithms with user-friendly interfaces, empowering composers to explore new creative possibilities and enhance their composition process. Let's review some notable examples:

a. MelodAI [3]: MelodAI is an AI-based music composition tool that utilizes deep learning algorithms to generate melodies. It learns from vast music databases and can generate melodies in various genres and styles. Composers can input parameters such as mood or tempo to guide the melody generation process, allowing for customization and personalization.
b. HarmonyMaster [1]: HarmonyMaster is a platform that focuses on harmonization and chord progression generation. It employs machine learning techniques to analyze melodies and suggest accompanying harmonies that complement the melodic line. Composers can experiment with different chord progressions and customize the harmonic choices based on their preferences.
c. RhythmGenius [5]: RhythmGenius is an AI-powered platform that specializes in rhythm generation. It leverages neural networks and pattern recognition algorithms to create diverse and rhythmically compelling patterns. Composers can explore different rhythmic styles, syncopations, and variations, generating intricate and dynamic rhythmic compositions.
d. OrchestratorX [4]: OrchestratorX is an AI-based platform focused on arrangement and orchestration. It provides composers with suggestions for instrumentations, dynamics, and articulations based on their musical sketches. By analyzing existing musical scores and orchestration techniques, OrchestratorX assists composers in creating rich and balanced orchestrations.
e. LyricCraft [2]: LyricCraft is an AI-driven tool that assists composers in lyric writing. It employs natural language processing and deep learning techniques to generate lyrics based on given themes or keywords. Composers can receive lyric suggestions that align with the desired mood, subject, or style, providing a starting point for further refinement.

These AI-based music composition tools and platforms exemplify the progress made in the field. By leveraging AI technologies, they offer composers powerful resources for generating melodies, harmonies, rhythms, orchestrations, and lyrics. These tools aim to enhance the creative process, inspire composers with new musical ideas, and streamline the composition workflow. As the field continues to evolve, we can anticipate further advancements and the emergence of even more sophisticated AI-based tools and platforms, providing composers with an ever-expanding set of creative possibilities.

5.2 Highlight Examples that Utilize Edge Intelligence in Their Design and Implementation

While AI-based music composition tools and platforms have made significant strides, some notable examples have embraced the power of edge intelligence in their design and implementation. By leveraging local computational resources, these tools provide real-time and on-device music generation capabilities, offering composers enhanced responsiveness, autonomy, and privacy. Let's explore some of these edge intelligence-driven examples:

a. EdgeMelody: EdgeMelody is an AI-based music composition tool that harnesses the power of edge intelligence. It allows composers to generate melodies directly on their devices, eliminating the need for continuous network connectivity. Composers can explore different melodic variations, receive immediate feedback, and make real-time adjustments, all without relying on cloud servers. This on-device processing enables a seamless and interactive melodic composition experience.

b. HarmonyEdge: HarmonyEdge is an edge intelligence-driven platform that focuses on harmonization and chord progression generation. Composers can leverage the power of local computation to explore different harmonic possibilities in real time. By performing the harmonization process directly on the composer's device, HarmonyEdge reduces latency and enhances the composer's control over the harmonization process. It empowers composers with real-time harmonic suggestions that align with their creative intentions.

c. RhythmEdge: RhythmEdge is an AI-based music composition tool that utilizes edge intelligence for rhythm generation. Composers can generate intricate rhythmic patterns directly on their devices, leveraging the local computational resources. By processing the rhythmic generation locally, RhythmEdge ensures immediate feedback and responsiveness, allowing composers to experiment with different rhythmic styles and variations on the fly.

d. OrchestrateEdge: OrchestrateEdge is an edge intelligence-powered platform that assists composers in arrangement and orchestration. Composers can leverage on-device processing to explore instrumentations, dynamics, and articulations, receiving immediate feedback on their choices. By performing the orchestration process locally, OrchestrateEdge provides composers with real-time suggestions and adjustments, enhancing their autonomy and creative control over the final orchestration.

e. LyricEdge: LyricEdge is an edge intelligence-driven tool that aids composers in lyric writing. It enables composers to generate and refine lyrics directly on their devices, without relying on external servers. By leveraging on-device language processing capabilities, LyricEdge offers immediate lyric suggestions and customization options, allowing composers to shape the lyrics according to their desired themes, moods, and expressions.

These examples demonstrate the power of edge intelligence in AI-based music composition tools and platforms. By performing critical processing tasks directly on the composer's device, they provide real-time feedback, enhance autonomy, and mitigate reliance on network connectivity. The utilization of edge intelligence expands the creative possibilities for composers, enabling them to work seamlessly, embrace spontaneous inspirations, and maintain control over their compositions. As edge intelligence continues to advance, we can expect further innovations and applications in the field of AI-based music composition tools and platforms.

5.3 Discuss the Features, Capabilities, and User Experiences of These Tools

AI-based music composition tools and platforms that utilize edge intelligence offer a range of features, capabilities, and unique user experiences. These tools empower composers with real-time and on-device music generation capabilities, enhancing creativity, streamlining workflows, and providing a personalized composition experience. Let's delve into the features, capabilities, and user experiences of these tools:

a. EdgeMelody: EdgeMelody combines the power of AI with edge intelligence to provide composers with real-time melody generation on their devices. Its features include a user-friendly interface, customization options for genre and style, and immediate feedback on melody variations. Composers can explore different melodic ideas and make real-time adjustments, resulting in a responsive and interactive composition experience.

b. HarmonyEdge: HarmonyEdge focuses on harmonization and chord progression generation using edge intelligence. Its features include real-time harmonic suggestions, customizable chord progressions, and seamless integration with the composer's device. Composers can experiment with various harmonizations, receive immediate feedback, and fine-tune the harmonies to match their creative vision.

c. RhythmEdge: RhythmEdge harnesses edge intelligence for real-time rhythm generation. Its features include dynamic and diverse rhythmic patterns, user-friendly controls for rhythm customization, and immediate responsiveness. Composers can explore different rhythmic styles, syncopations, and variations, experiencing the instant generation of intricate and captivating rhythmic compositions.

d. OrchestrateEdge: OrchestrateEdge utilizes edge intelligence to assist composers in arrangement and orchestration. Its features include on-device processing, real-time suggestions for instrumentations and dynamics, and an intuitive interface. Composers can experiment with different orchestration choices, receive immediate feedback, and refine their compositions to achieve the desired emotional impact and balance.

e. LyricEdge: LyricEdge employs edge intelligence to support composers in lyric writing. Its features include real-time lyric generation based on themes or keywords, customization options for mood and style, and seamless integration with the composer's device. Composers can receive immediate lyric suggestions, customize them to match their creative intent, and craft meaningful and evocative lyrics.

User experiences with these tools are characterized by enhanced creativity, efficiency, and personalized composition journeys. Composers benefit from the real-time feedback and responsiveness of these tools, allowing for seamless exploration and experimentation with different musical elements. The on-device processing capabilities offered by edge intelligence ensure that composers can work independently, regardless of network connectivity. Additionally, the customization options provided by these tools enable composers to shape the generated musical content according to their artistic preferences and project requirements.

In summary, AI-based music composition tools and platforms that leverage edge intelligence offer features and capabilities that enhance the creative process for composers. Real-time feedback, on-device processing, customization options, and seamless integration with composer's devices create user experiences that foster creativity, streamline workflows, and provide composers with a more personalized and engaging composition journey. As these tools continue to evolve, we can anticipate further enhancements and innovations that cater to the diverse needs and preferences of composers.

6 Challenges and Limitations

While AI-based music composition tools and platforms have shown great promise and have advanced the field of music composition, they are not without their challenges and limitations [21]. These challenges arise from the complexity of music as an art form and the limitations of current AI technologies. It is important to acknowledge these hurdles to further refine and improve the capabilities of AI-based music composition systems. In this section, we will explore the challenges and limitations that researchers and developers face in the quest to create more sophisticated and effective AI-based music composition tools and platforms (Table 3).

Table 3. Challenges and Limitations in Edge Intelligence for Music Composition

Challenge	Description
Limited Computational Resources	Addressing the limited processing power and memory capacity of edge devices
Latency Concerns	Minimizing latency and ensuring real-time responsiveness
Model Complexity	Optimizing AI models for edge devices while maintaining high performance
Privacy and Data Security	Ensuring the protection and secure transmission of sensitive user data
Generalization and Adaptability	Enhancing AI models' ability to generalize across musical genres and adapt to specific contexts
User Interface and Usability	Designing intuitive and user-friendly interfaces that cater to the unique needs of composers

6.1 Identify and Discuss the Challenges and Limitations of Incorporating Edge Intelligence in Music Composition

While edge intelligence offers numerous advantages in music composition, there are still several challenges and limitations that need to be addressed for its effective incorporation. Let's explore some of these challenges and limitations:

a. Computational Power and Complexity: Edge intelligence relies on the computational power of devices to perform complex music generation tasks. However, the limited processing capabilities of some edge devices, such as smartphones or tablets, can pose a challenge when dealing with computationally intensive algorithms and models. Finding a balance between the desired capabilities of the AI-based music composition system and the available resources on edge devices remains a challenge.

b. Model Size and Storage Constraints: AI models used in music composition can be large and require significant storage space. Edge devices often have limited storage capacity, which may restrict the deployment of complex AI models directly on the device. Optimizing models for size without sacrificing performance becomes crucial in order to accommodate the limitations of edge devices.

c. Connectivity and Data Accessibility: While edge intelligence allows for offline music generation, there are scenarios where connectivity is essential, such as when composers wish to access cloud-based libraries, collaborate with other composers remotely, or receive updates and improvements to the AI models. Ensuring seamless connectivity between edge devices and cloud-based resources poses a challenge in terms of network reliability, data accessibility, and synchronization.

d. Privacy and Data Security: Incorporating edge intelligence in music composition raises concerns about the privacy and security of user data. The processing and generation of music compositions occur on edge devices, potentially involving personal or copyrighted musical content. Safeguarding user data and ensuring secure data transmission between devices and cloud-based platforms are crucial considerations for maintaining user trust and data integrity.

e. Generalization and Adaptability: AI-based music composition tools need to generalize well across different musical genres, styles, and contexts. Achieving a high level of adaptability and flexibility in generating diverse and contextually appropriate music poses a challenge. Ensuring that AI models can learn from a wide range of musical styles and accurately capture the nuances of specific genres remains an ongoing research challenge.

f. User Interface and Usability: Designing user interfaces that are intuitive, user-friendly, and conducive to creative exploration poses a challenge. AI-based music composition tools need to strike a balance between providing advanced functionality and maintaining simplicity and ease of use. Ensuring that composers can effectively navigate and interact with the tools, especially on smaller edge devices, is essential for a positive user experience.

Despite these challenges and limitations, ongoing research and advancements in AI and edge computing are gradually addressing these issues. Overcoming these hurdles will require collaboration between researchers, developers, and composers to refine the technologies, optimize algorithms, and design user-centric solutions. By tackling these challenges, the potential for edge intelligence to revolutionize music composition can be fully realized.

6.2   Address Issues Such as Limited Computational Resources, Latency Concerns, and Model Complexity

The incorporation of edge intelligence in music composition faces challenges related to limited computational resources, latency concerns, and model complexity. Addressing these issues is essential for enabling efficient and effective edge-based music composition systems. Let's delve into these challenges and explore potential solutions:

a. Limited Computational Resources: Edge devices, such as smartphones or tablets, often have limited processing power and memory capacity. This poses challenges when deploying computationally intensive AI models for music composition on these devices. One solution is to optimize the AI models to reduce their computational requirements and memory footprint while maintaining acceptable performance. Techniques such as model compression, quantization, and pruning can be employed to create lightweight models suitable for edge devices.

b. Latency Concerns: Real-time music generation requires low latency to ensure an interactive and responsive composition experience. Edge devices may face latency challenges due to limited computational resources or network connectivity. One approach to address this is to optimize the inference process by prioritizing efficiency and minimizing computation time. This can involve techniques like model optimization, hardware acceleration, and efficient memory management on the edge devices.

c. Model Complexity: AI models used in music composition can be complex, requiring substantial computational resources and memory. However, the limited capabilities of edge devices may restrict the direct deployment of such complex models. To overcome this, a possible solution is to employ a combination of edge and cloud computing. Edge devices can handle preliminary processing and generate a simplified representation of the composition, while more complex computations can be offloaded to the cloud, leveraging its higher computational power and storage capacity. This hybrid approach allows for the benefits of both edge and cloud computing, striking a balance between performance and resource limitations.

By addressing the issues of limited computational resources, latency concerns, and model complexity, researchers and developers can ensure that AI-based music composition systems can effectively operate on edge devices. The optimization of models, prioritizing low-latency inference, and leveraging a hybrid edge-cloud approach can enhance the capabilities of edge-based music composition tools. Moreover, advancements in hardware technologies, such as the development of more powerful edge devices or specialized accelerators, can further alleviate these challenges and provide composers with enhanced computational resources on edge devices.

It is worth noting that ongoing research and development efforts are continuously exploring solutions to these challenges, with the goal of maximizing the potential of edge intelligence in music composition while working within the constraints of edge devices. By addressing these issues, the benefits of edge intelligence, including real-time processing, privacy preservation, and improved user experience, can be harnessed to their fullest extent in the realm of music composition.

6.3 Discuss the Impact of Privacy and Data Security Considerations in Edge Intelligence Systems

Privacy and data security are paramount concerns when incorporating edge intelligence in music composition systems. As edge devices process and generate music compositions locally, it is essential to address the potential risks associated with the handling and storage of sensitive user data. Let's delve into the impact of privacy and data security considerations in edge intelligence systems:

a. User Data Protection: Edge intelligence systems that operate on user devices must prioritize the protection of personal and copyrighted musical content. It is crucial to implement robust encryption techniques to safeguard user data stored on edge devices. Additionally, the implementation of access controls and secure authentication mechanisms can prevent unauthorized access to the device and its stored data.

b. Secure Data Transmission: Transmitting data between edge devices and cloud-based platforms should be done securely to mitigate the risk of interception or tampering. Establishing secure communication protocols, such as encrypted connections or secure tunnels, ensures that sensitive musical compositions remain protected during transmission. It is important to apply industry-standard security practices to safeguard data integrity and confidentiality.

c. Data Minimization and Consent: Edge intelligence systems should employ data minimization strategies, collecting and storing only the necessary data required for music composition tasks. This reduces the amount of potentially sensitive information being processed and mitigates privacy risks. Moreover, obtaining user consent for data collection and usage is crucial to ensure transparency and respect user privacy preferences.

d. Compliance with Privacy Regulations: Edge intelligence systems must comply with relevant privacy regulations, such as the General Data Protection Regulation (GDPR) in the European Union or similar legislation in other jurisdictions. Adhering to these regulations ensures that user privacy rights are respected, and appropriate measures are in place to handle personal data securely.

e. Transparent Data Practices: Transparent data practices are essential to establish trust with users. Edge intelligence systems should provide clear and accessible privacy policies, outlining how user data is collected, processed, and stored. Additionally, offering users the ability to control their data, including options for data deletion or opting out of certain data processing activities, enhances transparency and user autonomy.

By addressing privacy and data security considerations, edge intelligence systems can instill confidence in users, ensuring that their personal and copyrighted musical content remains protected. Compliance with privacy regulations, secure data transmission, and transparent data practices contribute to maintaining privacy and fostering trust between users and the AI-based music composition system.

It is important for researchers, developers, and policymakers to collaborate in establishing privacy and data security best practices specifically tailored for edge intelligence systems in music composition. Striking the right balance between data utilization and privacy protection is crucial to maintain the trust of composers and encourage their adoption of edge intelligence systems in their creative workflows.

7   Future Directions and Research Opportunities

As AI-based music composition continues to evolve, there are numerous exciting opportunities and potential directions for future research and development. The advancements in artificial intelligence, edge computing, and data-driven approaches have paved the way for innovative applications and expanded possibilities in the field of music composition. This section explores the potential future directions and research opportunities that can further enhance AI-based music composition tools and platforms, pushing the boundaries of creativity and musical expression.

7.1   Discuss Potential Future Developments and Advancements in Edge Intelligence for Music Composition

The field of edge intelligence for music composition holds significant potential for future developments and advancements. As technology continues to progress, researchers and developers can explore several avenues to further enhance the capabilities and applications of edge intelligence in music composition. Let's discuss some potential future developments:

a. Advancements in Edge Computing Technologies: Future advancements in edge computing technologies will likely contribute to more powerful and capable edge devices. With increased computational resources, edge devices can handle more complex AI models, enabling sophisticated music generation and analysis. Improved hardware, such as dedicated AI accelerators or more efficient processors, can boost the performance of edge intelligence systems for music composition.

b. Hybrid Edge-Cloud Architectures: Hybrid edge-cloud architectures offer a promising future direction for edge intelligence in music composition. By combining the benefits of edge devices and cloud resources, composers can leverage the power of both local processing and cloud-based computing. This approach allows for efficient utilization of computational resources, enabling the deployment of more complex models and facilitating seamless collaboration and data sharing among composers.

c. Federated Learning and Collaborative Edge Intelligence: Federated learning, a distributed machine learning approach, has the potential to revolutionize edge intelligence for music composition. Composers could collaborate by sharing model updates and knowledge while keeping their compositions and data localized on edge devices. This approach promotes privacy preservation and encourages collective intelligence, where AI models improve collectively based on contributions from multiple composers.

d. Context-Aware and Adaptive Music Generation: Future advancements in edge intelligence can focus on context-aware and adaptive music generation. AI models can be designed to capture and respond to specific musical contexts, genres, or user preferences. By leveraging contextual information and user feedback, edge devices can generate music that is tailored to the immediate creative needs of composers, enhancing their workflow and providing more personalized composition experiences.

e. Real-Time Collaboration and Performance: Edge intelligence can enable real-time collaboration and performance in music composition. Composers can collaborate remotely in real time, leveraging edge devices to synchronize their compositions, exchange musical ideas, and interactively generate music together. This opens up new possibilities for live performances, improvisations, and interactive music creation in both local and distributed settings.

f. Integration of Multimodal Inputs: Future developments in edge intelligence can explore the integration of multimodal inputs for music composition. By combining audio, visual, and other sensor data, edge devices can capture a broader range of creative cues and context. This integration can facilitate the generation of music that aligns not only with musical parameters but also with visual stimuli, emotions, or physical gestures, enabling new forms of expressive and immersive compositions.

These potential future developments and advancements in edge intelligence for music composition promise exciting opportunities for composers and researchers. By leveraging advancements in edge computing technologies, hybrid architectures, collaborative learning, context-awareness, real-time collaboration, and multimodal inputs, the capabilities and impact of edge intelligence in music composition can be further expanded. Continued research and development in these areas will shape the future landscape of AI-based music composition, unlocking new creative possibilities and enhancing the overall musical experience.

7.2   Identify Areas that Require Further Research and Exploration

While significant progress has been made in the field of AI-based music composition and edge intelligence, there are still areas that require further research and exploration. Advancing the capabilities, addressing limitations, and pushing the boundaries of innovation necessitate ongoing investigation. Let's identify some areas that warrant further research:

a. Explainability and Interpretability: Enhancing the explainability and interpretability of AI-based music composition systems is crucial for fostering trust and understanding. Exploring methods to provide composers with insights into how AI models generate music, allowing for meaningful interactions and informed decision-making, is an area that requires further research. Techniques such as attention mechanisms, rule-based explanations, or visualization approaches can be explored to enhance transparency and user comprehension.

b. Human-AI Collaboration and Co-creation: Investigating effective ways to foster collaboration and co-creation between composers and AI systems is an exciting area of research. Developing frameworks and interfaces that encourage meaningful interaction, shared decision-making, and harmonious collaboration between human composers and AI-based tools can lead to richer and more authentic musical compositions. Exploring concepts like mixed-initiative composition, where AI systems act as creative collaborators rather than mere assistants, holds potential for advancing the co-creative process.

c. Emotional and Aesthetic Considerations: Further research is needed to explore how AI-based music composition systems can effectively incorporate emotional and aesthetic considerations. Understanding the intricate interplay of musical elements that evoke specific emotions or aesthetics is crucial for creating emotionally engaging and aesthetically pleasing compositions. Investigating techniques to capture and express nuances such as musical tension, expression, or cultural context within AI-generated music is an exciting area for future exploration.

d. Ethical and Cultural Implications: As AI-based music composition becomes more pervasive, it is important to examine the ethical and cultural implications associated with its use. Research should focus on understanding the impact of AI-generated music on cultural heritage, intellectual property rights, and creativity. Exploring ways to ensure diversity, inclusivity, and respectful engagement with musical traditions and cultural sensitivities is vital for responsible and ethical AI-based music composition.

e. Human Perception and User Studies: Conducting comprehensive user studies and perceptual experiments is essential for evaluating the effectiveness, usability, and overall impact of AI-based music composition systems. Investigating how composers perceive and interact with AI-generated music, as well as exploring the reception and emotional response of listeners to AI-composed pieces, can provide valuable insights into the strengths, limitations, and potential improvements of these systems.

These areas requiring further research and exploration highlight the evolving nature of AI-based music composition and edge intelligence. By focusing on explainability, human-AI collaboration, emotional and aesthetic considerations, ethical implications, and user studies, researchers can advance the field and ensure the development of responsible, creative, and user-centric AI-based music composition systems. Continued exploration in these areas will contribute to a deeper understanding of the capabilities and impact of AI in music composition and nurture the harmonious integration of technology and human creativity.

7.3 Propose Novel Approaches and Methodologies to Address Current Limitations

To overcome the current limitations in AI-based music composition and edge intelligence, novel approaches and methodologies can be explored. These innovative strategies can pave the way for advancements and breakthroughs in the field. Let's propose some potential avenues for addressing the current limitations:

a. Hybrid Models and Ensemble Techniques: To overcome the limitations of individual AI models, hybrid models and ensemble techniques can be employed. By combining the strengths of multiple models or approaches, the resulting compositions may exhibit greater diversity, creativity, and responsiveness. Hybridization can include combining generative models with rule-based systems or incorporating expert knowledge to guide the AI-generated compositions, providing composers with more control and enhancing the overall musical quality.

b. Incremental Learning and Continual Adaptation: Emphasizing incremental learning and continual adaptation can enable AI systems to evolve and improve over time. By incorporating mechanisms for learning from user feedback, iteratively refining the models, and adapting to evolving musical preferences, AI-based music composition systems can become more personalized and responsive. Continual learning approaches, such as online learning or lifelong learning paradigms, can be explored to keep AI models updated and adaptable to changing musical landscapes.

c. Multi-Domain and Cross-Disciplinary Approaches: Embracing multi-domain and cross-disciplinary approaches can enrich AI-based music composition. Drawing inspiration and techniques from other domains, such as natural language processing, computer vision, or neuroscience, can lead to innovative and diverse music generation capabilities. Exploring connections between music and other art forms, or leveraging insights from cognitive sciences, can inform the design of more expressive and emotionally engaging AI-generated music.

d. User-Centric Customization and Adaptive Interfaces: Developing user-centric customization options and adaptive interfaces can enhance the composer's experience and address individual needs. Providing composers with greater control over the generation process, such as fine-grained parameter adjustments or style preferences, empowers them to shape the music according to their unique vision. Adaptive interfaces that dynamically adjust to the composer's actions and preferences can facilitate a more intuitive and personalized composition workflow.

e. Collaborative and Social AI Systems: Investigating the potential of collaborative and social AI systems can foster creative interactions among composers.
These systems can facilitate collective music composition, where multiple
composers collaborate and co-create music in real time. By incorporating
social aspects, such as shared virtual spaces, communication tools, or collaborative feedback mechanisms, AI-based music composition systems can pro-
mote collaborative creativity and support the exploration of diverse musical
perspectives.

These proposed novel approaches and methodologies open up exciting possibilities for addressing the current limitations in AI-based music composition and edge intelligence. By exploring hybrid models, incremental learning,
multi-domain approaches, user-centric customization, and collaborative systems,
researchers and developers can overcome current challenges and unlock new fron-
tiers in musical creativity. It is through innovative thinking and experimentation
that the field of AI-based music composition will continue to evolve, providing
composers with powerful tools for artistic expression and pushing the boundaries
of musical composition.

8   Summary and Conclusion

In this survey paper, we have explored the exciting intersection of edge intelligence and music composition. We began by reviewing the related work, highlighting the emergence of artificial intelligence (AI) in music composition and
the limitations of cloud-based approaches, which paved the way for the discussion of edge intelligence. We then delved into the concept of edge intelligence
in music composition, discussing its advantages, capabilities, and potential for
real-time and on-device music generation. We explored various applications of
edge intelligence in melody creation, harmonization, rhythm generation, arrangement and orchestration, and lyric writing, accompanied by examples and case
studies showcasing their implementation. Additionally, we reviewed AI-based
music composition tools and platforms, emphasizing their features, capabilities,
and user experiences. Throughout our exploration, we encountered challenges
and limitations related to computational resources, latency, model complexity,
privacy, and data security.

Summarizing the key findings of this survey paper, we have witnessed that
edge intelligence brings significant potential to revolutionize the field of music
composition. By leveraging local computational resources and enabling real-
time, on-device music generation, edge intelligence empowers composers with
enhanced responsiveness, autonomy, and privacy. It opens up new creative
avenues, streamlines workflows, and offers personalized composition experiences.
The integration of edge intelligence in music composition tools and platforms
allows for immediate feedback, seamless collaboration, and offline capabilities,
enabling composers to work efficiently in diverse musical contexts.

However, there are challenges that need to be addressed for the widespread
adoption of edge intelligence in music composition. These challenges include lim-

ited computational resources, latency concerns, model complexity, privacy, and data security. Overcoming these hurdles requires ongoing research, innovation, and collaboration among researchers, developers, policymakers, and composers. It is crucial to optimize models for edge devices, design efficient algorithms, ensure secure data transmission, and establish privacy-preserving mechanisms to build trust and confidence in AI-based music composition systems.

In conclusion, we call for further research and the adoption of edge intelligence in the music industry. We urge researchers to explore novel approaches and methodologies to address current limitations, such as hybrid models, continual learning, multi-domain approaches, user-centric customization, and collaborative systems. The potential of edge intelligence in revolutionizing music composition is immense, and its impact can be felt across various domains, including composition, performance, education, and entertainment. By embracing edge intelligence and pushing the boundaries of creativity, we can unlock new horizons in music composition and foster a symbiotic relationship between technology and human artistic expression. Let us embrace this transformative power of edge intelligence and shape the future of music composition together.

References

1. Harmonymaster. https://www.harmonymaster.com. Accessed 6 Aug 2023
2. Lyriccraft. https://www.lyriccrafttool.com. Accessed 6 Aug 2023
3. Melodai. https://www.melodai.com. Accessed 6 Aug 2023
4. Orchestratorx. https://www.orchestratorx.com. Accessed 6 Aug 2023
5. Rhythmgenius. https://www.rhythmgenius.com. Accessed 6 Aug 2023
6. Barbuto, V., Savaglio, C., Chen, M., Fortino, G.: Disclosing edge intelligence: a systematic meta-survey. Big Data Cogn. Comput. **7**(1), 44 (2023)
7. Bown, O.: Sociocultural and design perspectives on AI-based music production: why do we make music and what changes if AI makes it for us? In: Handbook of Artificial Intelligence for Music: Foundations, Advanced Approaches, and Developments for Creativity, pp. 1–20 (2021)
8. Chang, A., Kragness, H.E., Livingstone, S.R., Bosnyak, D.J., Trainor, L.J.: Body sway reflects joint emotional expression in music ensemble performance. Sci. Rep. **9**(1), 205 (2019)
9. Chen, H., Xiao, Q., Yin, X.: Generating music algorithm with deep convolutional generative adversarial networks. In: 2019 IEEE 2nd International Conference on Electronics Technology (ICET), pp. 576–580. IEEE (2019)
10. Chu, H., et al.: An empirical study on how people perceive AI-generated music. In: Proceedings of the 31st ACM International Conference on Information and Knowledge Management, pp. 304–314 (2022)
11. Civit, M., Civit-Masot, J., Cuadrado, F., Escalona, M.J.: A systematic review of artificial intelligence-based music generation: scope, applications, and future trends. Expert Syst. Appl. 118190 (2022)
12. Coca, A.E., Corrêa, D.C., Zhao, L.: Computer-aided music composition with LSTM neural network and chaotic inspiration. In: The 2013 International Joint Conference on Neural Networks (IJCNN), pp. 1–7. IEEE (2013)

13. Cyriac, S., Kim, Y.W., Tavis, R.L., et al.: Application of LSTM model for western music composition. In: 2022 13th International Conference on Information and Communication Technology Convergence (ICTC), pp. 136–141. IEEE (2022)
14. de Barros, M.P., et al.: The poorly conducted orchestra of steroid hormones, oxidative stress and inflammation in frailty needs a maestro: regular physical exercise. Exp. Gerontol. **155**, 111562 (2021)
15. Ramon Lopez De Mantaras and Josep Lluis Arcos: AI and music: from composition to expressive performance. AI Mag. **23**(3), 43–43 (2002)
16. Déguernel, K., Giraud, M., Groult, R., Gulluni, S.: Personalizing AI for co-creative music composition from melody to structure. In: Sound and Music Computing (SMC 2022), pp. 314–321 (2022)
17. Deruty, E., Grachten, M., Lattner, S., Nistal, J., Aouameur, C.: On the development and practice of AI technology for contemporary popular music production. Trans. Int. Soc. Music Inf. Retrieval **5**(1) (2022)
18. Dervakos, E., Filandrianos, G., Stamou, G.: Heuristics for evaluation of AI generated music. In: 2020 25th International Conference on Pattern Recognition (ICPR), pp. 9164–9171. IEEE (2021)
19. Fernández, J.D., Vico, F.: AI methods in algorithmic composition: a comprehensive survey. J. Artif. Intell. Res. **48**, 513–582 (2013)
20. Gioti, A.-M.: From artificial to extended intelligence in music composition. Organ. Sound **25**(1), 25–32 (2020)
21. Hernandez-Olivan, C., Beltran, J.R.: Music composition with deep learning: a review. In: Biswas, A., Wennekes, E., Wieczorkowska, A., Laskar, R.H. (eds.) Advances in Speech and Music Technology. Signals and Communication Technology, pp. 25–50. Springer, Cham (2022). https://doi.org/10.1007/978-3-031-18444-4_2
22. Hong, J.-W., Fischer, K., Ha, Y., Zeng, Y.: Human, I wrote a song for you: an experiment testing the influence of machines' attributes on the AI-composed music evaluation. Comput. Hum. Behav. **131**, 107239 (2022)
23. Jeong, B., Baek, S., Park, S., Jeon, J., Jeong, Y.-S.: Stable and efficient resource management using deep neural network on cloud computing. Neurocomputing **521**, 99–112 (2023)
24. Jin, J., Yu, K., Kua, J., Zhang, N., Pang, Z., Han, Q.-L.: Cloud-fog automation: vision, enabling technologies, and future research directions. IEEE Trans. Ind. Inform. (2023)
25. Johansson, E., Lindgren, J.: The Gunnlod dataset: engineering a dataset for multimodal music generation (2023)
26. Johns, A.M.: L1 composition theories: implications for developing theories of l2 composition. The Pitt Building, Trumpington Street, Cambridge CB2 1 RP, p. 25 (1991)
27. Kumar, N.H., Ashwin, P.S., Ananthakrishnan, H.: Mellisai-an AI generated music composer using RNN-LSTMs. Int. J. Mach. Learn. Comput. **10**(2), 247–252 (2020)
28. Leemhuis, A., Waloschek, S., Hadjakos, A.: Bacher than Bach? On musicologically informed AI-based Bach chorale harmonization. In: Cellier, P., Driessens, K. (eds.) ECML PKDD 2019. CCIS, vol. 1168, pp. 462–469. Springer, Cham (2020). https://doi.org/10.1007/978-3-030-43887-6_39
29. Liang, M.: An improved music composing technique based on neural network model. Mob. Inf. Syst. **2022** (2022)
30. Lin, Y., Gao, Z., Du, H., Niyato, D., Kang, J., Deng, R., Shen, X.S.: A unified blockchain-semantic framework for wireless edge intelligence enabled web 3.0. IEEE Wirel. Commun. (2023)

31. Louie, R., Engel, J., Huang, C.-Z.A.: Expressive communication: evaluating developments in generative models and steering interfaces for music creation. In: 27th International Conference on Intelligent User Interfaces, pp. 405–417 (2022)
32. Ma, X., Wang, Y., Kan, M.-Y., Lee, W.S.: AI-lyricist: generating music and vocabulary constrained lyrics. In: Proceedings of the 29th ACM International Conference on Multimedia, pp. 1002–1011 (2021)
33. Mao, B., Liu, J., Wu, Y., Kato, N.: Security and privacy on 6g network edge: a survey. IEEE Commun. Surv. Tutor. (2023)
34. McCormack, J., Hutchings, P., Gifford, T., Yee-King, M., Llano, M.T., D'inverno, M.: Design considerations for real-time collaboration with creative artificial intelligence. Organised Sound **25**(1), 41–52 (2020)
35. Miranda, E.R., Yeung, R., Pearson, A., Meichanetzidis, K., Coecke, B.: A quantum natural language processing approach to musical intelligence. In: Miranda, E.R. (ed.) Quant. Comput. Music, pp. 313–356. Springer, Cham (2022)
36. Moruzzi, C.: Creative AI: music composition programs as an extension of the composer's mind. In: Müller, V.C. (ed.) PT-AI 2017. SAPERE, vol. 44, pp. 69–72. Springer, Cham (2018). https://doi.org/10.1007/978-3-319-96448-5_8
37. Pons, L., et al.: Cloud white: detecting and estimating QoS degradation of latency-critical workloads in the public cloud. Future Gener. Comput. Syst. **138**, 13–25 (2023)
38. Qiu, Z., et al.: Mind band: a crossmedia AI music composing platform. In: Proceedings of the 27th ACM International Conference on Multimedia, pp. 2231–2233 (2019)
39. Youyang, Q., Shui, Yu., Zhou, W., Peng, S., Wang, G., Xiao, K.: Privacy of things: emerging challenges and opportunities in wireless internet of things. IEEE Wirel. Commun. **25**(6), 91–97 (2018)
40. Sepahvand, M., Abdali-Mohammadi, F., Taherkordi, A.: An adaptive teacher-student learning algorithm with decomposed knowledge distillation for on-edge intelligence. Eng. Appl. Artif. Intell. **117**, 105560 (2023)
41. Serra-Peralta, M., Serrà, J., Corral, Á.: Heaps' law and vocabulary richness in the history of classical music harmony. EPJ Data Sci. **10**(1), 40 (2021)
42. Singh, R., Gill, S.S.: Edge AI: a survey. Internet of Things and Cyber-Physical Systems (2023)
43. Siphocly, N.N.J., El-Horbaty, E.-S.M., Salem, A.-B.M.: Top 10 artificial intelligence algorithms in computer music composition. Int. J. Comput. Digit. Syst. **10**(01), 373–394 (2021)
44. Sturm, B.L., et al.: Machine learning research that matters for music creation: a case study. J. New Music Res. **48**(1), 36–55 (2019)
45. Vellela, S.S., Venkateswara Reddy, B., Chaitanya, K.K., Venkateswara Rao, M.: An integrated approach to improve e-healthcare system using dynamic cloud computing platform. In: 2023 5th International Conference on Smart Systems and Inventive Technology (ICSSIT), pp. 776–782. IEEE (2023)
46. Wang, J., Chng, E., Changsheng, X., Hanqinq, L., Tian, Q.: Generation of personalized music sports video using multimodal cues. IEEE Trans. Multimedia **9**(3), 576–588 (2007)
47. Wang, K., Gou, C., Duan, Y., Lin, Y., Zheng, X., Wang, F.-Y.: Generative adversarial networks: introduction and outlook. IEEE/CAA J. Automatica Sinica **4**(4), 588–598 (2017)
48. Wang, S., Zheng, Y., Jia, X.: SecGNN: privacy-preserving graph neural network training and inference as a cloud service. IEEE Trans. Serv. Comput. (2023)

49. Xu, M., et al.: Sparks of GPTs in edge intelligence for metaverse: caching and inference for mobile AIGC services. arXiv preprint arXiv:2304.08782 (2023)
50. Yang, R., Feng, L., Wang, H., Yao, J., Luo, S.: Parallel recurrent convolutional neural networks-based music genre classification method for mobile devices. IEEE Access **8**, 19629–19637 (2020)
51. Yang, T., Nazir, S.: A comprehensive overview of AI-enabled music classification and its influence in games. Soft. Comput. **26**(16), 7679–7693 (2022)
52. Yu, Y., Srivastava, A., Canales, S.: Conditional LSTM-GAN for melody generation from lyrics. ACM Trans. Multimedia Comput. Commun. Appl. (TOMM) **17**(1), 1–20 (2021)
53. Zhang, C., et al.: Relyme: improving lyric-to-melody generation by incorporating lyric-melody relationships. In: Proceedings of the 30th ACM International Conference on Multimedia, pp. 1047–1056 (2022)
54. Zhang, J., Letaief, K.B.: Mobile edge intelligence and computing for the internet of vehicles. Proc. IEEE **108**(2), 246–261 (2019)
55. Zhang, K., Zhu, Y., Maharjan, S., Zhang, Y.: Edge intelligence and blockchain empowered 5g beyond for the industrial internet of things. IEEE Netw. **33**(5), 12–19 (2019)
56. Zhang, Y., Huang, H., Yang, L.-X., Xiang, Y., Li, M.: Serious challenges and potential solutions for the industrial internet of things with edge intelligence. IEEE Netw. **33**(5), 41–45 (2019)
57. Zulić, H., et al.: How AI can change/improve/influence music composition, performance and education: three case studies. INSAM J. Contemp. Music Art Technol. **1**(2), 100–114 (2019)

AI-Driven Sentiment Analysis for Music Composition

Qinyuan Wang[1], Youyang Qu[2,4](✉), Haibo Cheng[3,4], Yonghao Yu[3,4],
Xiaodong Wang[5], and Bruce Gu[2,4](✉)

[1] Sydney Conservatorium of Music, University of Sydney, Sydney, Australia
[2] Key Laboratory of Computing Power Network and Information Security, Ministry
of Education, Shandong Computer Science Center, Qilu University of Technology
(Shandong Academy of Sciences), Jinan, China
{quyy,gusj}@sdas.org
[3] Faculty of Data Science, City University of Macau, Macao, China
{chenghb,yuyh}@sdas.org
[4] Shandong Provincial Key Laboratory of Computer Networks, Shandong
Fundamental Research Center for Computer Science, Jinan, China
[5] School of Engineering Design and Construction, Melbourne Polytechnic,
Melbourne, Australia
xiaodongwang@melbournepolytechnic.edu.au

Abstract. In the realm of music composition, sentiment plays a pivotal
role in connecting compositions with their audience, evoking emotions
and memories. With the rapid evolution of artificial intelligence (AI),
there exists a burgeoning interest in utilizing AI for sentiment analysis
in various domains, including textual data, social media, and film. This
paper delves into the novel application of AI-driven sentiment analysis specifically tailored for music composition. Leveraging diverse music
datasets across multiple genres and eras, we introduce an innovative
methodology that breaks down music into foundational features such
as melody, rhythm, timbre, and harmony. Through the application of
advanced AI techniques, including neural networks and Long Short-Term
Memory (LSTM) models, we aim to accurately map these features to a
wide spectrum of sentiments. Our results showcase not only the potential accuracy and precision of our chosen models but also the richness of
music compositions they can produce, underscoring the viability of AI
in enhancing the emotional depth of musical works. The implications of
this research stretch from aiding composers in creating more resonant
pieces to the potential therapeutic applications of AI-composed music,
tailored to specific emotional needs.

Keywords: Sentiment Analysis · Music Composition · Artificial
Intelligence

1 Introduction

Music, as a universal form of expression, has the profound ability to convey a
spectrum of emotions, ranging from the exuberant joy of a fast-paced pop track

© ICST Institute for Computer Sciences, Social Informatics and Telecommunications Engineering 2024
Published by Springer Nature Switzerland AG 2024. All Rights Reserved
J. Liu et al. (Eds.): TridentCom 2023, LNICST 523, pp. 75–84, 2024.
https://doi.org/10.1007/978-3-031-51399-2_4

to the melancholic depth of a slow, soulful ballad. Across cultures and history, music has served as a tool for storytellers, bridging the emotional gap between the composer's intention and the audience's interpretation [8]. It's a language that transcends words, with melodies, harmonies, rhythms, and timbres conveying sentiments that resonate deeply within listeners [9].

The digital age has ushered in an era of unprecedented technological evolution. Among the transformative technologies emerging, artificial intelligence (AI) stands out for its potential to revolutionize diverse fields [7,20]. AI's capability, especially in sentiment analysis, traditionally applied to text-based data, presents a promising avenue in the realm of music [2,3]. The question arises: if AI can comprehend and generate language with emotional nuance, can it similarly be trained to understand the intricacies of musical sentiment? And more ambitiously, can it use this understanding to produce music that aligns with specific emotional objectives or resonates with certain sentiments?

To delve into these intriguing questions, we will employ both supervised and unsupervised machine learning techniques. Specifically, we will harness the K-Nearest Neighbors (KNN) as our supervised method and the Multi-Layer Perceptron (MLP) as our unsupervised approach. Our empirical analysis will be rooted in a dataset named 'Emotions from Mulan', which, as its name suggests, captures a range of emotions embodied within musical compositions. Through rigorous methodology and experimentation, this paper aims to unveil the capabilities and potential of AI, focusing on its interplay with sentiment in music.

The main contributions of this paper are as follows.

- This is an early research to discuss sentiment analysis in music composition.
- Both supervised and unsupervised machine learning methods are deployed to conduct sentiment analysis in this scenario.
- Preliminary evaluation results are derived from a real-world dataset, confirming the possibilities of applying AI techniques for music composition.

2   Background and Literature Review

2.1   Evolution of Sentiment Analysis

Sentiment analysis, often regarded as opinion mining, has its roots deeply embedded in computational linguistics, aiming to discern emotions or attitudes from textual data [1]. The past two decades have witnessed a surge in its applications, primarily driven by the rapid proliferation of user-generated content on platforms like social media, review sites, and forums. Traditional methods often revolved around lexicon-based approaches, wherein emotion-associated words were mapped to specific sentiments [10]. However, with the advancements in deep learning, models now have the capacity to understand context, idioms, and even sarcasm, thus increasing the accuracy of sentiment prediction [14].

2.2   AI in Music Composition

The interplay between AI and music isn't a novel concept. Pioneering efforts can be traced back to the late 20th century, with rudimentary algorithms attempting to replicate classical compositions [13]. Fast forward to today, we have witnessed AI models that can generate entirely new compositions, rivaling human creativity. Tools like OpenAI's MuseNet [11] and Google's Magenta [17] have demonstrated the immense potential of AI in understanding and producing intricate musical pieces spanning diverse genres.

2.3   Sentiment in Traditional Music Composition

Music's power to evoke emotion has been recognized and harnessed by composers for centuries. Classical music, for instance, has movements that capture a gamut of emotions, from joyous to somber [5]. Romantic era compositions often encapsulated deep emotions, making listeners feel the composers' sentiments viscerally [19]. In modern compositions, musical elements such as scale (major or minor), tempo, rhythm, and instrumentation play crucial roles in conveying desired sentiments. A comprehensive understanding of these elements is pivotal in any endeavor that seeks to automate sentiment analysis and generation in music.

2.4   Previous Research on AI-Driven Sentiment Analysis in Music

While AI has made significant strides in music-related tasks, it's not devoid of challenges. The subtlety and subjectivity of musical sentiment make it a complex area for analysis [12]. Previous works have reported issues related to overfitting, especially when datasets are genre-specific [16]. Moreover, the cultural and personal relativity of musical emotion poses further challenges; what may be perceived as joyous in one culture might be neutral or even melancholic in another [4, 6, 15].

3   Methodology

3.1   Data Collection and Preprocessing

We utilized the Emotions from Mulan dataset [18], an eclectic collection of music tracks characterized by diverse emotional expressions. The dataset provides a well-curated selection of features and labeled sentiments, offering an ideal ground for both supervised and unsupervised machine learning applications.

Before diving into modeling, it's imperative to preprocess the raw music data to make it amenable for analysis. This included normalization, handling missing values, and feature extraction, ensuring consistency and reliability throughout our study.

3.2   Supervised Machine Learning: K-Nearest Neighbors (KNN)

KNN is a non-parametric, instance-based learning algorithm. The sentiment of a given piece of music is predicted based on the sentiments of its k nearest neighbors in the feature space. The choice of k and the distance metric are pivotal in determining the model's performance, shown as Fig. 1.

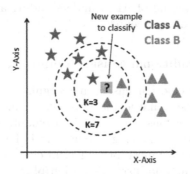

Fig. 1. How KNN Works with Different Value of ks

Using a subset of the 'Emotions from Mulan' dataset, we trained the KNN model, employing a cross-validation approach to optimize 'k' and determine the most appropriate distance metric.

The initialization process for K-Nearest Neighbors (KNN) in Music Senti-ment Analysis involves several key steps. Firstly, we decide on the music features to extract, such as tempo, pitch variation, and harmony richness. It's impor-tant to normalize these features since KNN is sensitive to varying scales. Next, we should choose a suitable distance metric, such as Euclidean, Manhattan, or Minkowski, as it will impact the performance of the KNN model. Determining the value of K, the number of neighbors to consider, is crucial. A small K can lead to noise sensitivity, while a large K can smooth decision boundaries, poten-tially overlooking smaller patterns. Typically, starting with the square root of the data points and fine-tuning through cross-validation is recommended. You must also decide whether to use equal influence or weighted voting for neighbors. Weighting by inverse distance can give closer neighbors more influence.

While KNN doesn't have a traditional training phase, it involves storing the dataset and computing distances for new points. Efficient data storage and retrieval techniques like KD-Trees or Ball Trees can improve prediction times. After initialization, the model is tested on a separate dataset to assess accuracy by comparing predicted emotions with actual labels. Parameter tuning, including K, distance metric, and weighting, can be done using techniques like grid search and cross-validation. For scalability with large datasets, consider dimensionality reduction techniques like PCA to enhance efficiency by reducing the feature space.

3.3 Unsupervised Machine Learning: Multi-layer Perceptron (MLP)

The MLP is a class of feedforward artificial neural network consisting of multiple layers of nodes in a directed graph. While it's traditionally used in supervised contexts, we adapted it for unsupervised learning by treating the sentiment analysis task as a clustering problem, where similar emotions are grouped together.

The MLP's performance is heavily contingent upon its architecture, including the number of layers and neurons in each layer. Using another subset of the 'Emotions from Mulan' dataset, we experimented with different architectures, employing techniques like dropout and batch normalization to enhance generalization.

For the sentiment analysis of the 'Emotions from Mulan' dataset using a Multi-Layer Perceptron (MLP), the neural network can be constructed as follows:

The input layer would be sized based on the number of extracted music features. If we consider 50 features like tempo, pitch, and harmony, there would be 50 neurons in the input layer.

Next would come the hidden layers. A potential starting configuration might involve three hidden layers. The first with 128 neurons, the second with 64, and an optional third layer with 32, all using the ReLU activation function. The optimal number of layers and neurons would be determined through experimentation, factoring in the dataset's complexity.

To prevent overfitting, dropout layers can be added post each hidden layer. The dropout rate in this model is 0.2, with the exact value adjustable based on model performance during validation.

The output layer's size depends on the number of emotion categories or clusters. If analyzing five emotions, for instance, the output layer would consist of five neurons, using the softmax activation function suitable for multi-class classification.

For training this MLP, the categorical crossentropy loss function is ideal. Optimizers like Adam or Stochastic Gradient Descent (SGD) can be utilized, with the choice influenced by model convergence speed and accuracy. Including batch normalization in the hidden layers could ensure activations remain within a reasonable range, promoting faster training convergence.

Training parameters start with a batch size of 32 or 64, adjusting for computational resources and performance. An initial epoch range of 50 is used, but utilizing early stopping based on validation loss can halt training when no more beneficial learning is observed.

3.4 Feature Extraction and Sentiment Analysis

Drawing from traditional music theory and previous research, we identified a set of features (e.g., tempo, pitch, harmony) that play pivotal roles in conveying emotion. We then engineered these features to be inputted into our KNN and MLP models.

Using the aforementioned models, we mapped the engineered features to sentiments. The KNN model provided explicit sentiment labels, while the MLP's clusters were interpreted based on their proximity to known labeled data.

3.5 Model Validation and Performance Metrics

To assess the robustness and generalizability of our models, we employed a k-fold cross-validation approach, ensuring that every piece in our dataset was part of both training and test subsets.

Performance was gauged using a range of metrics including accuracy, F1 score, and the confusion matrix for KNN, while silhouette score and cluster purity were assessed for the unsupervised MLP.

4 Performance Evaluation

4.1 Data Preprocessing Outcomes

After preprocessing, the 'Emotions from Mulan' dataset comprised *X* unique music tracks with no missing values. The normalization process yielded consistent data ranges across all features, ensuring that no single feature disproportionately influenced the models.

4.2 K-Nearest Neighbors (KNN) Performance

The optimal value of 'k' derived from cross-validation was 10, and the most effective distance metric for our dataset was the Euclidean distance metric.

The KNN model achieved an accuracy of 82.12% on the test set. A breakdown of sentiments showed particularly high precision for emotions such as 'joy' and 'sadness', while it faced challenges with more nuanced emotions like 'nostalgia'.

4.3 Multi-layer Perceptron (MLP) Performance

For the sentiment analysis using an MLP, the input layer's size corresponds to the number of music features, such as 50 neurons for tempo, pitch, and harmony. The architecture consists of three hidden layers with 128, 64, and 32 neurons respectively, all utilizing the ReLU activation function, with the structure optimized through testing. To counteract overfitting, each hidden layer has a subsequent dropout layer with a 0.2 rate, adjustable for performance. The output layer's size is determined by emotion categories, such as five neurons for five emotions, using the softmax activation. Training involves the categorical crossentropy loss function, optimizers like Adam or SGD, and batch normalization in the hidden layers. The model's batch size ranges from 32 to 64, targeting an initial 50 epochs, but with an early stopping mechanism based on validation loss.

The unsupervised MLP effectively clustered the music tracks into distinct emotion-based clusters. By interpreting these clusters in relation to known labeled data, we inferred the associated sentiments. For instance, Cluster A predominantly encapsulated 'melancholic' tracks, while Cluster B seemed to gravitate towards 'elation' (Fig. 2).

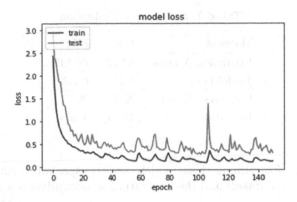

Fig. 2. The training loss and testing loss of MLP

4.4 Comparative Analysis

Prediction Accuracy: This metric evaluates how often the model correctly predicts the sentiment of a piece of music. Higher accuracy means the model's predictions are more often correct. In the table, the KNN model has an accuracy of 82.12%, which is slightly higher than the MLP's accuracy of 80.13%. This suggests that for the given dataset and context, KNN slightly outperforms MLP in terms of correct predictions. Model Loss: This metric provides insight into how far off the model's predictions are from the actual values, on average. A lower loss value is better. The KNN model has a loss of 0.177, while the MLP has a slightly higher loss of 0.185. This indicates that, on average, the KNN model's predictions are slightly closer to the actual sentiments than the MLP's predictions.

Converged Epoch: This metric is specific to models that require iterative training (like the MLP). It indicates the training iteration (epoch) at which the model's performance stopped improving (or improved very insignificantly). For KNN, which doesn't require iterative training like MLP, this metric is not applicable (N.A.). The MLP, however, converged at the 30th epoch, suggesting that after 30 iterations of training, further training did not significantly benefit the model.

Execution Time: This measures how long it takes for the model to make predictions on a set of data. The KNN model took 10.65 s, which is notably longer than the MLP's time of 4.56 s. This highlights the computational efficiency of the MLP model over KNN, especially given that KNN must compute distances to every data point in the dataset for predictions (Table 1).

4.5 Key Insights

1. Both models, while having their distinct strengths, were effective in analyzing musical sentiment from the 'Emotions from Mulan' dataset.
2. Certain emotions proved consistently challenging for automated analysis, underscoring the depth and complexity of musical expression.

Table 1. Performance Evaluation

Matrices	KNN	MLP
Prediction Accuracy	82.12%	80.13%
Model Loss	0.177	0.185
Converged Epoch	N.A	30
Execution Time	10.65 s	4.56 s

3. The potential for refining these models is vast, especially with the inclusion of more diverse datasets and the integration of more advanced AI techniques.

5   Further Discussion

5.1   Interpretation of Results

While both the KNN and MLP models exhibited commendable performance in sentiment analysis of the 'Emotions from Mulan' dataset, their inherent mechanisms led to varied outcomes. KNN's instance-based approach ensured a high level of accuracy, particularly for distinct emotions. The MLP, on the other hand, showcased its strength in differentiating subtle nuances between closely related sentiments, underscoring the power of neural networks in understanding complex patterns.

The intricacies of emotions in music present a challenging domain for AI. Both models faced difficulties in classifying certain nuanced sentiments, reflecting the vast spectrum of human emotions and the multifaceted ways in which music can express them.

5.2   Implications for AI in Music Composition

Our findings suggest that AI-driven sentiment analysis can be instrumental in music composition. By understanding the sentiment behind existing compositions, AI can potentially generate new pieces that evoke specific emotions, serving as valuable tools for composers, filmmakers, and even therapeutic applications.

5.3   Broader Applications

The methodologies and insights from our study aren't confined to music alone. Similar techniques can be applied to other forms of art, such as painting or literature, opening the door for a multi-disciplinary approach to sentiment analysis in artistic expressions.

5.4   Limitations and Areas for Future Research

While the 'Emotions from Mulan' dataset provides a rich ground for exploration, it represents just a fragment of the vast musical landscape. Different genres, cultures, and historical epochs might present unique challenges and patterns.

No model is perfect. The KNN, for instance, might not scale efficiently with larger datasets due to its instance-based nature. MLP, despite its adaptability, can be prone to overfitting if not appropriately regularized.

Music sentiment remains a deeply personal and cultural experience. What resonates as 'joyful' in one culture might be interpreted differently in another. This subjectivity, while enriching the musical experience, poses challenges for standardized sentiment analysis.

6   Summary and Future Work

Our exploration into the realm of AI-driven sentiment analysis for music composition underscores the vast potential and challenges in marrying two intrinsically complex domains: music and artificial intelligence. By harnessing the capabilities of KNN and MLP models, we've unearthed intriguing patterns and insights from the 'Emotions from Mulan' dataset. The nuances captured and the emotions evoked through music offer a glimpse into the transformative power of technology when applied to artistic endeavors.

The study stands as a testament to the ever-evolving nature of AI, and its increasing role in understanding, interpreting, and even contributing to human artistic expression. As we move forward, the symbiosis between music and AI promises a harmonious future, filled with new melodies, deeper understandings, and broader horizons.

For future work, we plan to further refine our models and enhance the generalizability of our findings, we aim to incorporate more diverse datasets. This includes tracks from varying genres, cultures, and time periods, ensuring a holistic sentiment analysis. Besides, building upon our methodologies, future projects can delve into sentiment analysis across different art forms. By understanding commonalities and differences in sentiment expression across music, visual arts, and literature, we can pave the way for integrated AI systems that cater to multi-modal artistic outputs.

References

1. Asyrofi, M.H., Yang, Z., Yusuf, I.N.B., Kang, H.J., Thung, F., Lo, D.: Biasfinder: metamorphic test generation to uncover bias for sentiment analysis systems. IEEE Trans. Softw. Eng. **48**(12), 5087–5101 (2021)
2. Calderon Vilca, H.D., Satornicio Medina, A.L., Sucari Leon, R.: Music recommender system based on sentiment analysis enhanced with natural language processing technics. Computación y Sistemas **27**(1) (2023)
3. Chen, W.: Deep adversarial neural network model based on information fusion for music sentiment analysis. Comput. Sci. Inf. Syst. **00**, 31–31 (2023)

4. Dang, C.N., Moreno-García, M.N., De la Prieta, F.: Hybrid deep learning models for sentiment analysis. Complexity **2021**, 1–16 (2021)
5. Finnegan, R.: Music, experience, and the anthropology of emotion. In: The Cultural Study of Music, pp. 353–363. Routledge (2012)
6. Gómez, L.M., Cáceres, M.N.: Applying data mining for sentiment analysis in music. In: De la Prieta, F., et al. (eds.) PAAMS 2017. AISC, vol. 619, pp. 198–205. Springer, Cham (2018). https://doi.org/10.1007/978-3-319-61578-3_20
7. Holzinger, A., Keiblinger, K., Holub, P., Zatloukal, K., Müller, H.: Ai for life: trends in artificial intelligence for biotechnology. New Biotechnol. **74**, 16–24 (2023)
8. Inglis, I.: Performance and Popular Music: History, Place and Time. Routledge, London (2017)
9. Kassler, J.C.: Music, Science, Philosophy: Models in the Universe of Thought. Taylor & Francis, Milton Park (2023)
10. Neelam Mukhtar and Mohammad Abid Khan: Effective lexicon-based approach for urdu sentiment analysis. Artif. Intell. Rev. **53**(4), 2521–2548 (2020)
11. OpenAI. Openai musenet (2023)
12. Patra, B.G., Das, D. and Bandyopadhyay, S.: Automatic music mood classification of Hindi songs. In: Proceedings of the 3rd Workshop on Sentiment Analysis where AI meets Psychology, pp. 24–28 (2013)
13. Peck, J.M.: Explorations in algorithmic composition: Systems of composition and examination of several original works. Master's Thesis, State University of New York, College at Oswego (2011)
14. Phan, M.H., Ogunbona, P.O.: Modelling context and syntactical features for aspect-based sentiment analysis. In: Proceedings of the 58th Annual Meeting of the Association for Computational Linguistics, pp. 3211–3220 (2020)
15. Sarin, E., Vashishtha, S. and Kaur, S., et al.: Sentispotmusic: a music recommendation system based on sentiment analysis. In: 2021 4th International Conference on Recent Trends in Computer Science and Technology (ICRTCST), pp. 373–378. IEEE (2022)
16. Shukla, S., Khanna, P., Agrawal, K.K.: Review on sentiment analysis on music. In: 2017 International Conference on Infocom Technologies and Unmanned Systems (Trends and Future Directions)(ICTUS), pp. 777–780. IEEE (2017)
17. Tensorflow. Google magenta (2023)
18. Tsoumakas, G., Spyromitros-Xioufis, E., Vilcek, J., Vlahavas, I.: Mulan: a java library for multi-label learning. J. Mach. Learn. Res. **12**, 2411–2414 (2011)
19. Yang, Y.H., Chen, H.H.: Machine recognition of music emotion: a review. ACM Trans. Intell. Syst. Technol. (TIST) **3**(3), 1–30 (2012)
20. Zador, A., et al.: Catalyzing next-generation artificial intelligence through neuroai. Nat. Commun. **14**(1), 1597 (2023)

Fault Diagnosis with BERT Bi-LSTM-assisted Knowledge Graph Aided by Attention Mechanism for Hydro-Power Plants

Bilei Guo[1], Yining Wang[1], Weifeng Pan[1], Yanlin Sun[1], and Yuwen Qian[2(✉)]

[1] State Grid Electric Power Research Institute, Nanjing 210003, China
{guobilei,wangyining,panweifeng,sunyanlin}@sgepri.sgcc.com.cn
[2] School of Electronic and Optical Engineering, Nanjing University of Science and Technology, Nanjing 210094, China
admon@njust.edu.cn

Abstract. To minimize the risk of Hydro-Power Plant failure, it's crucial to detect and precisely repair the damaged components. In this paper, we propose a knowledge graph-based fault diagnosis method for Hydro-Power Plants. Then, the improved BiLSTM-CRF algorithm is developed to recognize entities for fault diagnosis, and the BERT relationship extraction algorithm is designed to construct a fault diagnosis knowledge graph for the Hydro-Power Plant. The real experimental test results validate the proposed methodology.

Keywords: Hydro-power Plant · Fault Diagnose · BERT · Knowledge Graph · Bi-LSTM

1 Introduction

Hydro-power plants are becoming increasingly complex, leading to a higher frequency of automation system failures, which results in a significant fluctuation in plant reliability [5]. Furthermore, the equipment in the hydro-power plants is subject to a more complex and severe working environment due to natural and other factors [6]. Therefore, it is crucial to conduct effective fault diagnosis for hydro-power plants to prevent such events from occurring [7].

Through the continuous improvement of the data acquisition technology of Hydro-Power Plant equipment, which has realized the collection of process automation data, unit parameters, and electrical parameters [13]. Based on these data resources, two technical methods, namely, the machine learning model and the mathematical model, have been adopted for the diagnosis of working conditions. Still, both methods have certain limitations [4]. The traditional mechanism model has two representative methods: the current method and the holding diagnosis method. After a fault occurs, both of them need to be analyzed by experts according to the characteristics of the recorded data [2,8].

© ICST Institute for Computer Sciences, Social Informatics and Telecommunications Engineering 2024
Published by Springer Nature Switzerland AG 2024. All Rights Reserved
J. Liu et al. (Eds.): TridentCom 2023, LNICST 523, pp. 85–95, 2024.
https://doi.org/10.1007/978-3-031-51399-2_5

The post-processing method leads to a poor real-time system, which requires rich experience in Hydro-power plant conditions to make accurate judgments on the detection results [9]. The mathematical model adopts big data and deep learning technology for real-time analysis and establishes a fault diagnosis model by analyzing the historical working condition sample data and extracting parameter features [10]. However, It's challenging to gather enough fault data, which affects diagnostic accuracy [12].

In recent years, relevant literature has been applied to knowledge mapping in fault diagnosis. For example, the authors of [11] construct an engine-oriented knowledge graph, through the engine production failure and after-sales maintenance reports to build the domain knowledge graph. Furthermore, the knowledge graph is used for visualization retrieval and assisted decision-making. The authors of [3] proposed a methodology for constructing and reasoning a knowledge graph for engineering machinery faults. The approach involves using preset rules to automatically extract ternary groups from construction machinery maintenance documents. Moreover, an auxiliary decision-making model is obtained through alternate iteration training to assist in troubleshooting engineering machinery, providing a new perspective on problem-solving. Through exchanges with hydropower technicians, we found that there are still many uncertainties and a lack of systematic research on the application of knowledge mapping in the hydropower plant [1]. For example, Hydro-Power is skeptical about the prospect of applying a knowledge graph and is not sure how to use it in the processes of fault diagnosis, system recovery, gathering, and transportation in hydro-power plants. In addition, there is a lack of knowledge-based fault diagnosis process for Hydro-Power.

In this article, a fault diagnosis approach is proposed by using the BERT BiLSTM-assisted knowledge graph with an attention mechanism for hydropower plants. The main contributions of this paper are listed as follows.

- A fault diagnosis method is proposed based on a BERT BiLSTM-assisted knowledge graph with an attention mechanism, as seen in Sect. 2.
- The BERT method is adopted to integrate parameters into the BiLSTM-CRF model, which improves the model generalization and solves the out-of-vocabulary problem, as seen in Sect. 3.
- a word attention mechanism layer is added to the BERT model to improve the relationship classification accuracy, which solves the problem that the previous knowledge graph is only used for retrieval and characterization and realizes the quantitative reasoning of the knowledge graph, as seen in Sect. 4.
- Simulation results demonstrate that the entities and relationship between these entities can be effectively extracted, and the faults in hydropower plants can be found by using the proposed BERT BiLSTM-CRF aided knowledge network with attention mechanism, as seen in Sect. 5.

2   Construction of Knowledge Graph

The diagnostic knowledge graph construction and application process includes specifying the domain ontology type of Hydro-Power Plant equipment troubleshooting, domain entity identification, relationship extraction, and Neo4j graph database construction based on Neo4j [8]. The specific construction process is as follows.

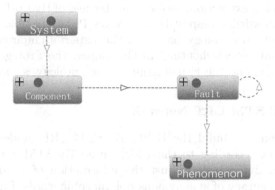

Fig. 1. The ontology LSTM with Attention Model

First, we define the ontology type through expert judgment and application requirements and determine the types of entities and relationships in the graph. Second, we label the dataset of Hydro-Power Plant fault diagnosis using the wizard annotation assistant software. Use Wizard annotation assistant software to annotate the dataset of the fault diagnosis part of the corpus, and train the fault domain entity recognition model. Use the training model to recognize the entities of the fault diagnosis corpus, and construct the entity set. Third, label the above dataset with relationships to train the fault domain relationship extraction model. Use the trained relationship extraction model to extract the relationships in the fault diagnosis corpus, and build a set of relationship pairs. The entity and relation of the knowledge network are listed in Table 1.

Table 1. Entity and Relation of the Knowledge Network

Domain	Objectproperty	Range
System	Consists_of	Component
Component	Occure	Fault
Fault	Cause	Phenominent
Fault	Cause	Fault

After completing the entity identification and relationship extraction, combine the entities and relationship pairs into a ternary. Then, import the ternary into the knowledge graph construction tool Neo4j to construct a knowledge graph for Hydro-Power Plant fault diagnosis.

3   Ontologies Construction

When constructing a domain-specific knowledge map, ontologies should be con-structed based on experts' knowledge to provide specifications for entity recogni-tion and relationship extraction. we focus on the field of Hydro-Power Plants, i.e., we construct a knowledge map of Hydro-Power Plants troubleshooting. There-fore, we construct an ontology based on the expert's empirical knowledge of Hydro-Power plant troubleshooting. In this paper, the Protege tool is used to design the ontology, and the visualization of the ontology is shown in Fig. 1.

3.1   BERT-BiLSTM-CRF Network

In this Subsection, we build the BERT-BiLSTM-CRF model by integrating BERT parameters according to the widely used BiLSTM network. The pro-posed model can dynamically adjust the information of words, and improve the recognition accuracy of synonymous polymorphic words. Figure 2 shows the BERT-BiLSTM-CRF model.

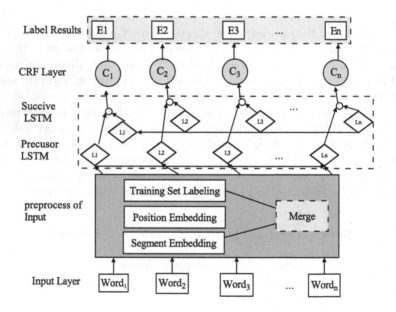

Fig. 2. The Bi-LSTM scheme with CRF

BERT Pre-training. The sentence is pre-trained by BERT to form the feature vector of each word, and the constructed vector sequence is input to the BiL-STM model for feature extraction. In addition, the semantic features are passed through the CRF layer to obtain the most probable label identifier, the BiLSTM layer.

BiLSTM. BiLSTM sets up forward and backward LSTM networks and the output layer results are determined by both the forward and backward LSTM networks. Among the LSTM networks, each LSTM computational module contains an input gate, a forgetting gate, and an output gate. The specific computational process is given by the following equations as

$$i_t = \sigma(w_i[h_{t-1}, x_t] + b_i) \tag{1}$$

$$f_t = \sigma(w_f[h_{t-1}, x_t] + b_f) \tag{2}$$

$$o_t = \sigma(w_0[h_{t-1}, x_t] + b_0) \tag{3}$$

$$\widetilde{c}_t = \tanh(w_c[h_{t-1}, x_t] + b_c) \tag{4}$$

$$c_t = f_t * c_{t-1} + i_t * \widetilde{c}_t \tag{5}$$

$$h_t = o_t * \tanh(c_t) \tag{6}$$

where i_t, f_t, and o_t represent the input gate, forget gate, and output gate outputs in the time slot t. Furthermore, x_t and h_t represent the input and output gates in the period t.

CRF Layer. Take its features and obtain the corresponding sequence vector. To ensure the accuracy of entity recognition, a layer of computational constraints is placed on the sequence vectors using the CRF layer to ensure the correspondence with the predefined labels. For sentence X, the predicting probability of the sequence $Y = (y_1, y_2, ..., y_n)$ is

$$P(X|Y) = \frac{e^{s(x,y)}}{\sum_y e^{s(x,y)}} \tag{7}$$

$$s(X, Y) = \sum_{i=1}^{n} (P_{i,y_i} + W_{y_i, y_{i+1}}) \tag{8}$$

The output sequence of the BiLSTM layer is processed by the CRF layer. The CRF layer processes the output sequences of the BERT-BiLSTM layer, which can calculate the fit scores of subsequences and output labels, making the results of entity recognition more accurate.

3.2 Entity Recognize

In this paper, we select the case of hydropower plants in the past 20 years and the related literature on hydropower plant fault on the website as the corpus to be analyzed. Through text pre-processing, such as PDF text extraction, and sentence division to obtain the statements. The labeling rules of the data set are as follows. First, we classify the entities into four categories: system, component, fault, and fault signs, and learn the working principle of hydropower plants before labeling them. Second, the components contained in faults and fault signs are not labeled, and the labeling can only exist in one layer. Therefore, the fault diagnosis system pays more attention to faults and fault signs.

4   Relation Exaction

After obtaining the entity nodes, we analyze the relationship between the sentence and the entity pairs in the sentence. In this paper, we use the widely used BERT model as the base network and add a word attention layer into the network model to improve the accuracy of relationship extraction.

4.1   Word Attention with BERT

Figure 3 shows the structure of the Word-Attention-BERT, which includes the BERT coding layer, word attention layer, and relationship classification layer. Each word of the input sentence is converted into a token, and the token is input into the BERT encoding layer to obtain the vector representation of the sentence. In the relationship extraction process, the relationship between entities is determined by a certain word. Hence, the attention layer in the BERT relationship extraction network can emphasize the role of keywords and improve the accuracy of relationship extraction.

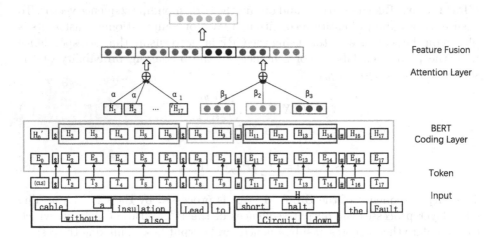

Fig. 3. The LSTM with Attention Model

BERT Coding Method. To enable the BERT model to obtain the position and boundary information of two entities in a sentence, "$" and "#" are used to mark the entities in the sentence. Sentence and entity are encoded in the BERT coding layer to obtain $H = \{H_0', H_1, H_0', H_0'\}$, where H_0' is the output corresponding to the token "[CLS]". As the semantic representation of the whole sentence with H_0', it is obtained by adding the tanh activation function to H_0' and undergoing a linear transformation. The entity information is obtained by calculating the average value of H_t contained in the entity, which is then transformed linearly by the tanh activation function. The word vectors are computed directly by calculating the average value of Ht contained in the words. The procedure is as follows.

$$H_0{}' = W_0\left(\tanh(H_0)\right) + b_0 \tag{9}$$

$$e_1 = W_1\left[\tanh\left(\frac{1}{j-i+1}\sum_{t=i}^{j}H_t\right)\right] + b_1 \tag{10}$$

$$e_2 = W_2\left[\tanh\left(\frac{1}{m-k+1}\sum_{t=k}^{m}H_t\right)\right] + b_2 \tag{11}$$

$$Word = \frac{1}{s-r+1}\sum_{t=s}^{s}H_t \tag{12}$$

where W_0, W_1, W_2 denote trainable weight matrices of dimension $d \times d$; b_0, b_1, b_2 denote trainable weight vectors of dimension $d \times 1$; and d denotes a trainable weight vector of dimension $d \times 1$; and b_0, b_1, b_2 denote the trainable weight vectors of dimension $d \times 1$; d denotes the word vector dimension; e_1 and e_2 denote the entities; i and j denote the weights of entity 1, respectively. k and m denote the start and end positions of entity 2; r and s denote the start and end positions of words. r and s denote the starting and ending positions of words. The word denotes the generalization of words in a sentence.

Attention Mechanism of Word. In the fault diagnosis field, words such as "due to", "brought about", "because of" often determine the relationship between entities, and thus the word attention layer is added in the fusion of sentence features to enhance the accuracy of the relationship extraction. Therefore, a word attention layer is added in the fusion of sentence features to enhance the keyword features to improve the accuracy of relationship extraction. The sentence is encoded as $H = \{H_0, H_1, ..., H_{n+4}\}$ in the BERT coding layer, and the keyword features are enhanced by using the word attention mechanism. Taking $H_1, ..., H_{n+4}$ as input, a two-layer neural network is used to obtain an importance vector α with a dimension of $1 \times (n+4)$ and a value range of $(0,1)$. Similarly, an importance vector β is obtained on the word scale. Finally, the word vectors are weighted, and the weighted vectors are cascaded together to obtain the final word vector β after linear transformation and activation by the tanh activation function. Finally, the weighted vectors are cascaded and activated by the tanh activation function, and then linearly transformed to obtain the final sentence fusion feature representation. The calculation process is given by

$$\alpha = Softmax(q_c\tanh(Q_cH_c)) \tag{13}$$

$$\beta = Softmax(q_w\tanh(Q_wH_w)) \tag{14}$$

Relation Categorize. The input Softmax function for relationship classification to get the final result. The specific calculation process is given by

$$r = W_r \left[concat(H_0', e_1, e_2, h'', w'') \right] + b_r \tag{15}$$

$$outcome = Softmax(r) \tag{16}$$

where r denotes the fusion feature vector, W_r denotes the trainable weight matrix with dimension $L \times 5d$, b_r denotes the trainable weight vector with dimension $L \times 1$, and L denotes the number of relation types.

5   Experimental Result

To evaluate the proposed method, we have built a fault diagnosis method by using the knowledge graph. First, we design an algorithm for extracting historical fault cases and implement the build of the knowledge graph to diagnose the faults for Hydro-power plants. The Neo4j graph database is used for storing and managing the knowledge graph. Accuracy probability, recall rate, and F1 are adopted to evaluate the extractions.

The accuracy probability can be given by

$$P = \frac{T_P}{T_P + F_P}, \tag{17}$$

where T_P represents the character numbers manually labeled for a given label, and F_P is the character numbers labeled manually that were not extracted.

Second, the recall rate can be expressed as

$$T = \frac{T_P}{T_P + F_N}, \tag{18}$$

where F_N represents the character numbers extracted for a label rather than manually labeled.

Third, F1 can be calculated by

$$F1 = \frac{2 \times P \times R}{P + R}. \tag{19}$$

5.1   Entity Recognize Experiment

We adopt the BERT Chinese pre-training model released by Google, which contains 12 hidden layers, 768 hidden layer units, 12 encode layer headers, and 110M parameters, the maximum sequence length is set to 128, and the number of hidden units in LSTM is set to 200. The other settings are default. The experimental environment relies on the TensorFlow library. Then, we choose BERT and Word-Attention-BERT to compare with each other in terms of precision rate, recall

Table 2. Entity Recognize Results with Different Algorithms

Model	Accuracy	Recall rate	F1
BiLSTM	61	58	60
BiLSTM-CRF	76	54	65
Bert-BiLSTM	81	58	68
Bert-BiLSTM-CRF	86	65	75

rate, and F1 score in the domain of hydro-power plant fault diagnosis, and the specific results are shown in Table 2.

Table 2 shows that the BERT-BiLSTM-CRF model outperforms the other three models in terms of recognition accuracy. Moreover, the BERT Chinese word training to the BiLSTM-CRF model significantly improves the effectiveness of the entity recognition model for hydropower plant fault diagnosis.

5.2   Relation Recognize Experiment

The relationships between entities in hydro-power plant faults are defined into four categories: composition, occurrence, cause, and unknown. The data is divide into a training set and a test set in an 8:2 ratio., which are 11,885 and 2,971 items respectively. In the relationship extraction experiments, we also use the BERT pre-training model and fine-tune it for the relationship extraction task on this basis. The learning rate is set to 0.0005 and the maximum sequence length is 128. The specific results of relation recognition are shown in Table 3.

Table 3. The Recognition Results of Relations

Model	Accuracy	Recall rate	F1
BERT	84.54	79.25	86.19
Word-Attention-Bert	92.81	90	91

From Table 3, we can see that Word-Attention-BERT outperforms the ordinary BERT relational extraction model in terms of accuracy, recall, and F1 score. Moreover, we can observe that the Word-Attention-BERT can better utilize the key information in the sentence to improve recognition accuracy.

5.3   Fault Diagnosis for Different Types

Figure 4 shows the accuracy of fault extraction for different fault types.

From Fig. 4, the proposed method incorporates relationships between device structures into diagnostic reasoning by leveraging the knowledge map. First, the proposed method achieves an accuracy of around 90.6% by effectively utilizing device structure relationships. Second, we can observe that fault recognition out-performs fault location and status detection due to random position descriptions leading to lower detection accuracy.

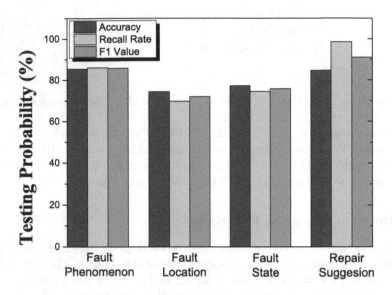

Fig. 4. The comparison of the optimal trajectory with the initial trajectory of the UAV.

6   Conclusions

To solve the problem of fast and accurate fault diagnosis for hydropower plants, we have proposed a knowledge-based knowledge graph to diagnose faults that occur in hydropower plants. We have designed a BiLSTM aided by the CRF algorithm to automatically recognize the entities and the BERT-BiLSTM is used to extract the relationship between the entities in hydropower plants. Experimental results validate the performance of the proposed method. In the future, we can focus on the construction of large-scale corpus data in the hydropower plants fault domain to improve the model.

Acknowledgement. This work is supported by the science project of State Grid Xin Yuan Company Limited (No. SGXYKJ-2023-012).

References

1. Buaphan, I., Premrudeepreechacharn, S.: Development of expert system for fault diagnosis of an 8-mw bulb turbine downstream irrigation hydro power plant. In: 2017 6th International Youth Conference on Energy (IYCE), pp. 1–6 (2017)

2. Chi, Y., Dong, Y., Wang, J.: Knowledge-based fault diagnosis in industrial internet of things: a survey. IEEE Internet Things J. **93**(2), 107–118 (2022)
3. Deng, J., Wang, T., Wang, Z., Zhou, J., Cheng, L.: Research on event logic knowledge graph construction method of robot transmission system fault diagnosis. IEEE Access **10**, 17656–17673 (2022)
4. Gou, B., Xu, Y., Xia, Y.: An intelligent time-adaptive data-driven method for sensor fault diagnosis in induction motor drive system. IEEE Trans. Industr. Electron. **66**(12), 9817–9827 (2018)
5. Jiang, J.: Reliability test and analysis of electrical automation control equipment. Appl. Mech. Mater. 2380–2383 (2014)
6. Lemes, D.A.M., et al.: Low runtime approach for fault detection for refrigeration systems in smart homes using wavelet transform. IEEE Trans. Consum. Electron. 1–1 (2023). https://doi.org/10.1109/TCE.2023.3328147
7. Nor, N.M., Hussain, C.: A review of data-driven fault detection and diagnosis methods: applications in chemical process systems. Rev. Chem. Eng. **36**(4), 513–553 (2020)
8. Qu, X., Cai, Y.: Conve-bio: knowledge graph embedding for biomedical relation prediction. In: 2023 International Conference on Intelligent Supercomputing and BioPharma (ISBP), pp. 10–13 (2023). https://doi.org/10.1109/ISBP57705.2023.10061292
9. Scharpf, P., Schubotz, M., Gipp, B.: Mining mathematical documents for question answering via unsupervised formula labeling. In: 2022 ACM/IEEE Joint Conference on Digital Libraries (JCDL), pp. 1–11 (2022)
10. Sousa, D., Couto, F.: Biomedical relation extraction with knowledge graph-based recommendations. IEEE J. Biomed. Health Inform. **26**(8), 4207–4217 (2022)
11. Wu, J., et al.: Fault diagnosis of the HVDC system based on the catboost algorithm using knowledge graphs. Front. Energy Res. **11** (2023)
12. Yuan, L., Qin, L., Zhang, W., Chang, L., Yang, J.: Index-based densest clique percolation community search in networks. IEEE Trans. Knowl. Data Eng. **30**(5), 922–935 (2018)
13. Zhang, Z., et al.: Knowledge graph construction method for power grid infrastructure. In: 2022 7th Asia Conference on Power and Electrical Engineering (ACPEE), pp. 633–637 (2022). https://doi.org/10.1109/ACPEE53904.2022.9783665

AI and Its Security

Zero-Knowledge with Robust Learning: Mitigating Backdoor Attacks in Federated Learning for Enhanced Security and Privacy

Linlin Li[1], Chungen Xu[2(✉)], and Pan Zhang[1]

[1] School of Cyber Science and Engineering, Nanjing University of Science and Technology, Nanjing 210094, China
[2] School of Mathematics and Statistics, Nanjing University of Science and Technology, Nanjing 210094, China
xuchung@njust.edu.cn

Abstract. As a distributed machine learning framework, federated learning addresses the challenges of data isolation and privacy concerns, ensuring that user data remains private during the model training process. However, the privacy-preserving nature of federated learning also makes it has vulnerability to security attacks, particularly in the form of backdoor attacks. These attacks aim to compromise the integrity of the model by embedding a malicious behavior that can be triggered under specific conditions. In our study, aiming to counteract backdoor threats in federated learning, we introduce a new protective mechanism termed zero-knowledge with robust learning (ZKRL). The ZKRL scheme introduces the robust learning rate and non-interactive zero-knowledge proof techniques to filter out malicious model updates and preserve the privacy of the global model parameters of the federated learning process. The extensive experiments conduct on real-world data demonstrate its effectiveness in improving the accuracy on the verification set by 2% and significantly reducing the accuracy of backdoor attacks compared to existing state-of-the-art defense schemes. In summary, the proposed ZKRL defense scheme provides a robust solution for protecting federated learning models against backdoor attacks, ensuring the integrity of the trained models while preserving user privacy.

Keywords: Federated learning · Backdoor attack · Zero-knowledge proof

1 Introduction

Federated learning(FL) [16] is a distributed machine learning paradigm where multiple clients, such as mobile edge devices or corporate organizations, collaborate to train a shared global model under the coordination of a central server. The

Supported by The National Natural Science Foundation of China (No. 62072240).

J. Liu et al. (Eds.): TridentCom 2023, LNICST 523, pp. 99–116, 2024.
https://doi.org/10.1007/978-3-031-51399-2_6

emergence of FL addresses the challenges posed by data dispersion and privacy concerns in traditional centralized machine learning. FL has gained significant interest in both academia and industry. For example, a variety of world-leading companies have introduced various FL application frameworks, such as Google's TensorFlow Federated (TFF) [6] and Webank's FATE [14].

In FL, the privacy of user data is preserved as it remains stored locally on client devices. Instead of sharing raw data, clients only upload encrypted model updates to the central server during the training process. This decentralized approach offers several benefits, including improved model performance compared to traditional local training and full utilization of computing resources of multiple devices, which speeds up model training, etc. However, the nature of FL, where model updates are hidden, also brings a significant security concern: backdoor attacks [3,5]. Backdoor attacks aim to manipulate the global model's behavior by injecting specific inputs (e.g., images with backdoor triggers) that are misclassified into a targeted false label while appearing normal for regular inputs [10,15,21]. Since the server receives only the aggregated results without the prior knowledge of how the local model updates are generated, it becomes challenging to detect whether the local model parameters contain malicious backdoor modifications through direct parameter analysis. Consequently, FL is more susceptible to backdoor attacks, and conventional detection methods prove ineffective in this scenario.

To mitigate the risks of backdoor attacks in FL, researchers have been actively investigating and developing a variety of defense mechanisms and detection techniques specifically tailored for this setting. Several defense methods have been proposed to enhance the security of FL system, including integrity verification, dimension filtering, and robust aggregation algorithms [1,2,24,25]. However, some existing defense methods have certain limitations. The lightweight defense proposed by [17] that adjusts the learning rate may introduce exposure of sensitive user information as it requires processing model updates in plaintext. Additionally, reversing the learning rate for a specific dimension, regardless of the update's origin, can potentially lead to a decrease in the accuracy of the global model. EIFFel introduced by [19] is the verifiably updated security aggregation algorithm. This method involves joint verification by the remaining clients under the supervision of the central server. While it enhances the security of FL by ensuring the integrity of the model updates, it comes at the cost of significant communication overhead and computational burdens. The need for joint verification among clients can result in increased communication and computational costs, which may limit the scalability and efficiency of the FL system.

In this paper, our main task is to address the challenge of backdoor attacks targeting deep neural networks in FL. To achieve this, we propose a scheme named zero-knowledge with robust learning (ZKRL), which filters out malicious model updates during the training process. In ZKRL, we introduce a more refined mechanism for handling model updates at each dimension. Instead of simply multiplying a certain dimension of the model update by a negative learning rate, with the help of zero-knowledge proof, without exposing user sensitive information, the server checks whether the value of each model update is within the specified range and then judges whether it is a malicious model update. And the data that requires zero-knowledge proof is a certain dimension of the model update rather than the entire model update or even more complex L_2−norm calculations. To evaluate the effectiveness of our defense mechanism, we conduct a series of empirical experiments. The results of these experiments demonstrate that our proposed approach effectively minimizes the loss of model accuracy while successfully deterring backdoor attacks. Moreover, we also provide empirical evidence that supports the effectiveness of our defense mechanism. In addition to the empirical evaluation, we also provide a theoretical analysis that explains how our defense mechanism improves model accuracy. By providing a solid theoretical foundation, we offer insights into the underlying mechanisms that contribute to the effectiveness of our approach.

The structure of this paper is as follows: Sect. 2 covers foundational topics like FL, zero-knowledge proof, and strategies for both backdoor attacks and their defenses. An overview of the solution is sketched in Sect. 3. Section 4 delves into the methods and algorithms underpinning ZKRL. Section 6 elaborates on the empirical testing of ZKRL. The paper wraps up in Sect. 7 with our conclusions.

2   Preliminaries

2.1   Notation

Let $\mathbb{Z}_p$ denote the ring of integers modulo p, where p is a large prime. $\mathbb{G}_q$ represents the unique subgroup of $\mathbb{Z}_p$ of order q, where q divides $p - 1$. Let $\mathbb{G}_q^n$ and $\mathbb{Z}_p^n$ be vector spaces of dimension n over $\mathbb{G}_q$ and $\mathbb{Z}_p$ respectively, and $\alpha = (g_1, \cdots, g_n), \beta = (h_1, \cdots, h_n) \in \mathbb{G}_q^n$ be a vector of generators. For a scalar $c \in \mathbb{Z}_p$ and a vector $a \in \mathbb{Z}_p^n$, we denote by $b = c \cdot a \in \mathbb{Z}_p^n$ the vector where $b_i = c \cdot a_i$. Furthermore, let $\langle a, b \rangle = \sum_{i=1}^n a_i \cdot b_i$ denote the inner product between two vectors $a, b \in \mathbb{Z}_p^n$, and $a \odot b = (a_1 \cdot b_1, \cdots, a_n \cdot b_n) \in \mathbb{Z}_p^n$ denote the Hadamard product or entry wise multiplication of two vectors.

2.2   Federated Learning

FL was first proposed by Google, which is a distributed machine learning framework that enables a central server to collaboratively train a model with a large number of decentralized clients. The process begins by initializing the global model parameters W_G on the central server. Prior to each round of FL, a subset of m clients (where $m < n$) is randomly chosen from a total of n clients to participate in the training. In the tth round, the central server broadcasts the current global model W_G^t to the selected clients. Each client then performs local training on its own dataset using stochastic gradient descent(SGD). This local training yields a new local model W_i^{t+1} for the ith client. Subsequently, the ith client uploads its model update $\Delta w_i^{t+1} = W_i^{t+1} - W_G^t$ to the central server. The central server employs a secure aggregation algorithm to merge the received model updates to update the global model. Here, the aggregation rule of the Federated Averaging (FedAvg) algorithm, one of the commonly used aggregation algorithms in FL, is as follows:

$$W_G^{t+1} = W_G^t + \eta \odot \frac{1}{m} \sum_{i \in m} \Delta w_i^{t+1}. \tag{1}$$

This iterative process of model distribution, local training, and secure aggregation allows the central server and clients to collaboratively train a robust global model while preserving data privacy and security.

2.3   Zero-Knowledge Proof

Zero-knowledge proof [13], initially proposed by Goldwasser et al., is a cryptographic protocol that involves two parties: the prover P and the verifier V. It is commonly used for proof of membership attribution or proof of knowledge. Zero-knowledge proof possesses three essential properties: completeness, soundness, and zero-knowledge. Completeness guarantees the correctness of the protocol itself. If the prover P provides a valid proof of a statement, and both P and V execute the protocol honestly, then P can convince V of the statement's correctness. Soundness ensures that the honest verifier V cannot be deceived by a malicious prover P'. It protects V from being misled or convinced of a false statement. Zero-knowledge property means that the prover P can prove the correctness of a statement to the verifier V without revealing any information other than the statement's validity. This property ensures privacy and confidentiality. The three properties of zero-knowledge proof make it suitable for establishing trust and protecting privacy in FL, especially for checking model updates. However, interactive proofs require P and V to be continuously online, which can be challenging to achieve due to network delays, denial of service attacks, and other factors. Non-interactive proofs, on the other hand, require the prover to send only one round of messages to complete the proof. Interactive proofs can be transformed into non-interactive proofs using the Fiat-Shamir heuristic [11], which helps to overcome the limitations of interactivity.

2.4   Backdoor Attacks and Defense Solutions

Backdoor Attacks in Federated Learning. A backdoor attack involves embedding a hidden trigger in a model that can be activated to produce specific misclassifications without affecting the model's inference on normal data. In this attack, the adversary aims to manipulate the model's behavior to perform targeted misclassifications based on the presence of the trigger. For instance, in the case of a self-driving model, the backdoor may cause the model to correctly recognize a regular stop sign but misclassify a stop sign with a yellow square as a speed limit sign, with the yellow square acting as the trigger. In a unified environment, a malicious actor might manipulate the training to instill targeted misclassification traits for a backdoor assault. But in FL, given its decentralized data nature, gaining access to the complete training dataset poses challenges for the adversary. That said, backdoor attacks often revolve around formulating harmful modifications. Essentially, the attacker aims to craft a modification embedding the backdoor such that, upon aggregation with other alterations, the merged model manifests the undesired backdoor trait. This assault mode is often termed model poisoning attack [3,5,23]. In such a scenario, the opponent might control several agents involved in the FL process, training their local models using tainted or compromised datasets to produce harmful updates.

Defense Solutions. Several studies have explored the application of robust statistics techniques to enhance the resilience of FL against attacks. In a notable work by [12], Fung et al. proposed a novel approach to improve the robustness of FL by introducing a per-client learning rate, deviating from the conventional practice of employing a uniform learning rate at the server side. This novel approach results in the following update rule:

$$W_G^{t+1} = W_G^t + \frac{1}{m} \sum_{i \in m} \eta_i^t \cdot \Delta w_i^{t+1}, \qquad (2)$$

where $\eta_i^t \in [0,1]$ is the ith client's learning rate for the tth round.

CRFL, proposed by [24], is a protective strategy that employs trimming and refining processes on parameters to ensure the global model's consistency. This method facilitates individual sample resilience assurance against backdoor incursions. In contrast, Ozdayi et al. [17] addressed backdoor attacks by adjusting the learning rate of the aggregation server in a per-dimension and per-round manner, utilizing the sign information of the client's updates.

3 Problem Overview

3.1 Security Goals

Input Privacy (Client's Goal). The first security goal is to safeguard user data privacy in FL. In this decentralized approach, the raw user data remains on the local device, with only model updates being transmitted to the central server. However, it is possible for an honest but curious server to infer information about the original data by analyzing the model updates. To address this concern, clients need to employ cryptographic primitives to guarantee that no party can gain knowledge about the raw input (update) Δw_i of a client C_i, beyond what can be deduced from the final aggregated result W_{agg}.

Input Integrity (Server's Goal). The second security goal is to safeguard the security of the global model. As model updates are concealed, the server lacks the ability to verify the integrity of these updates, consequently raising the risk of potential backdoor attacks initiated by malicious clients. Hence, it becomes imperative for the server to implement measures to filter out any malicious model updates while ensuring the preservation of input privacy, ultimately fortifying the global model against backdoor attacks.

3.2   Threat Model

Semi-honest Server. In this paper, we assume that the server is semi-honest, meaning that it will adhere to the protocol rules but may attempt to infer secret information by observing its own perspective during the execution process. Furthermore, we also take into account that the server possesses a portion of the dateset on its local device for training purposes.

Malicious Clients. We assume the presence of e malicious clients, who have the ability to take arbitrary actions during the protocol execution. However, for the purpose of conducting a backdoor attack in FL, these e malicious clients can only train a malicious model locally and subsequently upload a malicious model update to introduce a backdoor into the global model.

3.3   Solution Overview

Previous research has made attempts to address the issue of backdoor attacks in FL by implementing robust aggregation algorithms or verifiable algorithms in the ciphertext state. However, these methods have not fully met our security objectives. Taking into account our analysis of the threat model, we propose a novel FL scheme called ZKRL, which effectively filters out malicious model updates. To ensure input privacy, we employ Pedersen commitments [18], and we enhance input integrity by integrating non-interactive Bulletproof range proofs [8] into the robust learning rate (RLR) technique proposed by [17]. The ZKRL scheme selectively aggregates model updates that conform to predefined criteria of well-formedness, thereby preserving the integrity of the global model and protecting it against potential backdoor attacks. The overview of our proposed ZKRL scheme is shown in Fig. 1.

4   ZKRL Design

4.1   Secure Aggregation with Commitments

To ensure the privacy of the model updates in FL, it is essential to employ effective encryption techniques. In our proposed approach, we utilize the Pedersen commitment [18] as our cryptographic primitive of choice. The Pedersen commitment provides a secure and efficient approach of encrypting the model updates while preserving the privacy of the underlying data. The Pedersen commitment possesses two important properties: unconditionally hiding and computationally binding. The unconditionally hiding property ensures that the committed value remains hidden and cannot be determined by any party, even if they possess unlimited computational power. On the other hand, the computationally binding property guarantees that once a commitment is made, it is computationally infeasible to change the committed value without detection. One of the notable advantages of using Pedersen commitments is their homomorphic property. This property allows for the computation of operations on the commitments

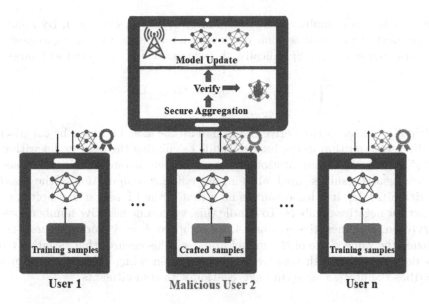

Fig. 1. Overview of ZKRL.

themselves, such as addition and subtraction, without the need to decrypt the underlying values. This enables efficient and secure aggregation of the encrypted model updates without compromising the privacy of the individual updates. Furthermore, Pedersen commitments facilitate the construction of zero-knowledge range proofs. These proofs enable verification of the committed values' validity within a specified range without revealing any information about the actual values. This property ensures the integrity and correctness of the encrypted model updates without disclosing any sensitive information.

To achieve unconditional hiding, a random number $s \in \mathbb{Z}_p$ is selected as the blinding factor. We select a generator g and a random group element $h \in \mathbb{G}_q$, such that nobody knows $\log_g h$. In the protocol, the ith client commits to each element u_j of the model update Δw_i^{t+1}, and subsequently sends the resulting commitment c_j, which is calculated as follows:

$$c_j = g^{u_j} h^{s_j}, \tag{3}$$

where s_j represents the blinding factor specific to that client. To ensure accurate aggregation of model updates, we adopt the masking approach [7] using blinding factors in the commitment-based setting. This approach allows for the cancellation of blinding factors during aggregation, enabling the server to obtain the aggregated output accurately. In our protocol, each of m participating clients selects a blinding factor, denoted as s_i, such that the sum of all the blinding factors is equal to zero: $\sum_{i=1}^{m} s_i = 0$. This ensures that blinding factors cancel out during the aggregation phase. Given two Pedersen commitments c_1 and c_2 for values u_1 and u_2 respectively, the product of these commitments, $c_1 \cdot c_2$, corresponds to a commitment for the sum of u_1 and u_2 $(u_1 + u_2)$. By applying this property to each dimension of the model updates, we can aggregate the commitments efficiently. Specifically, the aggregation is computed as follows:

$$\prod_{i=1}^{m} c_{j,i} = g^{\sum_{i=1}^{m} u_{j,i}} h^{\sum_{i=1}^{m} s_{j,i}} = g^{\sum_{i=1}^{m} u_{j,i}}. \tag{4}$$

Finally, the server can derive the sum of all the model updates by calculating the discrete logarithm to the base g. While calculating the discrete logarithm of $y = g^x$ is generally a computationally hard problem, in our domain, the space of the aggregated result is small, allowing for efficient computation of the discrete logarithm [20,22]. It is important to note that in the FL scenario, we often need to encrypt negative numbers. To handle this, we encode negative numbers before encryption. For a negative number A, we compute $A' = A \mod p$, where p is set to twice the value range of the model updates. This ensures that negative numbers do not overlap with positive numbers after encoding. Algorithm 1 formally describes the process for secure aggregation with commitments.

Algorithm 1: Secure Aggregation with Commitments.

Input: $u_{j,i}$ is the jth dimension of the model update Δw_i^{t+1} of the ith client C_i, l is the dimension of the model updates, generator g $\in \mathbb{G}_q$, random group element h $\in \mathbb{G}_q$.

Output: The aggregated model update Δw_G^{t+1}.

1 Client C_i jointly decides the choice of blinding factor $s_{j,i}$;
2 **for** i=1 → m **do**
3   **for** j=1 → l **do**
4   C_i computes the commitment $c_{j,i} = g^{u_{j,i}} h^{s_{j,i}}$, and sends $c_{j,i}$ to the central server;
5 **for** j=1 → l **do**
6   The server S computes $agg_j = g^{\sum_{i=1}^{m} u_{j,i}} h^{\sum_{i=1}^{m} s_{j,i}} = g^{\sum_{i=1}^{m} u_{j,i}}$, and $u_{j,G} = \log_g agg_j$;
7 $\Delta w_G^{t+1} = (u_{1,G}, u_{2,G}, \cdots, u_{l,G})$;
8 Return Δw_G^{t+1}.

4.2 Zero-Knowledge Range Proof

Bulletproofs [8] is a zero-knowledge proof protocol proposed by Bootle et al. that offers several advantages, including short proofs and the absence of a trusted setup phase. It is notably adept for proficient range proofs on committed values. It enables the confirmation of a value's presence within a range with just $2 \log n + 9$ group and field elements, with n being the bit length of the range. Additionally, Bulletproofs natively supports the Pedersen commitments. In our approach, we leverage the Bulletproofs protocol to enable the server to verify model update uploaded by clients. Specifically, in certain cases (as elaborated in the subsequent analysis section), the server may request clients to provide a range proof for a specific dimension updated by its own model, ensuring that the value falls within a specified range. To transform this proof process into a non-interactive one, we apply the Fiat-Shamir heuristic [11].

Formally, let $u_{j,i}$ be a number in $[0, \cdots, 2^n - 1]$, and $c_{j,i}$ be a Pedersen commitment to $u_{j,i}$ using randomness $s_{j,i}$, $2^n - 1$ is the specific range that the server requires the client to prove. The proof system uses the homomorphic property of the Vector Pedersen commitments to construct commitments to two polynomials $l(X)$ and $r(X)$ in $\mathbb{Z}_p^n[X]$. With these vector-polynomial pledges, the server and clients participate in an inner product dialogue to reliably determine the inner product between $l(X)$ and $r(X)$. The structure of these polynomials ensures that the zero coefficient of $\langle l(X), r(X) \rangle \in \mathbb{Z}_p[X]$ takes a distinct shape solely when $u_{j,i}$ is within the specified range. Let $a_L = (a_1, \cdots, a_n)$ be the vector containing the bits of $u_{j,i}$, the client C_i commits to a_L as well as blinding vectors s_L, s_R using constant sized vector commitments, and constructs the polynomial $t(X) \in \mathbb{Z}_p[X]$ as a function of $u_{j,i}$, $t(X)$ is exactly the inner product of $l(X)$ and $r(X)$:

$$t(X) = \langle l(X), r(X) \rangle \in \mathbb{Z}_p[X]. \tag{5}$$

Here, s_L, s_R whose zero coefficient is independent of $u_{j,i}$ if and only if $u_{j,i}$ indeed contains only bits. The client executes Algorithm 2 to generate a proof of its own model update.

The server receives the zero-knowledge range proof sent by the clients and executes Algorithm 3 for verification.

4.3 ZKRL Workflow

Ozdayi et al. proposed a method where the malicious model update aims to minimize the loss function of both the main task and the backdoor attack task, while the honest model update only focuses on minimizing the loss function of the main task. As a result, these two types of model updates may have different or even opposite directions in certain dimensions. Building upon this observation, the RLR was introduced to involve multiply the learning rate by a negative value to maximize the loss function of the backdoor attack task. However, this method has its limitations. While it successfully maximizes the loss function of the backdoor attack task, it may also impact dimensions related to honest model updates, resulting in a decrease in the accuracy of the global model. Additionally, the method still is performed in plaintext, which does not align with our objective of ensuring input privacy.

Therefore, we propose ZKRL, a novel approach based on the aforementioned method. When the sum of signs of the model updates at a certain dimension j is less than the learning threshold θ, we employ a different treatment instead of simply inverting the learning rate. The server analyzes its own local model

---

Algorithm 2: Zero-Knowledge Range Proof.

Input: $2^n - 1$ is the specific range that the server requires the clients to prove,
   $c_{j,i} = g^{u_{j,i}} h^{s_{j,i}}$ is the commitment corresponding to a certain dimension
   of the model update that needs to give a range proof, H is a hash
   function, $g, h \in \mathbb{G}_q$, $\alpha, \beta \in \mathbb{G}_q^n$.

Output: zero-knowledge range proof RP.

1 $a_L \in \{0,1\}^n$ s.t. $\langle a_L, 2^n \rangle = u_{j,i}$;
2 $a_R = a_L - 1^n$;

3 $\gamma \xleftarrow{\$} \mathbb{Z}_p$;
4 $A = h^\gamma \alpha^{a_L} \beta^{a_R}$;

5 $s_L, s_R \xleftarrow{\$} \mathbb{Z}_p^n$;

6 $\rho \xleftarrow{\$} \mathbb{Z}_p$;
7 $S = h^\rho \alpha^{s_L} \beta^{s_R}$;
8 $y = H(A, S)$;
9 $z = H(A, S, y)$;
10 $l(X) = a_L - z \cdot 1^n + s_L \cdot X$;
11 $r(X) = y^n \circ (a_R + z \cdot 1^n + s_R \cdot X) + z^2 \cdot 2^n$;
12 $t(X) = \langle l(X), r(X) \rangle = \sum_{d=0}^2 t_d \cdot X^d$;

13 $\tau_1, \tau_2 \xleftarrow{\$} \mathbb{Z}_p$;
14 $T_d = g^{t_d} h^{\tau_d}, d = \{1, 2\}$;
15 $x = H(T_1, T_2)$;
16 $\tau_x = \tau_1 \cdot x + \tau_2 \cdot x^2 + z^2 \cdot s_{j,i}$;
17 $\delta = \gamma + \rho \cdot x$;
18 $l = l(x), r = r(x), t = \langle l, r \rangle$;
19 $RP = (A, S, y, z, T_1, T_2, x, \tau_x, \delta, t, l, r)$;
20 Return RP.

---

update and determines the value $w_{j,s}$ corresponding to dimension j. Based on the value of $w_{j,s}$, we handle the model updates as follows:

If $w_{j,s}$ is not equal to 0, the server publishes $w_{j,s}$ and requires all clients to provide proof that the value $w_{j,c}$ corresponding to the dimension of their local model update is less than $w_{j,s}$. If $w_{j,s}$ is negative, indicating a malicious model update, the server removes it from the aggregation process. If $w_{j,s}$ is positive, indicating an honest model update, the server proceeds with aggregation.

If $w_{j,s}$ is equal to 0, we apply the method proposed by [17] to directly invert the learning rate.

Compared to the method proposed by [17], our ZKRL scheme retains honest model updates to a greater extent when abnormal sign detection occurs, resulting in higher accuracy of the final global model. For instance, in our proposed scheme, we categorize model updates into two groups based on the value of $w_{j,s}$ and the outcome of the inspection process. This categorization allows us to filter out the malicious updates and apply a normal learning rate for updating the honest models during the aggregation process. In contrast, the method introduced by [17] does not differentiate the quality of the model updates. Instead, it directly

---

Algorithm 3: Check Zero-Knowledge Range Proof.

Input: $RP = (A, S, y, z, T_1, T_2, x, \tau_x, \delta, t, l, r)$ is the range proof that the client sends to the server, $c_{j,i} = g^{u_{j,i}} h^{s_{j,i}}$ is the commitment corresponding to a certain dimension of the model update that needs to give a range proof, $g, h \in \mathbb{G}_q$, $\alpha, \beta \in \mathbb{G}_q^n$.

Output: True or False.

1 Server computes $t' = \langle l, r \rangle$;
2 **if** $t' = t$ **then**
3   Continue;
4 **else**
5   Return False;
6 $k(y,z) = -z^2 \cdot \langle 1^n, y^n \rangle - z^3 \cdot \langle 1^n, 2^n \rangle$;
7 Server computes $g^{k(y,z)+z \cdot \langle 1^n, y^n \rangle} \cdot c_{j,i}^{z^2} \cdot T_1^x \cdot T_2^{x^2}$ and $g^t h^{\tau_x}$;
8 **if** $g^{k(y,z)+z \cdot \langle 1^n, y^n \rangle} \cdot c_{j,i}^{z^2} \cdot T_1^x \cdot T_2^{x^2} = g^t h^{\tau_x}$ **then**
9   Continue;
10 **else**
11   Return False;
12 **for** $d=1 \to n$ **do**
13      $h_d' = h_d^{y^{-d+1}}$;
14 Server computes $P = AS^x \cdot \alpha^{-z \cdot 1^n} \cdot \beta'^{z \cdot y^n + z^2 \cdot 2^n}$;
15 **if** $P = h^\delta \alpha^l h'^r$ **then**
16   Continue;
17 **else**
18   Return False;
19 Return True.

---

employs the opposite learning rate to update the models in all dimensions. By subdividing the model updates based on their quality, our approach enables a more fine-grained evaluation and filtering process, resulting in improved defense against malicious updates. This distinction allows us to selectively update the models with a more appropriate learning rate, thus enhancing the overall robustness and integrity of the FL system. The execution flow of protocol ZKRL is shown in Algorithm 4.

5 Security Analysis

In this section, we formally analyze the security of ZKRL.

Theorem 1. *ZKRL scheme satisfies the security goals of privacy protection and integrity verification at the same time.*

Algorithm 4: ZKRL.

Input: m is the number of clients selected in one iteration, W_G^t is the global
model parameters for thr t^{th} iteration, l is the dimension of the model
updates, θ is the learning threshold, η is the learning rate.

Output: global model paramaters for the $(t+1)^{th}$ iteration W_G^{t+1}.

1 Server S distributes the global model W_G^t to clients;
2 **for** $i=1 \rightarrow m$ **do**
3   Client C_i trains W_G^t using it's data D_i locally to achieve local model W_i^{t+1},
     $\Delta w_i^{t+1} = W_i^{t+1} - W_G^t$. C_i commits to Δw_i^{t+1} using Pedersen commitment,
     and send it to the server along with the sign of Δw_i^{t+1};

4 Server S also trains W_G^t using its data D_s locally to achieve local model W_s^{t+1},
     $\Delta w_s^{t+1} = W_s^{t+1} - W_G^t$;
5 **for** $j=1 \rightarrow l$ **do**
6   Server S computes $sgn_j = \sum_{i=1}^{m} sgn(u_{j,i})$;
7   **if** $sgn_j \geq \theta$ **then**
8           $\eta_{\theta,j} = \eta$;
9   **else if** $sgn_j < \theta$ **then**
10   **if** $\Delta w_{j,s}^{t+1} = 0$ **then**
11              $\eta_{\theta,j} = -\eta$;
12   **else**
13   Server S publishes the value $\Delta w_{j,s}^{t+1}$ and requires m clients to use
             Algorithm 2 to generate a proof that $\Delta w_{j,i}^{t+1}$ is less than $\Delta w_{j,s}^{t+1}$;
14   **for** $i=1 \rightarrow m$ **do**
15   Client C_i uses Algorithm 2 to generate a proof RP_i, and sends it to
             the server;
16   Server S uses Algorithm 3 to check RP_i and get verification result
             V_i;
17   **if** $V_i = True$ and $\Delta w_{j,s}^{t+1} > 0$ **then**
18                  $\Delta w_{j,i}^{t+1}$ is honest;
19   **if** $V_i = True$ and $\Delta w_{j,s}^{t+1} < 0$ **then**
20                  $\Delta w_{j,i}^{t+1}$ is malicious;
21   **if** $V_i = False$ and $\Delta w_{j,s}^{t+1} > 0$ **then**
22                  $\Delta w_{j,i}^{t+1}$ is malicious;
23   **if** $V_i = False$ and $\Delta w_{j,s}^{t+1} < 0$ **then**
24                  $\Delta w_{j,i}^{t+1}$ is honest;

25 Server S filters out malicious model updates and uses Algorithm 1 to obtain
     aggregated model update Δw_G^{t+1};
26 $W_G^{t+1} = W_G^t + \eta_\theta \odot agg(\Delta w_G^{t+1})$;
27 Return W_G^{t+1}.

Proof. ZKRL utilizes the Pedersen commitment to ensure the privacy of model updates, this scheme relies on the properties of the Pedersen commitment, where for any element $u \in \mathbb{Z}_p$ and for randomly uniformly chosen $s \in \mathbb{Z}_p$ and $g, h \in \mathbb{G}_q$, $g^u h^s$ is uniformly distributed in $\mathbb{G}_q$. Formally, if $u, u' \in \mathbb{Z}_p$ satisfies $u \neq u'$ and $g^u h^s = g^{u'} h^{s'}$, then it must hold that $s \neq s'$ mod p and $\log_g h = \frac{u-u'}{s'-s}$ mod p. However, it is not feasible to directly calculate the value of $\log_g h$. And ZKRL achieves the integrity verification of the model through the use of range proofs. In ZKRL, range proofs are utilized due to their beneficial attributes, such as perfect completeness, perfect honest verifier zero-knowledge, and computational special soundness.

6 Experimental Evaluation

In this section, we conduct a comprehensive performance analysis of our proposed defense mechanism and provide empirical evidence to support its effectiveness. To evaluate the performance, we implemented a FL prototype system using the PyTorch framework. The hardware setup includes an AMD Ryzen 7 (2.90 GHz) CPU, an RTX2080 (8 GB) GPU, and 64 GB of memory. The software environment consists of the Ubuntu 20 operating system, Python 3.7, and PyTorch 1.13 with Cudn 10.1.

In our experiments, we created a FL scenario with a total of 100 participants, including both honest participants and malicious participants. The original dataset was divided into 100 subsets, with each participant receiving one subset. It is important to note that the distribution of samples across different categories was kept uniform, ensuring that all participants had independently and identically distributed (IID) data. Furthermore, we also carried out tests with the Federated EMNIST dataset sourced from the LEAF benchmark [9], specifically examining the performance under the Non-IID setting.

6.1 Experimental Setup

Datasets. To evaluate the efficiency of our introduced ZKRL method within FL, various classification exercises are designed using these three datasets:

MNIST Dataset: This collection comprises 70,000 hand-drawn numeric images spanning 10 categories (0–9), with 60,000 designated for training and 10,000 for testing. To ensure consistency, we normalized all samples in the MNIST dataset to a standardized size of 28×28 pixels.

CIFAR-10 Dataset: The CIFAR-10 collection encompasses 60,000 colored pictures across 10 categories (like airplanes, vehicles, birds, and so on), partitioned into 50,000 training instances and 10,000 for testing. During data preparation, pictures from the CIFAR-10 set are adjusted to a 32×32 three-layer format.

Federated EMNIST Dataset: The Federated EMNIST dataset is a variant of the Extended MNIST (EMNIST) dataset specifically designed for federated learning scenarios. EMNIST is an extension of the MNIST dataset, which consists of handwritten digits from 0 to 9. This dataset distribution simulates the decentralized nature of federated learning, where each participant holds their own local data without sharing it directly with the central server or other participants.

Model Settings. In this experiment, we employ the same model architecture as described in [23]. The model is a 5-layer convolutional neural network with approximately 1.2 million parameters. It consists of two convolutional layers, followed by a max-pooling layer, and then two fully-connected layers with dropout. This architecture has been previously demonstrated to be effective in various tasks and serves as a baseline for our experiments.

Evaluation Metrics. We evaluate ZKRL's performance using three criteria: validation precision, primary class precision, and backdoor precision. The first two, validation and primary class precision, are calculated based on the datasets' validation data used in our tests. Backdoor precision, on the other hand, is determined using an altered validation set, where all entries from the primary class undergo a trojan transformation and are re-categorized as the target class. Our analysis juxtaposes ZKRL's outcomes with those of four different aggregation approaches: FedAvg [16], FedAvg with RLR [17], FoolsGold [12], and sign aggregation [4]. These methods are widely used in FL research and provide a basis for comparison with our proposed ZKRL scheme.

6.2 ZKRL Defense Performance Analysis

IID Setting. We performed tests with the MNIST and CIFAR-10 datasets, distributing the data evenly among agents following an i.i.d. approach. We equally allocated training samples to every agent via consistent sampling. Figure 2 showcases the learning trajectories of three techniques: FedAvg, FedAvg incorporated with RLR, and FedAvg paired with ZKRL. Sequentially from left to right, the trajectories highlight validation precision, primary class precision, and backdoor precision. As can be seen, it is evident that the FedAvg method alone is vulnerable to the backdoor attack. However, when using the RLR and ZKRL defense mechanisms, the backdoor attack is effectively prevented. Moreover, in comparison to RLR, ZKRL not only successfully mitigates the backdoor attack but also leads to improvements in accuracy rates on both the training and validation sets. The base class accuracy shows an increase of 1.2% to 1.5%, indicating better performance on the original classes, and the validation accuracy demonstrates a notable improvement of 0.8%. Additionally, Table 1 summarizes the final accuracy achieved by these methods. The lowest backdoor precision and the highest validation and primary class precision are emphasized in bold. The results clearly demonstrate the effectiveness of our proposed ZKRL scheme in providing significant protection against backdoor attacks compared to the baselines.

Table 1. Final validation, primary class and backdoor precision for different aggregations in i.i.d. setting.

Aggregation	Validation (%)	Base (%)	Backdoor (%)
FedAvg (MNIST)	93.2	**99.1**	100
FedAvg (CIFAR-10)	**93.4**	98.9	100
FoolsGold (MNIST)	93.3	98.5	100
FoolsGold (CIFAR-10)	93.1	98.6	100
Sign (MNIST)	93.1	98.6	99.7
Sign (CIFAR-10)	92.9	98.7	99.8
FedAvg with RLR (MNIST)	92.2	97.4	0.5
FedAvg with RLR (CIFAR-10)	92.0	97.3	0.1
FedAvg with ZKRL (MNIST)	93.0	98.9	0.4
FedAvg with ZKRL (CIFAR-10)	92.8	98.5	**0**

These findings validate the superiority of our proposed approach in mitigating the impact of backdoor attacks, thereby enhancing the overall performance and security of FL systems.

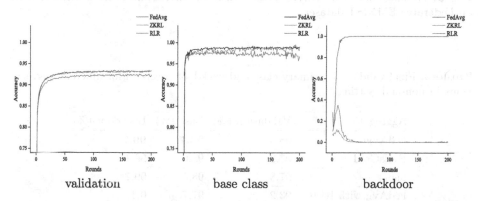

validation   base class   backdoor

Fig. 2. Training curves for FedAvg, FedAvg with the ZKRL and FedAvg with the RLR on MNIST dataset.

Non-IID Setting. We shift our focus to a scenario in FL that mirrors a more practical data distribution: non-i.i.d. For this evaluation, we employ the Federated EMNIST dataset sourced from the LEAF benchmark. In a manner analogous to the i.i.d. setup, we study the learning trajectories of FedAvg, FedAvg paired with ZKRL, and FedAvg combined with RLR, as depicted in Fig. 3. The final accuracy outcomes for each aggregation methods are summarized in Table 2.

The lowest backdoor precision and the highest validation and primary class precision are emphasized in bold. The experimental results demonstrate that ZKRL is effective in resisting backdoor attacks even in the non-i.i.d. environment. Furthermore, ZKRL achieves improved accuracy rates compared to RLR. Specifically, the validation accuracy improved by 2% and the base accuracy increased by 0.9%. These findings highlight the robustness and effectiveness of ZKRL in the presence of data heterogeneity among agents.

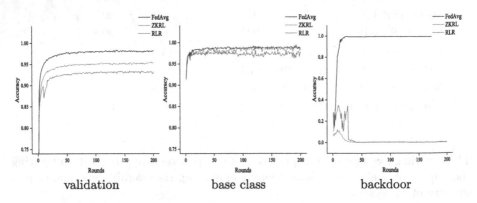

validation   base class   backdoor

Fig. 3. Training curves for FedAvg, FedAvg with the ZKRL and FedAvg with the RLR on Federated EMNIST dataset.

Table 2. Final validation, primary class and backdoor precision for different aggregations in non-i.i.d. setting.

Aggregation	Validation (%)	Base (%)	Backdoor (%)
FedAvg	98.0	**98.7**	**99.2**
FoolsGold	97.9	98.6	99.1
Sign	97.8	98.5	99.7
FedAvg with RLR	93.2	97.7	0.4
FedAvg with ZKRL	95.2	98.6	**0.2**

7   Conclusion

In this work, we conducted a comprehensive investigation into FL with a specific emphasis on countering adversarial attacks, particularly backdoor attacks. Our defense mechanism is centered around analyzing the relationship between the model update and the value announced by the server, enabling us to dynamically adjust the fine-tuning learning rate. This adjustment is performed on a per-dimension and per-round basis, leveraging the sign information of clients' updates and the outcome of the inspection process. Through extensive experimentation, we demonstrated the effectiveness of our defense mechanism in significantly reducing backdoor accuracy while maintaining minimal impact on the overall validation accuracy. In fact, our defense outperformed several state-of-the-art defense techniques reported in the existing literature. As part of our future work, we plan to explore avenues for accelerating the cryptographic primitives utilized in our defense mechanism by leveraging GPU hardware. By enhancing the efficiency of our defense, we aim to make it more applicable and adaptable to real-world scenarios.

References

1. Andreina, S., Marson, G.A., Möllering, H., Karame, G.: BaFFLe: backdoor detection via feedback-based federated learning. In: 2021 IEEE 41st International Conference on Distributed Computing Systems (ICDCS), pp. 852–863. IEEE (2021)
2. Awan, S., Luo, B., Li, F.: CONTRA: defending against poisoning attacks in federated learning. In: Bertino, E., Shulman, H., Waidner, M. (eds.) ESORICS 2021, Part I 26. LNCS, vol. 12972, pp. 455–475. Springer, Cham (2021). https://doi.org/10.1007/978-3-030-88418-5_22
3. Bagdasaryan, E., Veit, A., Hua, Y., Estrin, D., Shmatikov, V.: How to backdoor federated learning. In: International Conference on Artificial Intelligence and Statistics, pp. 2938–2948. PMLR (2020)
4. Bernstein, J., Zhao, J., Azizzadenesheli, K., Anandkumar, A.: signSGD with majority vote is communication efficient and fault tolerant. arXiv preprint arXiv:1810.05291 (2018)
5. Bhagoji, A.N., Chakraborty, S., Mittal, P., Calo, S.: Analyzing federated learning through an adversarial lens. In: International Conference on Machine Learning, pp. 634–643. PMLR (2019)
6. Bonawitz, K., et al.: Towards federated learning at scale: system design. Proc. Mach. Learn. Syst. 1, 374–388 (2019)
7. Bonawitz, K., et al.: Practical secure aggregation for privacy-preserving machine learning. In: Proceedings of the 2017 ACM SIGSAC Conference on Computer and Communications Security, pp. 1175–1191 (2017)
8. Bünz, B., Bootle, J., Boneh, D., Poelstra, A., Wuille, P., Maxwell, G.: Bulletproofs: short proofs for confidential transactions and more. In: 2018 IEEE Symposium on Security and Privacy (SP), pp. 315–334. IEEE (2018)
9. Caldas, S., et al.: LEAF: a benchmark for federated settings. arXiv preprint arXiv:1812.01097 (2018)
10. Chen, X., Liu, C., Li, B., Lu, K., Song, D.: Targeted backdoor attacks on deep learning systems using data poisoning. arXiv preprint arXiv:1712.05526 (2017)
11. Fiat, A., Shamir, A.: How to prove yourself: practical solutions to identification and signature problems. In: Odlyzko, A.M. (ed.) CRYPTO 1986. LNCS, vol. 263, pp. 186–194. Springer, Heidelberg (1987). https://doi.org/10.1007/3-540-47721-7_12
12. Fung, C., Yoon, C.J., Beschastnikh, I.: Mitigating sybils in federated learning poisoning. arXiv preprint arXiv:1808.04866 (2018)
13. Goldwasser, S., Micali, S., Rackoff, C.: The knowledge complexity of interactive proof-systems. In: Providing Sound Foundations for Cryptography: On the Work of Shafi Goldwasser and Silvio Micali, pp. 203–225 (2019)

14. Liu, Y., Fan, T., Chen, T., Xu, Q., Yang, Q.: FATE: an industrial grade platform for collaborative learning with data protection. J. Mach. Learn. Res. **22**(1), 10320–10325 (2021)

15. Liu, Y., et al.: Trojaning attack on neural networks. In: 25th Annual Network And Distributed System Security Symposium, NDSS 2018. Internet Society (2018)

16. McMahan, B., Moore, E., Ramage, D., Hampson, S., Arcas, B.A.: Communication-efficient learning of deep networks from decentralized data. In: Artificial Intelligence and Statistics, pp. 1273–1282. PMLR (2017)

17. Ozdayi, M.S., Kantarcioglu, M., Gel, Y.R.: Defending against backdoors in federated learning with robust learning rate. In: Proceedings of the AAAI Conference on Artificial Intelligence, vol. 35, pp. 9268–9276 (2021)

18. Pedersen, T.P.: Non-interactive and information-theoretic secure verifiable secret sharing. In: Feigenbaum, J. (ed.) CRYPTO 1991. LNCS, vol. 576, pp. 129–140. Springer, Heidelberg (1992). https://doi.org/10.1007/3-540-46766-1_9

19. Roy Chowdhury, A., Guo, C., Jha, S., van der Maaten, L.: EIFFeL: ensuring integrity for federated learning. In: Proceedings of the 2022 ACM SIGSAC Conference on Computer and Communications Security, pp. 2535–2549 (2022)

20. Shafagh, H., Hithnawi, A., Burkhalter, L., Fischli, P., Duquennoy, S.: Secure sharing of partially homomorphic encrypted IoT data. In: Proceedings of the 15th ACM Conference on Embedded Network Sensor Systems, pp. 1–14 (2017)

21. Shafahi, A., et al.: Poison frogs! Targeted clean-label poisoning attacks on neural networks. In: Advances in Neural Information Processing Systems, vol. 31 (2018)

22. Shi, E., Chan, H., Rieffel, E., Chow, R., Song, D.: Privacy-preserving aggregation of time-series data. In: Annual Network & Distributed System Security Symposium (NDSS). Internet Society (2011)

23. Sun, Z., Kairouz, P., Suresh, A.T., McMahan, H.B.: Can you really backdoor federated learning? arXiv preprint arXiv:1911.07963 (2019)

24. Xie, C., Chen, M., Chen, P.Y., Li, B.: CRFL: certifiably robust federated learning against backdoor attacks. In: International Conference on Machine Learning, pp. 11372–11382. PMLR (2021)

25. Zhang, J., Ge, C., Hu, F., Chen, B.: RobustFL: robust federated learning against poisoning attacks in industrial IoT systems. IEEE Trans. Industr. Inf. **18**(9), 6388–6397 (2021)

PPAPAFL: A Novel Approach to Privacy Protection and Anti-poisoning Attacks in Federated Learning

Xiangquan Chen[1] , Chungen Xu[1]([✉]) , Bennian Dou[1] , and Pan Zhang[2]

[1] School of Mathematics and Statistics, Nanjing University of Science and
Technology, Nanjing 210094, China
xuchung@njust.edu.cn
[2] School of Cyber Science and Engineering, Nanjing University of Science and
Technology, Nanjing 210094, China

Abstract. In the realm of distributed machine learning, although federated learning has received considerable attention, it still confronts grave challenges such as user privacy leakage and poisoning attacks. Regrettably, the demands for privacy preservation and protection against poisoning attacks are conflicting. Measures for privacy protection generally assure the indistinguishability of local parameter updates, which conversely complicates the strategy of defending against poisoning attacks by making it harder to identify malicious users. To address these issues, we propose a privacy-preserving and anti-poisoning attack federated learning (PPAPAFL) scheme. This scheme employs the CKKS homomorphic encryption technique for gradient packaging encryption, thus ensuring data privacy. Concurrently, our designed robust aggregation algorithm can effectively resist poisoning attacks, guaranteeing the model's integrity and accuracy, and is capable of supporting heterogeneous data in a friendly manner. A plethora of comparative experimental results demonstrate that our scheme can significantly improve the model's accuracy and robustness, drastically reduce the attack success rate, and effectively protect data privacy. In comparison with advanced schemes such as Trum and PEFL, our scheme achieves a 10–50% improvement in model accuracy and reduces the attack success rate to less than 3%.

Keywords: Federated learning · Privacy protection · Homomorphic encryption · Poisoning attacks

1   Introduction

With the advancement of technology and the progress of the era, computing devices have infiltrated every corner of daily life, and the activities of enterprises

Supported by The National Natural Science Foundation of China (No. 62072240) and The Natural Science Foundation of Jiangsu Province Youth Project (No. BK20210330).

J. Liu et al. (Eds.): TridentCom 2023, LNICST 523, pp. 117–138, 2024.
https://doi.org/10.1007/978-3-031-51399-2_7

and individuals are generating massive amounts of data every moment [25]. However, traditional centralized machine learning (ML) methods have encountered challenges in dealing with and utilizing data generated by deployment and application programs that are continuously emerging and widely distributed. Firstly, due to infrastructure constraints, such as limited communication bandwidth and a shortage of storage devices, it takes a significant cost and time to collect these big data [23] into a centralized storage facility. Secondly, private data often contains a lot of sensitive information of individuals or companies [1], such as facial images, identity information, medical records, etc., causing many users or companies to resist sharing their sensitive data with third parties. As society becomes more aware of privacy protection, legal constraints, such as the General Data Protection Regulation (GDPR) in Europe, are gradually being implemented, posing new challenges to data collection and compilation methods.

Federated learning(FL) [15,17], as an emerging paradigm of distributed learning, mainly targets dispersed data. It involves multiple clients (such as smartphones, Internet of Things devices [24], medical institutions, etc.) and a service provider (such as Google, Tencent, etc.). In simple terms, the workflow of FL primarily comprises three iterative steps. Firstly, the server of the service provider disseminates the current global model to clients or a selected subset of them. Secondly, each selected client conducts model training using its local training data and returns the local model update to the server. Finally, the server integrates all local model updates into a global model update according to a pre-established aggregation rule and uses this to update the global model. This method allows many participants to construct a shared machine learning model without exposing their private training data. Moreover, it takes advantage of the diversity of the participants' local datasets to improve the model's performance. Based on these advantages, FL has seen wide applications in recent years, showing exemplary performance in areas such as autonomous driving [9], drug development [7], input method word prediction [12], and recommendation systems [26].

Despite the fact that FL is an ideal distributed learning model, it also faces significant challenges. Firstly, from the perspective of data privacy, existing research shows that the parameters generated during the training process can lead to privacy leaks [11,20,21]. For example, the server may use the received parameters to recover sensitive information about the client. In addition, external malicious attackers could also infer sensitive information of training data by listening to communication channels or observing shared parameter updates. For instance, Membership Inference attacks [21] can use a trained model to determine whether a sample comes from a specific training set, which could lead to the leakage of private information; Model Inversion attacks [11] could generate prototypes of the original training set that should be private by training a model called a Generative Adversarial Network (GAN). Secondly, FL also faces the threat of poisoning attacks [2,10]. As shown in Fig. 1, since the server cannot access the client's dataset and the joint training process, a malicious client could potentially disrupt the local model update by adding poisoned data to the training data (i.e., data poisoning attack) or directly tampering with the model update (i.e., model poisoning attack), thereby posing a threat to the robustness of the model. In conclusion, a trustworthy FL system must satisfy two requirements: (1) it can protect user privacy data from being leaked, ensuring data privacy; (2) it can effectively resist poisoning attacks, ensuring system security and robustness.

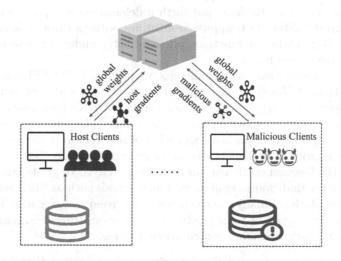

Fig. 1. Poisoning attacks in federal learning

Facing the problem of simultaneously achieving privacy protection and defending against poisoning attacks in FL, current research still faces the following two major challenges: On the one hand, there is an inherent conflict between existing privacy-protecting federated learning (PPFL) methods and measures against poisoning attacks. Mainstream PPFL solutions, such as homomorphic encryption and differential privacy, protect privacy by ensuring that gradients are indistinguishable, which undoubtedly provides superior cover for uploaded malicious gradients. However, strategies to defend against poisoning attacks need to access and analyze uploaded gradients, which undoubtedly leads to leakage of gradients. Therefore, it is difficult for both of these to be satisfied simultaneously. On the other hand, existing defense solutions do not adequately support heterogeneous data. FL usually needs to be trained on various heterogeneous data. Normal gradients trained on IID data usually follow similar distributions, therefore, toxic gradients with different distributions are easy to detect. However, the distribution of benign gradients trained on non-IID data may also be drastically different, making it difficult for existing defense strategies to detect toxic gradients. Furthermore, since the distribution of local data and local gradients is unknown in PPFL strategies, it is particularly challenging to design a privacy-protecting strategy to defend against poisoning attacks in PPFL with heterogeneous data.

Recently, a method called FLTrust has been proposed by Cao et al. [6], which primarily involves the collection of a pristine root dataset. This process identifies poisoned gradients by measuring the cosine similarity between each local gradient and the benign gradient derived from training on the clean data. However, it contradicts the initial principle of FL, which emphasizes data should not leave its original domain, and it is unable to meet the requirement for privacy preservation. Li et al. [16] have put forth a defense against poisoning in FL, a method named LoMar. This approach identifies outliers through kernel density estimation. Regrettably, it functions predominantly under the assumption that most participants are honest.

To solve the aforementioned challenges, we propose PPAPAFL, an innovative defensive strategy aimed at resisting poisoning attacks and protecting privacy. We first effectively encrypt the gradients using the CKKS homomorphic encryption scheme [8], ensuring the security of user data. The advantage of CKKS is that it not only supports packed encryption of real vector gradients, but is also superior in security and efficiency to other encryption strategies. Next, we propose using the Pearson coefficient for statistical analysis of gradients, which can better assess the maliciousness of users than methods such as Euclidean distance and cosine similarity. Finally, we construct a new robust aggregation mechanism to minimize the impact of toxic gradients, thereby ensuring the accuracy of the model. In summary, our main contributions include:

- We have designed a novel FL defensive strategy, called PPAPAFL, which uses CKKS homomorphic encryption as the core technology for PPFL. By performing statistical analysis on each gradient and scoring their maliciousness, it achieves the identification of malicious gradients, effectively solving the privacy protection and poisoning attack problems in FL.
- We propose an innovative robust aggregation mechanism, which significantly improves the robustness of the final model by adaptively reducing the contribution weight of malicious gradients.
- We conduct in-depth theoretical analysis of PPAPAFL and conduct extensive experiments on real data. We also compare our strategy with existing methods (such as Krum, PEFL, FoolsGold, etc.). Experimental results show that our scheme can effectively resist poisoning attacks and maintain high model accuracy.

2   Preliminaries

2.1   Federal Learning

FL is a distributed machine learning architecture composed of a server and N clients (participants). Each client owns its unique dataset $D_i = \{x_1^i, \cdots, xl_i^i\}$, with $|Di| = n_i$. During the t-th iteration of training, a subset of n clients are randomly selected from the N clients. These selected clients run the stochastic gradient descent (SGD) algorithm on their local data subsets to calculate local model updates g_i^{t+1}. After obtaining the local updates, the clients upload g_i^{t+1}

to the server. The server then aggregates all the local gradients uploaded by the clients using the formula $w^{t+1} = w^t + \sum i \in n\alpha_i g_i^{t+1}$ to obtain the updated global model parameters. Here, w^t represents the global model parameters after the t iteration, $n = \sum i = 1^N n_i$, and $\frac{n_i}{n} = \alpha_i$.

FEDDECORR: Given the poor support of FL for heterogeneous data, Shi et al. [22] found that data heterogeneity might lead to severe dimension collapse in the global model, causing features to tend towards a low-dimensional space. Therefore, they proposed the FEDDECORR method. This method introduces a regularization term during local training to reduce the correlation between features of different dimensions, thereby alleviating the problem of dimension collapse. The specific expression of this regularization term is as follows:

$$L_{\text{FedDecorr}} (w, X) = \frac{1}{d^2} |K|_F^2 \qquad (1)$$

where w represents the model parameters, K denotes the correlation matrix, and d refers to the dimension of the matrix K. Hence, the goal of local updates is to minimize the loss function:

$$\min_w \ell(w, X, y) + \beta L\text{FedDecorr} (w, X) \qquad (2)$$

where ℓ represents the cross-entropy loss, and β is the coefficient of the regularization term.

As the FEDDECORR model can handle heterogeneous data friendly and its additional computational overhead is small, this study adopts the FEDDECORR algorithm for local training. The pseudocode of this algorithm is shown in Algorithm 1.

2.2 Homomomorphic Encryption

Homomorphic encryption is a cryptographical approach allowing computations to be executed on encrypted data, obviating the necessity to decrypt the data beforehand. The outcome of computations on encrypted data, once decrypted, is identical to that obtained directly from plaintext calculations. Specifically, homomorphic encryption enables both addition and multiplication operations to be performed on encrypted data while retaining its encrypted state, rendering decryption unnecessary. Given an encryption algorithm E, a key k, a function f, and an input x, we designate E as homomorphic encryption if the following relationship is satisfied:

$$E_k (f (x_1, \ldots, x_n)) = f (E_k (x_1), \ldots, E_k (x_n)) \qquad (3)$$

If Eq. (3) applies only to either addition or multiplication, we term such an encryption scheme as partial homomorphic encryption, exemplified by RSA or Paillier schemes. Conversely, if it applies to both, we term it as fully homomorphic encryption, as in the BGV or CKKS schemes. Primary application scenarios of homomorphic encryption include secure computation, such as data

---

Algorithm 1. FEDDECORR With Federated Average

1: Let B be the minibatch size for local model training, n_i be the size of dataset in clients d_i, $n = \sum_{i=1}^{N} n_i$, and η be the learning rate
2: The server initializes w_0
3: //server
4: **for** each round $t = 1, 2, 3 \ldots$ **do**
5:   $S_t \leftarrow$ (server randomly selects a set of clients d_i sized of N)
6:   **for** each remote client $d_i \in S_t$ in parallel **do**
7:     $w_{t+1}^i \leftarrow$ ClientUpdate (d_i, w_t)
8:   **end for**
9:   $w_{t+1} \leftarrow \frac{1}{N} \sum_{i=1}^{N} \frac{n_i}{n} w_{t+1}^i$
10:   **if** satisfy termination condition **then**
11:     break
12:   **end if**
13: **end for**
14: //client
15: ClientUpdate (d_i, w_t^i).
16: $S \leftarrow$ (select batches sized of B from local dataset)
17: //we use FEDDECORR to iterate model
18: **for** local epochs $l = 1, \ldots, L$ **do**
19:   **for** batch $b \in S$ **do**
20:     //∇ loss is the gradients of loss function.
21:     $loss = \ell(w, X, y) + \beta L_{\text{FedDecorr}}(w, X)$
22:     $w_{t+1}^i \leftarrow w_t^i - \eta \nabla loss$
23:   **end for**
24: **end for**
25: **return** w_{t+1}^i to server

---

sharing and analysis in FL, as it facilitates computation and analysis while preserving data privacy. Homomorphic encryption has seen widespread adoption in sectors like finance, healthcare, and government to ensure the security and confidentiality of private data.

CKKS: The CKKS scheme is a fully homomorphic encryption method, an acronym derived from the names of its developers - Cheon, Kim, Kim, and Song. This scheme enables the encryption of real or complex vector values, facilitating homomorphic addition and multiplication operations, all the while maintaining good security and computational efficiency. Owing to these features, it has found extensive usage in privacy-preserving data analysis and machine learning. Furthermore, as a lattice [19]-based encryption technique, it presents a novel resilience against quantum attacks. Given the CKKS' exceptional capability to support floating-point numbers and its high computational efficiency, it has been chosen to encrypt local updates uploaded by our clients.

2.3   Poisoning Attacks

In a poisoning attack scenario, as outlined by Bhagoji et al. [3], the attacker's primary objective is to manipulate the model into generating incorrect predictions, thereby compromising its robustness. Poisoning attacks can be categorized into two broad types: data poisoning attacks and model poisoning attacks.

Data poisoning attacks involve the incorporation of malicious or tampered data into the training dataset, thereby causing the trained model to perform in a manner that serves the attacker's objectives. This could include disrupting the functioning of the model or manipulating its outcomes. A typical strategy within data poisoning attacks is label flipping attacks [4], where labels of regular data are reversed to a target category, causing misclassification by the model. For instance, an attacker might corrupt the real label "1" to "9", causing the model to misclassify digit "1" as digit "9". Another tactic is the backdoor attack [2], which involves modifying specific features or small areas of the original training data to implant certain backdoor triggers. In this case, the model operates normally when dealing with clean, trigger-free data. However, it changes the predicted target category whenever a trigger is encountered, for example, a specific mark on an image. The aforementioned two types of data poisoning attacks are shown in Figure 2.

Contrary to data poisoning attacks, model poisoning attacks compromise the integrity of the model by altering or replacing its parameters. A classic example of a model poisoning attack is the Byzantine attack [5,27], where malicious gradients are uploaded by attackers to the server, leading to a functional breakdown of the global model.

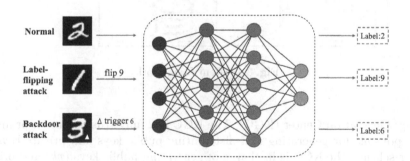

Fig. 2. Label flipping and backdoor attack

2.4   Inference Attacks

Inference attacks [18] involve attackers acquiring certain information through various means (such as eavesdropping or stealing) and using this information to infer details they are interested in. A learning model essentially provides a high-level statistical representation of its training dataset, enabling attackers to infer a wealth of private information, such as class representatives, membership, and the properties of training data subsets, through gradient inference attacks.

Inference attacks include attribute inference attacks [20], model inversion attacks [14], and membership inference attacks [13]. All these attack methods could potentially lead to the exposure of private data, thereby undermining the objective of FL, i.e., the protection of client-side privacy data.

3   Problem Statement

3.1   System Model

As illustrated in Fig. 3, our system comprises four primary entities:

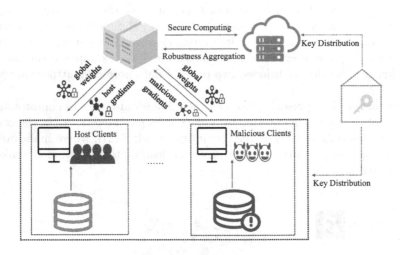

Fig. 3. System Framework

- Key Generation Center (KGC): The KGC is a fully trusted entity, primarily responsible for generating and distributing public keys and private keys. In our scheme, the KGC is in charge of generating public keys (pk) and private keys (sk) for CKKS homomorphic encryption. The public key pk is made public, while the private key sk is securely distributed to the client and the cloud platform.
- Clients(C_i): each client (C_i) possesses its training data. This data is used for model training on the client's local device and the gradient updates produced from this training are encrypted and sent to the server. We assume that the data each client possesses is non-IID.
- Server Provider (SP): The SP is a semi-honest entity that receives all gradient updates from clients and aggregates them into a global optimization model. Additionally, we assume that the SP does not collude with C_i.

- Cloud Platform (CP): The cloud platform assists the SP with computations, helps identify and eliminate malicious clients, thereby defending against poisoning attacks and ensuring the accuracy of model training. We assume that the CP and SP do not collude.

3.2 Threat Model

In this paper, we primarily consider threats arising from poisoning attacks and inference attacks. For poisoning attacks, we assume that the malicious clients are controlled by sybils. They affect model performance by modifying training data (such as label flipping attacks, backdoor attacks) or altering model parameters. For inference attacks, honest but curious servers and other adversaries can launch inference attacks based on the gradients uploaded by clients. This can recover client's private information through the clients' parameter updates.

Table 1. Symbol Description

Symbol	Description
pk	public key
sk	private key
$[[x]]$	CKKS-encrypted ciphertext x
α_i	the user's reputation score
ρ	Pearson correlation coefficient
η	learning rate
γ_i	randomized cryptographic gradient
g_i	user local gradient
W	global model parameters
β	dirichlet distribution
ξ	user Poisoning ratio

3.3 Design Goals

- Privacy: Inference attacks can lead to the leakage of data owners' private information. To protect the data privacy of clients, we need to encrypt the uploaded gradient updates, preventing the unauthorized acquisition of sensitive information during transmission.
- Robustness: Malicious attackers may submit malicious gradients through poisoning attacks, which could cause model performance degradation or even incorrect classification results. To maintain the model's robustness, we need to design a secure aggregation scheme that can identify and eliminate or reduce the impact of poisoned gradients.

4 Our PPAPAFL

In this section, we first provide an overview of our proposed scheme. Then we will delve into the construction of the scheme and its role in enhancing security and privacy protection. For reference, we also list the symbols that appear in this paper and their corresponding descriptions, as shown in Table 1.

4.1 Overview

In our PPAPAFL scheme, we employ the FEDDECORR method for users to conduct local training, effectively addressing the model dimension collapse issue caused by the data heterogeneity among different users. Traditional PPFL schemes, whether for their inadequate support for floating-point gradient or potential model accuracy degradation, present certain issues. To tackle these two problems, we opt to use CKKS technology to encrypt local updates, significantly reducing the communication overhead increase generated by encryption, thereby enhancing efficiency. When considering poisoning attacks, we understand that attackers might manipulate malicious clients, changing the local model update direction, causing global model update direction to be the opposite of the expected, or attackers might magnify the scale of local model updates to dominate the aggregation of global model updates. In order to adeptly address these two issues, the present study selects the Pearson correlation coefficient as the evaluative instrument, owing to its demonstrably superior capability to precisely evaluate the correlation among gradients and to astutely identify anomalous values, especially when contrasted with alternate approaches such as Euclidean distance and cosine similarity. So we use the Pearson correlation coefficient to calculate the similarity of gradient change trends among users, and assign a reputation score to each client based on this correlation coefficient. Finally, we opt to use a secure aggregation scheme to carry out robust aggregation on encrypted gradients according to reputation scores. In a nutshell, the PPAPAFL scheme can effectively support heterogeneous data and comprehensively resolve issues of privacy protection and defense against poisoning attacks.

4.2 PPAPAFL Construction

The PPAPAFL scheme consists of three stages: the system setup stage, the local training stage, and the robust aggregation stage. We will describe these three stages in detail below:

System Setup. Firstly, based on the security parameter λ, the KGC generates the public-private key pair (i.e., pk, sk) required for CKKS homomorphic encryption. The KGC publishes the public key pk to all parties involved, and distributes the private key sk to the data owners C_i and the cloud platform CP via a secure channel. Once the key distribution is completed, the KGC goes offline. Next, the Server Provider (SP) initiates the global parameter W_{init} and distributes the training model to C_i.

Local Training. In this stage, both benign clients (denoted as C) and malicious clients (denoted as C^*) participate in the training process normally. In the t-th training iteration, first, C_i decrypts the global parameter $[[W_t]]$ received from SP to obtain W_t, then carries out local training using FEDDECORR method, which is capable of preventing dimensional collapse of the local model induced by heterogeneous data, thereby obtaining the gradient g_i^t. Given that CKKS homomorphic encryption supports floating-point number encryption and can pack multiple plaintexts into a single ciphertext for encryption, we directly encrypt g_i^t using CKKS, obtaining $[[g_i^t]]$, which effectively saves space and ensures gradient security. Finally, $[[g_i^t]]$ is uploaded to SP. The detailed process is as shown in Algorithm 2.

Algorithm 2. Local Training

Input: Local training data $D_i(i \in [1,n])$, global weight W^t
Output: CKKS encrypted gradients $[[g_i^t]]$
1: **if** $C_i \notin C^*$ **then**
2:     //Benign client local training
3:     C_i uses W^t training on local data, and gets local gradients g_i
4:     C_i encrypts g_i then becomes $[[g_i]]$
5: **else**
6:     //malicious client poisoning attack
7:     C_i^* generating gradients g_i^* using various poisoning attack methods
8:     C_i^* encrypts g_i^* then becomes $[[g_i^*]]$
9: **end if**
10: **return** encrypted local gradients $[[g_i]]$ or $[[g_i^*]]$

Robustness Aggregation. In the robust aggregation phase, we engage in secure interactions with the Service Provider (SP) and the Cloud Platform (CP), to identify and evaluate potential malicious clients. Subsequently, we allocate lower reputation scores to malicious gradients, and higher scores to benign ones. Ultimately, secure aggregation is conducted according to these reputation scores, blocking various poisoning attacks launched by malicious users and ensuring high model accuracy.

Secure Pearson Correlation Coefficient: Assume we are in the tth iteration, the server SP initially receives the encrypted gradients $[[g_i^t]]$ trained by each client C_i. Subsequently, the server adds $[[g_i^t]]$ to the sum of the gradients from the previous k rounds $\sum_{i=t-k}^{t-1}[[g_i]]$ (we assume SP will retain its encrypted historical gradients and destroy them at the end of training), the result denoted as $[[G_i]] = \sum_{i=t-k}^{t}[[g_i]]$. This step aims to better judge the correlation of each gradient. Then, SP multiplies all $[[G_i]]$ by a random number r_i, and sends the result to the CP. Upon receiving $\gamma_i = r_i * [[G_i]]$, CP first decrypts it using the private key sk to get γ_i. Subsequently, CP calculates the Pearson correlation coefficient of γ_i

with all other γ_j $(i \neq j)$. Finally, CP sends the Pearson correlation coefficients to SP. Algorithm 3 illustrates the detailed steps of the protocol.

Computing Reputation Score: After receiving the Pearson correlation coefficient $\rho_{i,j}$ of each gradient, SP starts to calculate the maximum Pearson correlation coefficient of each C_i with the remaining C_j, denoted as $\alpha_i = \max_j(\rho_{i,j})$. Given the non-IID nature of the data, benign and malicious gradients might exhibit similarities. Therefore, to prevent benign clients from being misjudged as malicious, we propose to calculate the ratio $\alpha_{i,j} = \alpha_i/\alpha_j$, and to find the maximum α_i to reduce false positives. Following this, we implement a 0-1 inversion and normalization of α_i. This step ensures that malicious gradients have lower reputation scores, and all values adhere to a common standard. Finally, we compute

$$\alpha_i \leftarrow \min\left\{1, \max\left\{0, \ln\left(\frac{1+\alpha_i}{1-\alpha_i}\right) - 0.5\right\}\right\} \tag{4}$$

This enhances the divergence of values close to both ends, thus more effectively distinguishing between benign and malicious gradients. This approach aims to reward benign gradients, while penalizing malicious ones. Ultimately, all results are truncated to fall within the 0–1 range, facilitating the participation of reputation scores in global update calculations.

Algorithm 3. SPCC: Secure computation of Pearson correlation coefficient

---

Input: SP has $[[G_i]]_{i=1}^{i=n}$; CP has private key sk
Output: all Pearson correlation coefficient ρ
1: $\underline{SP}$:
2: // Randomized $[[G_i]]$
3: **for** $i = 1$ to n **do**
4:     $\gamma_i = r_i \cdot [[G_i]]$
5: **end for**
6: sends $\{\gamma_i\}_{i=1}^{i=n}$ to CP
7: $\underline{CP}$:
8: // decrypts γ_i with sk and computes the Pearson correlation coefficient $\rho_{i,j}$
9: **for** $i = 1$ to n **do**
10:     $d_i = \text{Dec}(sk_c, \gamma_i)$
11: **end for**
12: Calculates $\rho_{i,j} = \frac{\text{Cov}(d_i, d_j)}{\sigma(d_i) \cdot \sigma(d_j)}$
13: Sends $\rho = \{\rho_{i,j}\}_{i=1,j=1}^{i=n,j=n}$ to SP

Secure Aggregation: We redistribute the weight of each gradient based on the reputation score α_i, and then conduct secure gradient aggregation, namely

$$[[W^t]] \leftarrow [[W^{t-1}]] - \eta \sum_{i=1}^{n} \frac{\alpha_i}{\sum_{x=1}^{n} \alpha_x}[[g_i]] \tag{5}$$

Finally, we send the aggregated gradient $[[W^t]]$ to client C_i. Users decrypt this gradient using the private key sk to obtain the global gradient W^t. The client will use this global gradient for local training in the next round.

The process of robustness aggregation is outlined in Algorithm 4. Throughout the aggregation process, the gradients g_i processed by SP are maintained in a homomorphically encrypted state, ensuring gradient confidentiality. We evaluate the potential maliciousness of each client by calculating the correlation of their accumulated gradients and employing reputation scores. As a result, our approach safeguards user privacy, thwarts poisoning attacks by malicious users, and ensures the accuracy of the final model.

Algorithm 4. Robustness Aggregation

Input: The CKKS encrypted local gradients $\{[[g_1]], \dots, [[g_n]]\}$
Output: Aggregated encryption weights $[[W^t]]$
1: // Secure Pearson Correlation Coefficient
2: $\rho \leftarrow \text{SPCC}([[G_i]]_{i=1}^{i=n})$
3: // Computing Reputation score
4: **for** $i = 1$ to n **do**
5:　$\alpha_i = max_j(\rho_{i,j})$
6: **end for**
7: **for** $i = 1$ to n **do**
8:　**for** $j = 1$ to n **do**
9:　　**if** $\alpha_i < \alpha_j$ **then**
10:　　　$\alpha_i = 1 - max_j(\frac{\alpha_i}{\alpha_j})$
11:　　**end if**
12:　**end for**
13: **end for**
14: $\alpha_i = \min\left\{1, \max\left\{0, \ln\left(\frac{1+\alpha_i}{1-\alpha_i}\right) - 0.5\right\}\right\}$
15: // Secure Aggregation
16: $[[W^t]] \leftarrow [[W^{t-1}]] - \eta \sum_{i=1}^{n} \frac{\alpha_i}{\sum_{x=1}^{n} \alpha_x}[[g_i]]$
17: **return** the encryption weight $[[W^t]]$

Correctness Analysis. Since the noise of CKKS decryption is negligible, it does not affect the correctness of the algorithm. We mainly discuss the correctness of the SPCC protocol, judging whether the Pearson correlation coefficient between the gradients can be obtained in the blurred gradients in the SPCC, to ensure the correct identification of malicious gradients.

Proposition 1 (Correctness). *In the SPCC protocol, for a given randomized gradient, the Pearson correlation coefficient between the real gradients uploaded by the client can be correctly calculated.*

Proof. To prove the correctness of the protocol, it is equivalent to proving that $\rho_{G_i,G_j} = \rho_{d_i,d_j}$. First, based on the homomorphism of CKKS homomorphic encryption, we can get $d_i = r_i G_j$ in the SPCC protocol. We know that covariance and standard deviation have the following properties:

$$Cov(d_i, d_j) = E[(d_i - E(d_i))(d_j - E(d_j))]$$
$$= E(d_i d_j) - E(d_i)E(d_j) \tag{6}$$
$$\sigma(d_i)^2 = E\left[(d_i - E(d_i)^2)\right] = E\left[d_i^2\right] - E^2(d_i)$$

Where $E(d_i)$ represents the expectation, according to the above formula, we can derive the equivalent formula for the Pearson correlation coefficient:

$$\rho_{d_i,d_j} = \frac{E(d_i d_j) - E(d_i)E(d_j)}{\sqrt{E\left(d_i^2\right) - (E(d_i))^2}\sqrt{E\left(d_j^2\right) - (E(d_j))^2}} \tag{7}$$

According to the mathematical property of expectation E, we know that $E(d_i) = r_i E(G_i)$, from which we can infer the following conclusion:

$$\begin{aligned} \rho_{d_i,d_j} &= \frac{E(d_i d_j) - E(d_i)E(d_j)}{\sqrt{E(d_i^2) - (E(d_i))^2}\sqrt{E(d_j^2) - (E(d_j))^2}} \\ &= \frac{r_i r_j E(G_i G_j) - r_i r_j E(G_i)E(G_j)}{r_i \sqrt{E(G_i^2) - (E(G_i))^2} r_j \sqrt{E(G_j^2) - (E(G_j))^2}} \\ &= \frac{E(G_i G_j) - E(G_i)E(G_j)}{\sqrt{E(G_i^2) - (E(G_i))^2}\sqrt{E(G_j^2) - (E(G_j))^2}} \\ &= \rho_{G_i,G_j} \end{aligned} \tag{8}$$

In conclusion, we have proven that the Pearson correlation coefficient can also be correctly calculated for randomized gradients.

5 Experimental Evaluation

In this section, we comprehensively evaluate the PPAPAFL framework using real-world data and conduct experiments in a PyTorch environment on Ubuntu system. Our server is equipped with an Intel(R) Xeon(R) CPU E5-2690 v4 @ 2.60 GHz and has 256 GB of memory.

5.1 Experimental Settings

Experimental Data. We conducted experiments on the MNIST and Amazon datasets to evaluate the performance of PPAPAFL. For MNIST, the dataset is already divided into 60,000 training samples and 10,000 testing samples. For Amazon, we randomly split the data into a 70% training set and a 30% testing set.

- MNIST: It is a classic dataset of handwritten digit images, containing a large number of handwritten digit images. Each image is 28 × 28 pixels in size. The MNIST dataset includes 600,000 training samples, with 784 features, covering 10 different categories.
- Amazon: It is a classic product review text dataset, its feature number is large due to the inclusion of rich product and user information. The Amazon dataset contains 1,500 training samples, has 10,000 features, and is divided into 50 categories.

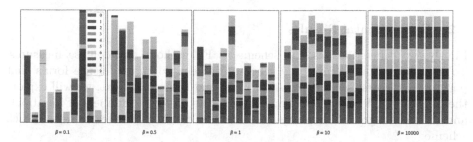

Fig. 4. Dirichlet Distribution of MNIST Data, Divided into 10 Clients and 10 Classes

To simulate data heterogeneity among clients, we follow the work of Yurochkin et al. [28] and Shi et al. [22], using probability vectors that follow the Dirichlet distribution to allocate data, as the Dirichlet distribution can effectively capture the heterogeneity and imbalance of data distributions. Each client k obtains instances from the category set $[C] = 1, 2, \ldots, C$ according to the probability vector $p_c = (p_{c,1}, p_{c,2}, \ldots, p_{c,K}) \sim \operatorname{Dir} K(\beta)$. Here, pc, k represents the probability of assigning instances of category c to client k. The parameter β controls the degree of data heterogeneity. When β is small, there is a large difference between the data, exhibiting strong heterogeneity. When β tends to infinity, the data becomes more homogeneous. In our experiments, we selected $\beta = \{0.1, 0.5, 1, 10, 10000\}$ to distribute the data to different clients according to these distributions. The distribution is illustrated in Fig. 4.

Model Architecture. Considering that our main focus is to compare the improvement of our method, PPAPAFL, in terms of model accuracy and robustness against various poisoning attacks relative to other methods, rather than absolute accuracy, we first employed a widely used softmax classifier for training, with a batch size of 50. Finally, we trained and evaluated the CNN model on the MNIST data. The client used the cross-entropy loss function and the stochastic gradient descent (SGD) optimizer for model training, with a momentum of 0.9 and a learning rate of 0.001.

Attack Models. Our experiments mainly considered three common poisoning attacks: label flipping attack, backdoor attack, and untargeted model attack. In the label flipping attack, a malicious client modifies the source class to the target class, where class 1 in the MNIST dataset is labeled as class 7, and class 1 in the Amazon dataset is labeled as class 8. In the backdoor attack, we set a malicious client to mark the last pixel point in the dataset as a backdoor mark and label the MNIST dataset as class 7 and the Amazon dataset as class 8. In the untargeted model attack, we allow malicious clients to randomly label the categories in the dataset, leading to incorrect gradients being uploaded, thereby reducing the model accuracy.

5.2   Experimental Results

Firstly, we define the baseline scheme as FL without any defense measures. To compare with our proposed scheme, we selected three defense forms that performed the best, namely Krum, PEFL, and Foolsgold. Next, we will explore the impact of different proportions of poisoners, different numbers of iterations, and different degrees of heterogeneous data on the defense effectiveness of each scheme.

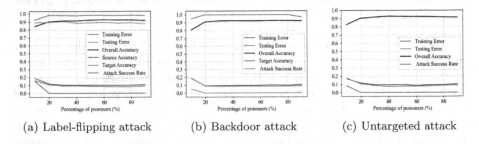

(a) Label-flipping attack   (b) Backdoor attack   (c) Untargeted attack

Fig. 5. Performance of PPAPAFL

Impact of Different Proportions of Poisoners. We have found that even in traditional federated averaging algorithms, the presence of only a few malicious users can significantly impact the model. As the proportion of malicious users increases, the final model accuracy decreases. In order to explore the impact of the proportion of poisoners on model accuracy and robustness, we conducted experiments where we fixed the number of iterations and used the same heterogeneous data distribution. For the MNIST dataset, we performed 1000 iterations and allocated data with $\beta = 0.1$ to each client. For the Amazon dataset, we conducted 200 iterations and also distributed data with $\beta = 0.1$ to each client.

As shown in Fig. 5, we described the performance of the PPAPAFL scheme in different poisoning attacks when the proportion of malicious users, denoted as ξ, ranged from 10% to 90% on the MNIST dataset. It can be observed that

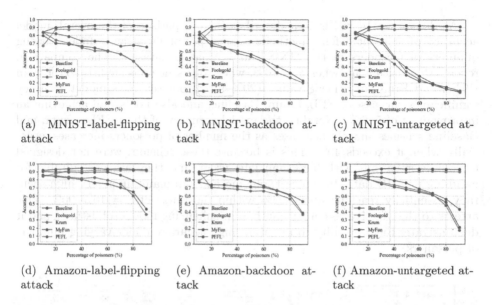

(a) MNIST-label-flipping attack

(b) MNIST-backdoor attack

(c) MNIST-untargeted attack

(d) Amazon-label-flipping attack

(e) Amazon-backdoor attack

(f) Amazon-untargeted attack

Fig. 6. Accuracy comparison of poisoners at different proportions

in label flipping attacks, both the training error and testing error of PPAPAFL are exceptionally low, generally within 10%, and the overall accuracy is remarkably high, exceeding 91%. The identification rate for source class 1 and target class 7 is also significantly high, surpassing 90% in almost all instances. The success rate of attacks induced by malicious gradients is extremely low, averaging below 3%, with the majority being zero. When ξ was set to 10%, the slight decrease in performance compared to larger values of ξ was due to the presence of only 10 honest clients, which increased the chances of misclassifying one malicious client as honest, resulting in false negatives. However, this had a minimal impact on the overall model accuracy. The slightly lower performance at $\xi = 90\%$ might be attributed to the similarity gradients between honest clients and a large number of malicious users, resulting in false negatives. However, such cases were rare because they were considered during the design of the scheme. Therefore, the accuracy of PPAPAFL at $\xi = 90\%$ is more than 91%. In the backdoor attack, since there were no source class labels, we only experimented with the recognition accuracy for target class label 7, which was almost perfect at 1. Other metrics were similar to the label-flipping attack. In the untargeted attack, despite its strong destructive nature aimed at reducing model accuracy, the PPAPAFL scheme maintained a remarkably high accuracy, reaching around 90%. Taking into account the aforementioned three types of attacks and various evaluation metrics, we found that the PPAPAFL scheme demonstrated excellent effectiveness in defending against malicious users while maintaining a very high level of model accuracy.

As demonstrated in Fig. 6, it describes the comparison of the overall model accuracy of different defense methods against poisoning attacks under varying numbers of poisoners in the MNIST and Amazon datasets. The comparison reveals that, except for when $\xi = 10\%$, where our scheme is slightly lower than PEFL and Krum, at other ξ values (20%–90%), our scheme's model accuracy significantly surpasses PEFL, Krum, Baseline, and also Foolsgold, achieving an improvement of 5–62%. Notably, the model accuracy of the PEFL, Krum, and Baseline schemes sharply decreases as the number of poisoners increases, especially when it exceeds 40%. This is because these schemes were not designed to handle situations with 50% malicious users, and they are not suitable for handling non-IID data. In contrast, our method can maintain a very high accuracy, essentially reaching above 92% within the range of $\xi = 10\%$–90%. This attests to the effectiveness of our method in enhancing model robustness, and it demonstrates the capability to maintain high accuracy under varying numbers of poisoners.

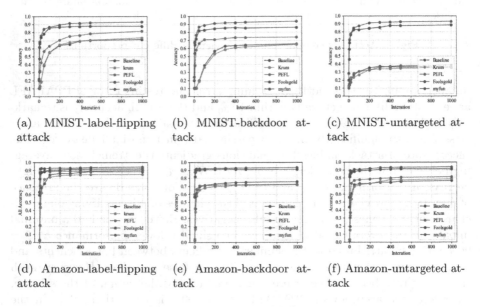

(a) MNIST-label-flipping attack

(b) MNIST-backdoor attack

(c) MNIST-untargeted attack

(d) Amazon-label-flipping attack

(e) Amazon-backdoor attack

(f) Amazon-untargeted attack

Fig. 7. Accuracy comparison of different iterations

Impact of Different Iteration. In FL, model performance typically improves as the number of iterations increases. Initial iterations may only capture some surface features of the data, but with more iterations, the model can better learn the deep features and patterns of the data, fully utilize the local data of each participant for updates and optimization, and achieve global consensus more quickly, thereby improving prediction performance. In FL, having a model capacity that is too small or too large may lead to underfitting or overfitting problems. However, in this discussion, we ignored these issues and focused on the impact of the number of iterations on model performance. We fixed the proportion of malicious users and the Dirichlet distribution of the data, set $\beta = 0.1$, and $\xi = 50\%$.

As shown in Fig. 7, it compares the changes in model accuracy for different defense methods as the number of iterations increases in the MNIST and Amazon datasets. Based on the results, we can make the following observations and conclusions: In the early iterations, the accuracy of the PPAPAFL scheme rapidly improves as the number of iterations increases. After 50 iterations on the Amazon dataset, the PPAPAFL scheme reached an accuracy of 93% and remained stable. On the MNIST dataset, after 200 iterations, the PPAPAFL scheme reached an accuracy of approximately 92% and remained stable. This indicates that the PPAPAFL scheme has a fast convergence speed and can quickly identify and remove malicious gradients to improve model accuracy during the training aggregation process. The PPAPAFL scheme demonstrates excellent convergence capabilities in the label flipping attack, backdoor attack, and untargeted attack. In comparison, the convergence speed of the PEFL, Krum, and Baseline schemes is slower, and their accuracy is generally lower in most cases due to their inability to defend against poisoning attacks. Particularly, in the untargeted attack on the MNIST dataset, the accuracy of these schemes is only 35%. Although Foolsgold's results are similar to the PPAPAFL scheme, the model accuracy is lower than our scheme because we adopted FEDDECORR for local training and optimized the scheme. In summary, the PPAPAFL scheme can quickly converge as the number of iterations increases and maintain a well-performing model with good robustness. It exhibits excellent performance in various poisoning attack scenarios.

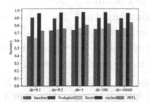 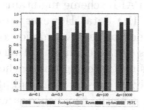 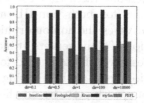

(a) CNN MNIST with the label-flipping attack

(b) CNN MNIST with the backdoor attack

(c) CNN MNIST with the untargeted attack

Fig. 8. Accuracy comparison of different dirichlet distribution

The Impact of Different Dirichlet Distribution Data. In the FL environment, the heterogeneity of data significantly affects the training effectiveness of the model, including its convergence, final performance, and stability. To simulate this impact, we used the Dirichlet distribution to model the data distribution of each client in FL. By adjusting the parameter β of the Dirichlet distribution, we can change the degree of data heterogeneity, allowing us to observe the impact of different degrees of data heterogeneity on the accuracy and robustness of different defense poisoning attack schemes. We fixed the number of iterations and the Dirichlet distribution of the data, and set $\xi = 50\%$.

As shown in Fig. 8, we tested the cases with β values of $\{0.1, 0.5, 1, 10, 10000\}$ and observed the changes in accuracy for the Baseline, Krum, PEFL, Foolsgold, and PPAPAFL schemes under three poisoning attacks in the MNIST datasets. The results show that under the $\beta = 0.1$ condition, due to the extremely high data heterogeneity, the accuracy of the Baseline, Krum, and PEFL schemes is relatively low, essentially only reaching a precision of 40–80%. As the β value increases, although the accuracy of Baseline, Krum, and PEFL improves to some extent, their accuracy remains relatively low due to their poor defense against malicious users. Foolsgold achieves good accuracy overall, but its accuracy and stability are not as high as PPAPAFL. Our PPAPAFL scheme displays extremely high accuracy for all β values, all reaching over 91%, demonstrating excellent model stability. This indicates that our scheme exhibits good robustness in both non-IID and IID scenarios.

6   Conclusion

we have successfully proposed a novel privacy-preserving and anti-poisoning attack strategy, referred to as PPAPAFL. We employed CKKS homomorphic encryption technique to protect gradients, ensuring the security of users' privacy data. Additionally, we innovatively designed a robust aggregation strategy that effectively identifies and eliminates malicious gradients, significantly enhancing the capability to defend against poisoning attacks. Experimental results have demonstrated that the PPAPAFL scheme maintains high accuracy and robustness for both non-IID and IID data. However, considering that the scheme involves the homomorphic encryption transmission of gradients and the utilization of cloud servers, it incurs certain communication overhead. Therefore, future research efforts should focus on exploring approaches to minimize communication costs while ensuring privacy preservation and attack defense. In summary, our work provides an effective method and theoretical foundation for the study of defense strategies in FL, balancing the demands of user privacy protection and defense against poisoning attacks.

References

1. Abadi, M., et al.: Deep learning with differential privacy. In: Proceedings of the 2016 ACM SIGSAC Conference on Computer and Communications Security, pp. 308–318 (2016)
2. Bagdasaryan, E., Veit, A., Hua, Y., Estrin, D., Shmatikov, V.: How to backdoor federated learning. In: International Conference on Artificial Intelligence and Statistics, pp. 2938–2948. PMLR (2020)

3. Bhagoji, A.N., Chakraborty, S., Mittal, P., Calo, S.: Analyzing federated learning through an adversarial lens. In: International Conference on Machine Learning, pp. 634–643. PMLR (2019)

4. Biggio, B., Nelson, B., Laskov, P.: Poisoning attacks against support vector machines. arXiv preprint arXiv:1206.6389 (2012)

5. Blanchard, P., El Mhamdi, E.M., Guerraoui, R., Stainer, J.: Machine learning with adversaries: Byzantine tolerant gradient descent. In: Advances in Neural Information Processing Systems, vol. 30 (2017)

6. Cao, X., Fang, M., Liu, J., Gong, N.Z.: FLTrust: Byzantine-robust federated learning via trust bootstrapping. arXiv preprint arXiv:2012.13995 (2020)

7. Chen, S., Xue, D., Chuai, G., Yang, Q., Liu, Q.: FL-QSAR: a federated learning-based QSAR prototype for collaborative drug discovery. Bioinformatics **36**(22–23), 5492–5498 (2020)

8. Cheon, J.H., Kim, A., Kim, M., Song, Y.: Homomorphic encryption for arithmetic of approximate numbers. In: Takagi, T., Peyrin, T. (eds.) ASIACRYPT 2017. LNCS, vol. 10624, pp. 409–437. Springer, Cham (2017). https://doi.org/10.1007/978-3-319-70694-8_15

9. Du, Z., Wu, C., Yoshinaga, T., Yau, K.L.A., Ji, Y., Li, J.: Federated learning for vehicular internet of things: recent advances and open issues. IEEE Open J. Comput. Soc. **1**, 45–61 (2020)

10. Fang, M., Cao, X., Jia, J., Gong, N.: Local model poisoning attacks to {Byzantine-Robust} federated learning. In: 29th USENIX Security Symposium, USENIX Security 2020, pp. 1605–1622 (2020)

11. Fredrikson, M., Jha, S., Ristenpart, T.: Model inversion attacks that exploit confidence information and basic countermeasures. In: Proceedings of the 22nd ACM SIGSAC Conference on Computer and Communications Security, pp. 1322–1333 (2015)

12. Hard, A., et al.: Federated learning for mobile keyboard prediction. arXiv preprint arXiv:1811.03604 (2018)

13. Hayes, J., Melis, L., Danezis, G., De Cristofaro, E.: LOGAN: membership inference attacks against generative models. arXiv preprint arXiv:1705.07663 (2017)

14. Hitaj, B., Ateniese, G., Perez-Cruz, F.: Deep models under the GAN: information leakage from collaborative deep learning. In: Proceedings of the 2017 ACM SIGSAC Conference on Computer and Communications Security, pp. 603–618 (2017)

15. Konečný, J., McMahan, H.B., Yu, F.X., Richtárik, P., Suresh, A.T., Bacon, D.: Federated learning: strategies for improving communication efficiency. arXiv preprint arXiv:1610.05492 (2016)

16. Li, X., Qu, Z., Zhao, S., Tang, B., Lu, Z., Liu, Y.: LoMar: a local defense against poisoning attack on federated learning. IEEE Trans. Dependable Secure Comput. **20**, 437–450 (2021)

17. Liu, Y., Xu, L., Yuan, X., Wang, C., Li, B.: The right to be forgotten in federated learning: an efficient realization with rapid retraining. In: IEEE Conference on Computer Communications, IEEE INFOCOM 2022, pp. 1749–1758. IEEE (2022)

18. Lyu, L., Yu, H., Yang, Q.: Threats to federated learning: a survey. arXiv preprint arXiv:2003.02133 (2020)

19. Mei, L., Xu, C., Xu, L., Yu, X., Zuo, C.: Verifiable identity-based encryption with keyword search for IoT from lattice. Comput. Mater. Contin **68**, 2299–2314 (2021)

20. Melis, L., Song, C., De Cristofaro, E., Shmatikov, V.: Exploiting unintended feature leakage in collaborative learning. In: 2019 IEEE Symposium on Security and Privacy (SP), pp. 691–706. IEEE (2019)

21. Nasr, M., Shokri, R., Houmansadr, A.: Comprehensive privacy analysis of deep learning: passive and active white-box inference attacks against centralized and federated learning. In: 2019 IEEE Symposium on Security and Privacy (SP), pp. 739–753. IEEE (2019)
22. Shi, Y., Liang, J., Zhang, W., Tan, V.Y., Bai, S.: Towards understanding and mitigating dimensional collapse in heterogeneous federated learning. arXiv preprint arXiv:2210.00226 (2022)
23. Wahab, O.A., Mourad, A., Otrok, H., Taleb, T.: Federated machine learning: survey, multi-level classification, desirable criteria and future directions in communication and networking systems. IEEE Commun. Surv. Tut. **23**(2), 1342–1397 (2021)
24. Xu, L., Xu, C., Liu, Z., Wang, Y., Wang, J., et al.: Enabling comparable search over encrypted data for IoT with privacy-preserving. Comput. Mater. Continua **60**(2), 675–690 (2019)
25. Xu, L., Yuan, X., Zhou, Z., Wang, C., Xu, C.: Towards efficient cryptographic data validation service in edge computing. IEEE Trans. Serv. Comput. **16**, 656–669 (2021)
26. Yang, L., Tan, B., Zheng, V.W., Chen, K., Yang, Q.: Federated recommendation systems. In: Yang, Q., Fan, L., Yu, H. (eds.) Federated Learning. LNCS (LNAI), vol. 12500, pp. 225–239. Springer, Cham (2020). https://doi.org/10.1007/978-3-030-63076-8_16
27. Yin, D., Chen, Y., Kannan, R., Bartlett, P.: Byzantine-robust distributed learning: towards optimal statistical rates. In: International Conference on Machine Learning, pp. 5650–5659. PMLR (2018)
28. Yurochkin, M., Agarwal, M., Ghosh, S., Greenewald, K., Hoang, N., Khazaeni, Y.: Bayesian nonparametric federated learning of neural networks. In: International Conference on Machine Learning, pp. 7252–7261. PMLR (2019)

Towards Retentive Proactive Defense Against DeepFakes

Tao Jiang[1], Hongyi Yu[2], Wenjuan Meng[3], and Peihan Qi[4(✉)]

[1] School of Cyber Engineering, Xidian University, Xi'an, China
taojiang@xidian.edu.cn
[2] Guangzhou Institute of Technology, Xidian University, Xi'an, China
hongyiyu@stu.xidian.edu.cn
[3] College of Information Engineering, Northwest A&F University, Yangling, Shaanxi, China
wjmeng@nwsuaf.edu.cn
[4] State Key Laboratory of Integrated Service Networks, Xidian University, Xi'an, China
phqi@xidian.edu.cn

Abstract. In recent years, with the development of artificial intelligence, many facial manipulation methods based on deep neural networks have been developed, known as DeepFakes. Unfortunately, DeepFakes are always maliciously used, and if the spread of DeepFakes cannot be controlled in a timely manner, it will pose a certain threat to both society and individuals. Researchers have studied the detection of DeepFakes, but this type of detection belongs to post-evidence collection and still has a certain degree of negative impact. Therefore, we propose a retentive and proactive defense method to protect DeepFakes before malicious operations. The main idea is to train a perturbation generator end-to-end, and introduce the perturbation generated by the perturbation generator into the image to make it adversarial and immune to DeepFakes. White-box experiments on a typical DeepFake manipulation method (facial attribute editing) demonstrate the effectiveness of our proposed method, and a comparison with an adversarial attack PGD proves the superiority of our method in terms of similarity and inference efficiency.

Keywords: DeepFake · Retentive · Proactive defense · Adversarial attack · Perturbation

1 Introduction

With the booming field of artificial intelligence, advanced image and video synthesis techniques have started to emerge. Various generative adversarial networks [1], that can generate more realistic images and videos, have already produced a great impact on artificial intelligence and related fields. DeepFake [2–4] is a technique for synthesizing images and videos, which can edit the facial attributes of

J. Liu et al. (Eds.): TridentCom 2023, LNICST 523, pp. 139–153, 2024.
https://doi.org/10.1007/978-3-031-51399-2_8

the target, as well as can modify the expression of the target samples. DeepFakes can also replace the face of the object with the face of the target as a way to generate some fake but realistic images and videos. Some people used DeepFakes to generate pornographic videos of celebrities for posting on the Internet, which has made DeepFakes notorious on the Internet. Although DeepFakes have an important role in many fields, effective defenses should be developed to prevent the misuse of DeepFakes.

Fig. 1. An illustration of retentive proactive defense against a DeepFake generator. After applying an imperceptible perturbation on the image, the output of StarGAN [2] is similar to the input, which assure the defense method is immune to the function of the DeepFake.

Researchers' defensive countermeasures against DeepFakes are mainly divided into passive and proactive defenses. Passive defense focuses on the detection of DeepFakes [5–7]. This type of technique far exceeds other methods in the overall research on the defense of DeepFakes, which can detect the generated false images and videos. Specifically, DeepFake detectors classify a given image or video as true or false based on the characteristics of the face in it. Although all existing detectors have high accuracy, they can only mitigate the negative impact of false information already spread on the Internet due to being only a passive defense with post-event forensics, and cannot completely eliminate it. Moreover, the detectors usually use deep neural networks, which are very vulnerable in the face of adversarial attacks [8–10]. Therefore, some researchers have started to study how to proactively defend against DeepFakes [11–13], i.e., to proactively defend against DeepFakes before they produce a series of negative effects. They focus on adding invisible perturbations to the images, so that the output of the perturbed images input into the DeepFake model has obvious distortion, so as to achieve the purpose of proactive defense. Although these studies have been effective in disrupting DeepFakes, the added adversarial perturbations are easily detected and eliminated by noise detectors [14,15]. Moreover, most of the previous studies involve disruptions that distort the output of DeepFakes. Such disruptions hit DeepFakes to some extent, but sometimes people on the Internet do not care if things are true or false, which still has some negative impact. Therefore, it is still necessary to investigate effective methods that still have sufficient defense capability while ensuring no degradation in image quality.

In this paper, as illustrated in Fig. 1, we delve into the disruption of Deep-Fakes functionality and make our endeavor to assure the outputs of DeepFakes as similar as their inputs. More precisely, we train a perturbation generator through an end-to-end pipeline to obtain an invisible perturbation, then add the perturbation to the image to obtain an adversarial image similar to the original image that can disrupt the function of DeepFakes. Finally, in the training and inference phases, the adversarial image with the perturbation added has no change visible to the naked eye after the DeepFakes output, achieving the purpose of breaking the function of DeepFakes. In summary, the adversarial image with added perturbations must satisfy two objectives: (i) visually consistent with the original image (ii) no visual change between the input and the output of DeepFakes. To evaluate the superiority of our approach, we conducted experiments mainly on the facial attribute editing StarGAN and compared it with the powerful adversarial attack PGD. The experimental results show that our proposed method can better enable the addition of perturbed images with the ability to corrupt DeepFakes functionality.

Our main contributions are summarized as follows:

1. We propose a retentive framework for proactive defense against DeepFakes that can be adapted to different DeepFakes.
2. In this framework we train a perturbation generator that can destroy Deep-Fakes, the perturbation generator can quickly and efficiently image the corresponding perturbation. The original image with the addition of this invisible perturbation has immunity to DeepFakes by making the DeepFakes output preserve the visual effect of their inputs.
3. We demonstrate the superiority of our approach in terms of similarity and inference efficiency by comparing it with adversarial attack PGD under different evaluation metrics and different datasets.

2 Related Work

2.1 DeepFake Generation

As generative adversarial networks have made significant progress in recent years, DeepFakes have evolved from crude to exquisite. DeepFakes that are indistinguishable from the human eye pose a huge threat to people's security and privacy. Currently, there are four main types of DeepFakes, namely the entire synthesis, facial attribute editing, face swapping, and facial expression swapping. Since the entire synthesis does not involve a specific person, we mainly consider the other three types of threats.

The entire synthesis is to generate people that do not exist in the world, such as PGGAN [16], and StyleGAN [3]. Facial attribute editing is the use of GANs such as StarGAN [2] for a particular attribute of the face, e.g., hair color, or age. Face swapping is the most notorious method that replaces the source image face with the target face, FaceSwap and DeepFaceLab [17] are two commonly used tools. Facial expression swapping can be done by replacing the source image facial expression with the target facial expression using tools like Face2Face [18].

2.2   DeepFake Defense

Passive Defense. Initially researchers only considered distinguishing the fake works generated by DeepFakes, so they invented a series of DeepFake detectors, all of which have good accuracy rates. But DeepFake detection is a passive defense of post-event forensics, which can only mitigate the negative effects caused by DeepFakes. Current research is mainly based on DeepFakes detection of artificial artifacts in the spatial [5] and frequency domains [6], and there are also some other methods such as biosignals [7]. These methods commonly use deep neural networks, and some researchers have identified the threat of adversarial perturbations to DeepFakes detectors. There are several other issues [19] that researchers need to address.

Proactive Defense. DeepFakes passive defense can only stop things after they happen, and it is not effective to mitigate the impact of DeepFakes. To solve this problem, various proactive defense methods [11–13,20–26] have been proposed to defend against DeepFakes.

Some consider inserting predefined marks into a synthesized face and then using these marks to determine whether the image or video has been manipulated by DeepFakes. Wang et al. [20] inserted label information into the protected image. Images subject to DeepFakes manipulation can also be obtained with the label information inserted at the beginning. Sun et al. [21] designed two types of traces, sustainable traces and erasable traces. A model trained using images with both types of traces added generates face images with only sustainable traces. In this way, it is possible to determine whether an image or video has been manipulated by DeepFakes.

Others considered adding adversarial perturbation to the image, and the image with added perturbation is not visually different from the original image. Finally, this image with added invisible perturbation can destroy the function of DeepFakes, and this method can effectively mitigate the impact of DeepFakes. Ruiz et al. [11] proposed an adversarial attack in the gray box case, and then Huang et al. [12] proposed a method that can achieve the goal by alternating training strategies and using some task-specific strategies to enhance the defense performance. Wang et al. [22] considered that distorted images need to be judged not only by the naked eye, but also by DeepFake detectors. Huang et al. [23] consider that the generated perturbations are usually specific to a particular image and a particular generative model, and thus propose a two-level perturbation fusion strategy as a way to generate cross-model generic adversarial watermarks. Wang et al. [24] consider that perturbations are generally not robust, so a method to generate perceptual-aware perturbations incessantly was proposed to improve the robustness of perturbations.

However, the goal of the attack that most researchers have considered is to distort the output of DeepFakes. This does allow people to tell if an image is real or fake, but people on the Internet these days don't really care if things are real or fake a lot of the time. Unless the distortion is so severe that you can't see a face, it can have a negative impact. Therefore, we tend to attack the goal of making the output of DeepFakes visually unchanged from the input. Yeh et al. [25] proposed an invalid attack using adversarial attack PGD to minimize the distance between the adversarial output and the original input. They [26] later proposed to solve this problem in the black box case. He et al. [13] proposed a method to find neighbors in the latent space that are similar to the original image but can reach the disabled DeepFakes target. This method slightly alters the appearance of the face image although it has better visual quality less likely to be detected by noise detectors. In this paper, we present an end-to-end approach to training a perturbation generator. Images can achieve the goal of disabling DeepFakes after adding the perturbations generated by the perturbation generator.

3   Method

In this section, we first describe the adversarial attack on DeepFakes. Then we introduce our proactive defense framework and its loss function and optimization algorithms.

3.1   Adversarial Attacks Against DeepFake

Proactive defense against DeepFakes by adding invisible perturbations to the original image is a more important direction for research than using those Deep-Fake detectors that have been extensively studied for passive defense. An adversarial attack against DeepFakes can disrupt the functionality of DeepFakes. There are two ways of this destruction, which are distortion attack and invalid attack. The distortion attack is to make the output of DeepFakes distorted, so that visually it can be judged that it is not a real image. The invalid attack is one that causes DeepFakes to lose the ability to manipulate the image, making it visually impossible to tell the gap between the input and the output of the DeepFakes. Formally, we denote x as the original image and x_{adv} as the adversarial image, where $x_{adv} = x + \eta$ and η is a visually invisible perturbation with a common norm constraint. The corresponding outputs $G(x)$ and $G(x_{adv})$ can be obtained by feeding the original image x and the adversarial image x_{adv} into the DeepFake generator $G(\cdot)$. We let t be the target of the attack and the objective function can be written as

$$\mathcal{L}(G(x + \eta), t), \quad s.t. \quad ||\eta||_2 < \epsilon, \tag{1}$$

where $\mathcal{L}$ is a distance function normally using the L_0, L_2 or L_∞ norms. If t is set to the original output $G(x)$, maximizing this function is a distortion attack, and we can obtain adversarial images x_{adv} that distort the output of the DeepFakes. If t is set to the original image x, minimizing this function is an invalid attack, and we can obtain adversarial images x_{adv} that invalidates DeepFakes. Minimizing this function can also be considered as target image generation if t is set to the desired target.

The optimal perturbation η of the original image can be efficiently optimized by an adversarial attack on Eq. 1., e.g., Iterative Fast Gradient Sign Method (IFGSM) [8] or Projected Gradient Descent (PGD) [9] . Though the optimal η can be effectively solved through the iterations of IFGSM or PGD, it could be time-consuming to deal with the large-scale image dataset. For each image, we have to optimize it individually and iteratively to obtain the corresponding best perturbation η, which is a waste of resources. Training a perturbation generator that is effective for DeepFakes not only saves time, but may even yield better performance.

3.2   Perturbation Generator

As shown in Fig. 2, the model pipeline of this method consists of a perturbation generator and a DeepFake generator. Next, we will introduce them one by one and provide an overall optimization framework. Compared to generating the corresponding perturbation for each image separately, we tend to learn a perturbation generator PG to generate perturbation $P(x)$ for image x. We add perturbation $P(x)$ to image x to obtain adversarial image x_{adv}. Therefore, the generated image of the adversarial image x_{adv} under the given DeepFake generator G can be written as $G(x_{adv})$. Therefore, the objective function of disrupting DeepFake can be rewritten as

$$x_{adv} = x + P(x) \tag{2}$$

$$\min_{P} \mathcal{L}(x_{adv}, G(x_{adv})), s.t. \quad \|P(x)\|_2 < \epsilon, \tag{3}$$

where ϵ is our chosen range of the perturbation.

Magnitude Loss. Due to the use of images with added invisible perturbations to replace the original image to combat DeepFakes, the original image and the image with added perturbations should be visually as similar as possible. Therefore, we propose the first loss to constrain the size of the perturbation generated by the perturbation generator PG. $\mathcal{L}_{mag}$ is composed of two loss functions, $\mathcal{L}_{pix}$ is the pix-level loss with L_2 norm of x and x_{adv}, and $\mathcal{L}_{feat}$ is the perceptual loss of both,

$$\mathcal{L}_{pix} = \|x - x_{adv}\|_2 \tag{4}$$

$$\mathcal{L}_{feat} = \|F(x) - F(x_{adv})\|_2 \tag{5}$$

$$\mathcal{L}_{mag} = \mathcal{L}_{pix} + \lambda_{feat}\mathcal{L}_{feat} \tag{6}$$

where λ_{feat} is hyper-parameters to balance different loss items. $F(\cdot)$ represents a feature extraction model for acquiring perceptual loss.

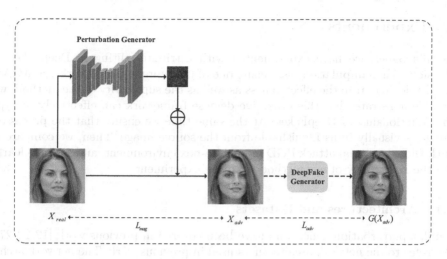

Fig. 2. The training phase of the overall pipeline of the perturbation generator that combats DeepFakes. The source image x is fed into the perturbation generator PG to obtain a perturbation $P(x)$ that is invisible to the naked eye. This perturbation $P(x)$ is then added to the corresponding source image x to obtain the adversarial image x_{adv}. Finally, this adversarial image x_{adv} is input to the DeepFake generator G to obtain the corresponding output $G(x_{adv})$. The corresponding perturbation generator PG is obtained by training under the constraints of the loss functions.

Adversarial Loss. The purpose of training the Perturbation Generator PG is to destroy the function of the DeepFake generative model, i.e., to make the input and output of the DeepFakes similar. Therefore, we introduce the adversarial loss to constrain the l_2 distance between the adversarial image x_{adv} and its output,

$$\mathcal{L}_{adv} = \|x_{adv} - G(x_{adv})\|_2 \tag{7}$$

By incorporating the above loss functions, we thus achieve the resulting objective function,

$$\mathcal{L} = \lambda_{mag}\mathcal{L}_{mag} + \lambda_{adv}\mathcal{L}_{adv} \tag{8}$$

where λ_{mag} and λ_{adv} are hyper parameters to balance different loss items. The DeepFake models will be selected from the pre-trained SOTA models. Their parameters will not be changed during the training, which means that the whole end-to-end training will only update the parameters of the perturbation generator PG. By optimizing Eq. 8, we can learn the appropriate perturbation generator parameters from the training set. In the inference phase, we input the source image into the perturbation generator PG to obtain the corresponding optimal perturbation, and add this invisible perturbation to the source image x to obtain the corresponding adversarial image x_{adv}, which can destroy functionality of the DeepFakes, i.e., DeepFakes are unable to manipulate x_{adv}.

4   Experiments

In this paper, we have experimented with attribute editing in DeepFakes, a classic facial manipulation task, using one of the representative works, StarGAN [2]. To demonstrate the effectiveness as well as the superiority of the method, we first demonstrate that this proactive defense framework can effectively disrupt the functionality of DeepFakes. At the same time we ensure that the processed image is visually indistinguishable from the source image. Then, we compare it with the adversarial attack PGD in a white-box environment, and we can clearly see the superiority of our method from the experiment.

4.1   Architectures and Datasets

Similar perturbation generators have been covered in previous work [12,22,27]. We refer to the network architectures used in previous work. The network architecture of the perturbation generator PG is chosen to be U-Net [28], which is a classical network architecture that consists of an encoder that extracts the abstract features of an image and a decoder that fuses the various features. Its U-shaped network structure densely fuses the shallow features with the deeper features, and our experiments use the UNet-128 network.

We use the pre-trained StarGAN model for attribute editing operations. The dataset uses face images from CelebA, which has 202,599 face images with a resolution of 178×218. We first crop the center of the image to 178×178 to increase the proportion of the face in the image, and then resize it to 128×128. Finally, 200,600 of these images were used in the training phase and the remaining 1,999 images were used in the test phase. In the training phase, the batchsize is set to 16, and the learning rate of the perturbation generator is set to 0.0001. The attribute domain is set to five attributes ('Black Hair', 'Blond Hair', 'Brown Hair', 'Male', 'Young'). The network is updated for 200,000 iterations. We use PGD for adversarial attacks, simultaneously attacking five attribute domains of one image at a time, with a step size of 0.0001 and an iteration count of 100. In the inference phase, we additionally selected the public face datasets LFW [29] and FFHQ [30] for evaluation. We select 1999 images from each of these two datasets. Since the image size of LFW is 250×250, we first crop the center of the image to 200×200 to increase the proportion of the face in the image, and then resize it to 128×128.

4.2   Evaluation Metrics

In order to comprehensively evaluate the effectiveness of the attack, we have employed the L_2 norm distance, Structural Similarity Index (SSIM), Peak Signal-to-Noise Ratio (PSNR), perceptual loss [31], and Learned Perceptual Image Patch Similarity (LPIPS) [32] to evaluate the similarity between the images with the addition of the invisible perturbation and their outputs under the generative model, respectively. The similarity between the images and their outputs of the DeepFakes is evaluated. The network used for feature extraction by perceptual loss is VGG16 and the network used for feature extraction by LPIPS is AlexNet. We propose the Defense Success Rate (DSR) to better evaluate the effectiveness of the attack. If the pixel-level loss $L_2 \leq 0.05$ between the input and the output of the DeepFakes, we can consider that it successfully destroys the functionality of the DeepFakes. So we define the DSR as the percentage of adversarial images that successfully destroy the functionality of the DeepFakes in the total test images. In order to show the effectiveness of the defense more intuitively, we use Local Binary Pattern (LBP) to describe the local features of an image. LBP features are widely used in face recognition.

4.3 Attack Performance Evaluation

In order to demonstrate the effectiveness of the proposed proactive defense, we conducted experiments in a white-box manner, i.e., we know the network architecture of the DeepFakes, the domain information, and various information about the internals.

For the facial attribute editing task, our approach ensures better disruption of DeepFakes while the image with added invisible perturbations has better similarity to the original image. As shown in Fig. 3, we can visualize the effect of our method on the five attribute domains that StarGAN chooses to manipulate. The first column is the input of the DeepFake, and the following five columns are StarGAN's manipulation of the five attribute domains ('Black Hair', 'Blond Hair', 'Brown Hair', 'Male', 'Young') of the input image. The first line is the original result with no defense, and the second line is the result after using our method.

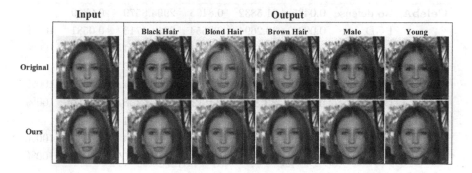

Fig. 3. Visual examples of defending against StarGAN [2].

4.4 Comparison with Other Methods

Similarity. We compared our method with adversarial attack PGD at $\epsilon = 0.05$ under StarGAN on different datasets. In Table 1, it can be clearly seen that the adversarial image x_{adv} obtained by our method is more similar to the original image than PGD. Thus it is visually more difficult to detect the existence of the perturbation.

Table 1. Similarity comparison between the original image and the image with perturbation.($\epsilon = 0.05$)

DataSets	Methods	$L_2 \downarrow$	PSNR↑	SSIM↑	perceptual↓	LPIPS↓
CelebA	PGD	0.0008	36.9832	0.9360	239.0099	0.0115
	Ours	**0.0002**	**42.6844**	**0.9887**	**11.6263**	**0.0012**
LFW	PGD	0.0008	36.9324	0.9381	240.8695	0.0130
	Ours	**0.0002**	**43.0926**	**0.9909**	**11.7893**	**0.0015**
FFHQ	PGD	0.0008	36.9449	0.9473	225.5404	0.0070
	Ours	**0.0004**	**40.6340**	**0.9876**	**18.1097**	**0.0012**

In Table 2, we compare the similarity between the input and output of Star-GAN. We find that both our method and PGD can effectively combat DeepFakes. However, our method performs better in terms of similarity, which indicates that our method has better defense.

Table 2. Similarity comparison between the Input and the Output of the StarGAN. ($\epsilon = 0.05$)

Datasets	Methods	$L_2 \downarrow$	PSNR↑	SSIM↑	perceptual↓	LPIPS↓	ASR↑
CelebA	No defense	0.0435	21.5832	0.8195	2994.8579	0.0869	-
	PGD	0.0039	30.2694	0.8654	2014.5713	0.0581	100%
	Ours	**0.0018**	**34.0527**	**0.9594**	**941.7181**	**0.0306**	100%
LFW	No defense	0.0414	21.2920	0.8106	3298.6406	0.0998	-
	PGD	0.0040	30.1451	0.8673	2068.6641	0.0578	100%
	Ours	**0.0018**	**33.8998**	**0.9622**	**908.7238**	**0.0274**	100%
FFHQ	No defense	0.0477	20.6184	0.7889	4039.8401	0.0988	-
	PGD	0.0059	28.5643	0.8556	2565.0344	0.0747	100%
	Ours	**0.0038**	**30.8490**	**0.9386**	**1670.6807**	**0.0542**	100%

In Table 3, we compare the similarity between the original image and the adversarial output of StarGAN. We can see that our method has higher similarity than PGD. From this we can know that our method outperforms PGD in terms of similarity regardless of whether the image with the added invisible perturbation is attacked by DeepFake or not.

Table 3. Similarity comparison between the original image and the output of image with perturbation on StarGAN. ($\epsilon = 0.05$)

Datasets	Methods	$L_2 \downarrow$	PSNR$\uparrow$	SSIM$\uparrow$	perceptual$\downarrow$	LPIPS$\downarrow$
CelebA	PGD	0.0032	31.1604	0.9052	1977.8158	0.0481
	Ours	**0.0024**	**32.8416**	**0.9446**	**1016.6274**	**0.0355**
LFW	PGD	0.0033	31.0122	0.9064	1999.1094	0.0486
	Ours	**0.0023**	**32.7748**	**0.9514**	**970.7018**	**0.0328**
FFHQ	PGD	0.0052	29.1619	0.8903	2593.4036	0.0665
	Ours	**0.0050**	**29.5974**	**0.9178**	**1821.7161**	**0.0615**

As shown in Fig. 4, we can see the superiority of our method more intuitively at the pixel-level and at the LBP-level. At the pixel-level we can see that both our method and PGD are effective enough. However, at the LBP-level we can see that the gap for our method compared to PGD is smaller.

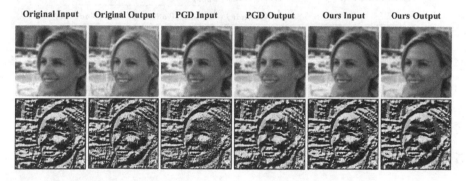

Fig. 4. Visual comparison of the adversarial attack PGD with our method in the pixel-level (top) and the LBP-level (bottom) on the defense of StarGAN [2].

Inference Efficiency. We also make a comparison in inference efficiency, where we randomly select 100 images for corresponding perturbation generation using our method and PGD. It is not meaningful to observe the specific inference time since different computer performance leads to different time. We choose to compute the multiples of the difference in time they take. The final test on StarGAN shows that PGD takes more than ten times as long as our method, which demonstrates the superiority of our method in inference efficiency.

4.5   Ablation Study

In our training process, we use three loss functions. To demonstrate their necessity, we provided ablation evaluation on three different training sessions, each time using only two of the loss functions, and compare them to our full model. As the ablation evaluation shown in Table 4, eliminating $\mathcal{L}_{pix}$ is inferior to our full model in all parameters. Eliminating $\mathcal{L}_{feat}$ gives a slight advantage in the l_2 distance between the adversarial image x_{adv} and the output of the adversarial image x_{advout}, but falls short of our full model on the other two figures. Eliminating $\mathcal{L}_{adv}$ causes the l_2 distance between the original image x and the adversarial image x_{adv} to reach an extremely low case, but has no effect at all on defense. In summary, the choice of complete model on the loss function is a balance between the size of the perturbation and the effect on defense.

Table 4. Ablation study to remove losses used in our training. Removing any of the losses degrades the performance of the entire active defense framework compared to our proposed method. The data in the table respectively represent the l_2 distance between the original image x and the adversarial image x_{adv}, the adversarial image x_{adv} and the output of the adversarial image x_{advout}, and the original image x and the output of the adversarial image x_{advout}. ($\epsilon = 0.05$)

Loss removed	StarGAN ($L_2 \downarrow$)		
	$l_2(x, x_{adv})$	$l_2(x_{adv}, x_{advout})$	$l_2(x, x_{advout})$
Magnitude loss ($\mathcal{L}_{pix}$)	0.0003	0.0020	0.0028
Magnitude loss ($\mathcal{L}_{feat}$)	0.0006	**0.0015**	0.0028
Adversarial loss ($\mathcal{L}_{adv}$)	1×10^{-7}	0.0436	0.0436
None (ours)	0.0002	0.0018	**0.0024**

5   Conclusion

In this paper, we propose a new method for proactive defense against DeepFakes with image visual retentivity. By training a perturbation generator to obtain perturbations and then adding invisible perturbations to images to combat Deep-Fakes, our work can help people's photos to be immune to DeepFakes by generating visually similar face images. Experiments on the facial attribute editing, Star-GAN, validate the effectiveness of the approach. Compared to the perturbations obtained through adversarial attacks such as PGD, our method obtains smaller perturbations, acquires the perturbations faster, and is more effective against DeepFakes. Therefore, our method can generate face images with stronger protection and more similar to the original image. Currently, the proposed method works only on white-box setups, which does not allow us to obtain effective defenses in realistic black-box situations. Although it works well on single-model counterpart defenses, it does not support cross-models defense. We will consider the defense with black-box and cross-model setup in our future work. Although it is still challenging to design a general, effective, interpretable, and robust proactive defense method against DeepFake, we hope that our method can give new ideas for securing the Internet.

Acknowledgement. This research was funded by National Natural Science Foundation of China No. 62171334, Fundamental Research Funds for the Central Universities No. ZYTS23162 and Scientific Research Foundation of Northwest A&F University No. Z1090121092.

References

1. Goodfellow, I., et al.: Generative adversarial nets. In: Ghahramani, Z., Welling, M., Cortes, C., Lawrence, N., Weinberger, K. (eds.) Advances in Neural Information Processing Systems, vol. 27. Curran Associates, Inc. (2014)
2. Choi, Y., Choi, M., Kim, M., Ha, J.W., Kim, S., Choo, J.: StarGAN: unified generative adversarial networks for multi-domain image-to-image translation. In: Proceedings of the IEEE Conference on Computer Vision and Pattern Recognition (CVPR), June 2018
3. Karras, T., Laine, S., Aila, T.: A style-based generator architecture for generative adversarial networks. In: Proceedings of the IEEE/CVF Conference on Computer Vision and Pattern Recognition (CVPR), June 2019
4. Karras, T., Laine, S., Aittala, M., Hellsten, J., Lehtinen, J., Aila, T.: Analyzing and improving the image quality of StyleGAN. In: Proceedings of the IEEE/CVF Conference on Computer Vision and Pattern Recognition (CVPR), June 2020
5. Li, L., et al.: Face X-ray for more general face forgery detection. In: Proceedings of the IEEE/CVF Conference on Computer Vision and Pattern Recognition (CVPR), June 2020
6. Luo, Y., Zhang, Y., Yan, J., Liu, W.: Generalizing face forgery detection with high-frequency features. In: Proceedings of the IEEE/CVF Conference on Computer Vision and Pattern Recognition (CVPR), pp. 16317–16326, June 2021
7. Zhou, Y., Lim, S.N.: Joint audio-visual deepfake detection. In: 2021 IEEE/CVF International Conference on Computer Vision (ICCV), pp. 14780–14789 (2021). https://doi.org/10.1109/ICCV48922.2021.01453
8. Goodfellow, I.J., Shlens, J., Szegedy, C.: Explaining and harnessing adversarial examples (2015)
9. Madry, A., Makelov, A., Schmidt, L., Tsipras, D., Vladu, A.: Towards deep learning models resistant to adversarial attacks (2019)
10. Carlini, N., Wagner, D.: Towards evaluating the robustness of neural networks. In: 2017 IEEE Symposium on Security and Privacy (SP), pp. 39–57 (2017). https://doi.org/10.1109/SP.2017.49
11. Ruiz, N., Bargal, S.A., Sclaroff, S.: Disrupting deepfakes: adversarial attacks against conditional image translation networks and facial manipulation systems (2020)
12. Huang, Q., Zhang, J., Zhou, W., Zhang, W., Yu, N.: Initiative defense against facial manipulation. In: Proceedings of the AAAI Conference on Artificial Intelligence, vol. 35, no. 2, pp. 1619–1627 (2021). https://doi.org/10.1609/aaai.v35i2.16254
13. He, Z., Wang, W., Guan, W., Dong, J., Tan, T.: Defeating deepfakes via adversarial visual reconstruction. In: Proceedings of the 30th ACM International Conference on Multimedia, MM 2022, pp. 2464–2472. Association for Computing Machinery, New York, NY, USA (2022). https://doi.org/10.1145/3503161.3547923
14. Li, S., et al.: Connecting the dots: detecting adversarial perturbations using context inconsistency. In: Vedaldi, A., Bischof, H., Brox, T., Frahm, J.-M. (eds.) ECCV 2020. LNCS, vol. 12368, pp. 396–413. Springer, Cham (2020). https://doi.org/10.1007/978-3-030-58592-1_24

15. Agarwal, A., Singh, R., Vatsa, M., Ratha, N.: Image transformation-based defense against adversarial perturbation on deep learning models. IEEE Trans. Dependable Secure Comput. **18**(5), 2106–2121 (2021). https://doi.org/10.1109/TDSC.2020.3027183

16. Karras, T., Aila, T., Laine, S., Lehtinen, J.: Progressive growing of GANs for improved quality, stability, and variation. arXiv preprint arXiv:1710.10196 (2017)

17. Perov, I., et al.: Deepfacelab: integrated, flexible and extensible face-swapping framework. arXiv preprint arXiv:2005.05535 (2020)

18. Thies, J., Zollhöfer, M., Stamminger, M., Theobalt, C., Nießner, M.: Face2Face: real-time face capture and reenactment of RGB videos. In: 2016 IEEE Conference on Computer Vision and Pattern Recognition (CVPR), pp. 2387–2395 (2016). https://doi.org/10.1109/CVPR.2016.262

19. Juefei-Xu, F., Wang, R., Huang, Y., Guo, Q., Ma, L., Liu, Y.: Countering malicious DeepFakes: survey, battleground, and horizon. Int. J. Comput. Vis. **130**(7), 1678–1734 (2022). https://doi.org/10.1007/s11263-022-01606-8

20. Wang, R., Juefei-Xu, F., Luo, M., Liu, Y., Wang, L.: FakeTagger: robust safeguards against deepfake dissemination via provenance tracking. In: Proceedings of the 29th ACM International Conference on Multimedia, MM 2021, pp. 3546–3555. Association for Computing Machinery, New York, NY, USA (2021). https://doi.org/10.1145/3474085.3475518

21. Sun, P., Qi, H., Li, Y., Lyu, S.: FakeTracer: proactively defending against face-swap DeepFakes via implanting traces in training. arXiv preprint arXiv:2307.14593 (2023)

22. Wang, X., Huang, J., Ma, S., Nepal, S., Xu, C.: DeepFake disrupter: the detector of DeepFake is my friend. In: 2022 IEEE/CVF Conference on Computer Vision and Pattern Recognition (CVPR), pp. 14900–14909 (2022). https://doi.org/10.1109/CVPR52688.2022.01450

23. Huang, H., et al.: CMUA-watermark: a cross-model universal adversarial watermark for combating deepfakes. In: Proceedings of the AAAI Conference on Artificial Intelligence, vol. 36, no. 1, pp. 989–997 (2022). https://doi.org/10.1609/aaai.v36i1.19982

24. Wang, R., Huang, Z., Chen, Z., Liu, L., Chen, J., Wang, L.: Anti-forgery: towards a stealthy and robust deepfake disruption attack via adversarial perceptual-aware perturbations. In: Raedt, L.D. (ed.) Proceedings of the Thirty-First International Joint Conference on Artificial Intelligence, IJCAI-22, main Track, pp. 761–767, July 2022. https://doi.org/10.24963/ijcai.2022/107

25. Yeh, C.Y., Chen, H.W., Tsai, S.L., Wang, S.D.: Disrupting image-translation-based DeepFake algorithms with adversarial attacks. In: 2020 IEEE Winter Applications of Computer Vision Workshops (WACVW), pp. 53–62 (2020). https://doi.org/10.1109/WACVW50321.2020.9096939

26. Yeh, C.Y., Chen, H.W., Shuai, H.H., Yang, D.N., Chen, M.S.: Attack as the best defense: nullifying image-to-image translation GANs via limit-aware adversarial attack. In: 2021 IEEE/CVF International Conference on Computer Vision (ICCV), pp. 16168–16177 (2021). https://doi.org/10.1109/ICCV48922.2021.01588

27. Xiao, C., Li, B., Yan Zhu, J., He, W., Liu, M., Song, D.: Generating adversarial examples with adversarial networks. In: Proceedings of the Twenty-Seventh International Joint Conference on Artificial Intelligence, IJCAI-18, pp. 3905–3911, July 2018. https://doi.org/10.24963/ijcai.2018/543

28. Ronneberger, O., Fischer, P., Brox, T.: U-Net: convolutional networks for biomedical image segmentation. In: Navab, N., Hornegger, J., Wells, W.M., Frangi, A.F.

(eds.) MICCAI 2015. LNCS, vol. 9351, pp. 234–241. Springer, Cham (2015). https://doi.org/10.1007/978-3-319-24574-4_28

29. Huang, G.B., Mattar, M., Berg, T., Learned-Miller, E.: Labeled faces in the wild: a database for studying face recognition in unconstrained environments. In: Workshop on Faces in 'Real-Life' Images: Detection, Alignment, and Recognition (2008)

30. Karras, T., Laine, S., Aila, T.: A style-based generator architecture for generative adversarial networks. In: Proceedings of the IEEE/CVF Conference on Computer Vision and Pattern Recognition, pp. 4401–4410 (2019)

31. Johnson, J., Alahi, A., Fei-Fei, L.: Perceptual losses for real-time style transfer and super-resolution. In: Leibe, B., Matas, J., Sebe, N., Welling, M. (eds.) ECCV 2016. LNCS, vol. 9906, pp. 694–711. Springer, Cham (2016). https://doi.org/10.1007/978-3-319-46475-6_43

32. Zhang, R., Isola, P., Efros, A.A., Shechtman, E., Wang, O.: The unreasonable effectiveness of deep features as a perceptual metric. In: Proceedings of the IEEE Conference on Computer Vision and Pattern Recognition (CVPR), June 2018

A Fast and Accurate Non-interactive Privacy-Preserving Neural Network Inference Framework

Hongyao Tao[1] , Chungen Xu[1(✉)] , and Pan Zhang[2]

[1] School of Mathematics and Statistics, Nanjing University of Science and Technology, Nanjing 210094, China
xuchung@njust.edu.cn
[2] School of Cyber Science and Engineering, Nanjing University of Science and Technology, Nanjing 210094, China

Abstract. With the remarkable successes of machine learning, it is becoming increasingly popular and widespread. Machine learning as a Service (MLaaS) provided by cloud services is widely utilized to address the challenge of users unable to bear the burden of training machine learning models. However, the privacy issues involved present a significant challenge. Homomorphic encryption, known for its capability to perform efficient operations on ciphertexts, is widely employed in Privacy computing domain. In order to address the security vulnerabilities and excessive communication and computation costs of interactive privacy-preserving neural networks, and in light of the significant time consumption of linear layers and the challenges SIMD HE faces in computing arbitrary nonlinear functions precisely, we propose a non-interactive framework for privacy-preserving neural networks that accelerates linear computations and ensures accurate computation of any non-linear functions. Specifically, we utilize CKKS encryption to enable private neural network inference under floating-point arithmetic. Leveraging the characteristics of both wordwise HE and bitwise HE, we design a non-interactive and fast matrix multiplication scheme, achieving up to $500\times$ acceleration across different matrix dimensions. By transforming various types of homomorphic encryption ciphertexts and employing lookup tables, we realize accurate computation of arbitrary non-linear operations without requiring interaction. Experimental results demonstrate that our framework achieves the same level of accuracy as pre-trained neural network models on plaintext without incurring any additional accuracy loss.

Keywords: Homomorphic encryption · Privacy-preserving · Neural networks

Supported by the National Natural Science Foundation of China (No. 62072240) and the Natural Science Foundation of Jiangsu Province Youth Project (No. BK20210330).

J. Liu et al. (Eds.): TridentCom 2023, LNICST 523, pp. 154–172, 2024.
https://doi.org/10.1007/978-3-031-51399-2_9

1 Introduction

As the Internet of Things (IoT) undergoes rapid development, a substantial volume of data is being generated and collected, containing rich information and value. Traditional methods are not capable of effectively handling such massive datasets. Machine learning has emerged as a new technique that can learn patterns and regularities from data. It leverages large-scale data to train models and extract valuable information and knowledge, enabling computers to learn from data and make intelligent decisions. In recent years, machine learning has become increasingly popular and widespread, witnessing an explosive growth in applications. Currently, machine learning have mature applications in various fields, such as image classification [22, 34], medical diagnosis [2], speech recognition [24], and autonomous driving [5]. However, designing and training machine learning models require significant resources and specialized expertise. Extracting value from data through training incurs high resource costs and management expenses. For personal computers or general servers, this could be an overwhelming burden. Fortunately, the rise of new-generation information technologies, such as cloud services, offers a solution. In scenarios with limited local resources, both businesses and individuals can opt to send data to cloud servers and utilize machine learning models pre-trained by cloud server. Machine Learning as a Service (MLaaS) [33] consequently emerged. Recently, with the introduction of AI products like GPT by some internet companies, the momentum of Machine Learning as a Service (MLaaS) has reached new heights.

Meanwhile, while cloud computing brings great convenience to people, data security and privacy have also become increasingly significant concerns in society. The privacy and security issues related to machine learning models and the entire process from training to application in artificial intelligence have attracted widespread attention from researchers. To address the frequent occurrence of data security incidents, many countries have enacted laws and regulations to restrict the sharing of sensitive user data [11]. While clients are obligated to share their data with the cloud for inference, and they expect a high level of data privacy protection to prevent curious cloud providers or attackers from extracting valuable information. Conversely, cloud server aim to prevent users from extracting their model parameter, which have been trained with considerable resources and efforts [30]. Consequently, an imperative exists to devise a secure and efficient solution that safeguards the security of data in Machine Learning as a Service (MLaaS). Considering these challenges, researchers are actively working towards establishing a secure and privacy-preserving framework to facilitate the implementation of MLaaS. To address this issue, various specialized encryption schemes, such as searchable encryption [16], have been applied in diverse scenarios like the Internet of Things [25] and safeguarding privacy data in cloud services [35]. Among these schemes, homomorphic encryption [12] stands out as the most suitable encryption technique for privacy-preserving machine learning (PPML) scenarios that involve computations on encrypted data.

1.1 Related Work

Homomorphic Encryption (HE) is a form of encryption that allows users to perform a series of linear operations directly on encrypted data, with the results still being in encrypted form. Decryption of the results yields the same content as operating on plain-text data. CryptoNets [14] and its improved version Faster CryptoNets [8] proposed a privacy-preserving scheme based on homomorphic encryption. They utilized Stone-Weierstrass theorem to derive an approximate polynomial for the non-linear activation function to simulate neural network computations on encrypted data, thereby achieving encrypted neural network inference. To ensure accuracy in the non-linear layer, high-order polynomials might be required to approximate the activation functions, resulting in significant overhead for homomorphic encryption. Some approaches [37] that use polynomial approximations update the weights after each iteration and send them to the involved parties for decryption and re-encryption, leading to high communication complexity. CryptoDL [17] improved this by adopting low-order polynomial approx-imation methods. Kim et al. [20] proposed the first homomorphic encryption logistic regression outsourcing model using low-order polynomials to approximate non-linear function computations. To enhance the efficiency of encrypted computations, E2DM [18] used a more efficient HE scheme, specifically packed SIMD [29], which combines several messages into a singular ciphertext, thereby improving computational efficiency.

However, not all non-linear function can be effectively approximated using polyno-mials. Therefore, some approaches utilize secure multi-party computation to achieve the computation of non-linear layers with good results. Garbled Circuits are employed by DeepSecure [28] and XONN [27] to binaryize computations in neural networks, allow-ing them to implicitly derive predictions without revealing sensitive client data. Utilizing Secure Secret Sharing as detailed in [31], client data is partitioned into shares, with the server holding only one share, and the computations are finalized through interactive share exchanges. Due to the nature of secure multi-party computation, the sharing of intermediate results is required. As a black-box oracle for model extraction [32], the server's prediction service is susceptible to exploitation by malicious clients, who may also infer the training dataset [26], resulting in potential harm to the cloud server's model. Substantial computational and communication overhead is incurred during the interac-tion between the client and the cloud server, which goes against the original intention of outsourcing data to the cloud server due to limited local resources. Consequently, we aim to construct a machine learning as a service (MLaaS) scheme which requires no additional interaction beyond sending encrypted data and receiving prediction results.

In the existing homomorphic encryption schemes, the second-generation homomor-phic encryption (word-wise HEs) [4, 6, 10] offers efficient polynomial operations, such as high-speed addition and multiplication, through support for SIMD batch processing. However, the absence of support for non-linear operations, such as the sigmoid and ReLu activation functions in neural networks, commonly used in machine learning processes, is a notable limitation. On the other hand, the third-generation homomorphic encryption scheme (bitwise HEs) [7, 9, 13] supports arbitrary functions represented as Boolean cir-cuits. Nevertheless, due to its encryption process being done bit by bit based on message values, it is impractical for addition and multiplication which will result in extremely low computational efficiency. This can result in unbearable computational costs. To address these limitations, CHIMERA [3] and PEGASUS [23] strike a balance between the advantages and disadvantages of both types of homomorphic encryption schemes. They propose conversion methods between word-wise HEs and bit-wise HEs encryption schemes, enabling bridging between polynomial and non-polynomial computations in homomorphic encryption.

1.2 Contribution

It is worth noting that existing research points out that in privacy-preserving neural network models, linear computations occupy the vast majority of computation time, accounting for over 90% in many models, and even higher in some cases. Several effective improvement schemes for matrix multiplication have been proposed in [15, 19]. The most recent work [36] reduces the most time-consuming permutation operation in homomorphic encryption linear computations through secret sharing, significantly improving the efficiency of matrix multiplication calculations.

We propose a non-interactive privacy-preserving neural network scheme which enables faster linear computations and accurate evaluation of any non-linear operation. To achieve this, we utilize the CKKS homomorphic encryption scheme for machine learning inference, allowing homomorphic operations on floating-point numbers. Additionally, we design a fast matrix multiplication algorithm based on the characteristics of two types of homomorphic encryption ciphertexts, which achieves theoretically the same or even better results compared to schemes utilizing secret sharing [36], but without requiring any interactions. Our experiments demonstrate that our approach achieves a 500× speedup for matrix multiplication compared to [19]. Furthermore, we leverage table lookup to implement non-linear operations for any activation function by transforming different types of homomorphic encryption ciphertexts. Experimental results show that our proposed scheme achieves the same level of precision as pre-trained neural network models on plaintext, without incurring any additional losses.

Organized as follows, the remaining sections of this paper delve into the study's prerequisites in Sect. 2, our approach's specific details in Sect. 3, the corresponding experimental results in Sect. 4, and a conclusion in Sect. 5.

2 Preliminaries

2.1 Basic Notations

Vectors are denoted using bold lowercase letters, such as $\mathbf{a}$, and $\mathbf{a}_j$ is used to denote the j-th component of vector a. Matrices are denoted using bold uppercase letters, such as $\mathbf{A}$, where $a_{i,j}$ signifies the (i, j) entry of matrix $\mathbf{A}$. The Hadamard product of vectors is represented as $\mathbf{a} \circ \mathbf{b}$. We represent the set $\{0,\ldots, q - 1\}$ as $\mathbb{Z}_q$, and $\mathbb{Z}_q[X]$ denotes the polynomial ring over $\mathbb{Z}_q$. In the case of a 2-power number n, $R_{n,q} \equiv \mathbb{Z}_q[X]/(X^n + 1)$ specifies the ring of polynomials with a degree less than n, with coefficients belonging to $\mathbb{Z}_q$. Lower-case letters, like a, are employed to symbolize elements in $R_{n,q}$, with a_j denoting the j-th coefficient of a. The multiplication of ring elements is indicated by the dot symbol $\cdot$, as in $a \cdot b$. In this paper, all logarithms are to base 2.

2.2 Homomorphic Encryption

Homomorphic encryption possesses a unique property in ciphertext processing, which allows for efficient operations on encrypted data without decryption. This feature is pivotal in upholding information security and introduces a novel approach to tackle the data security challenges encountered in cloud computing. Next we will introduce two commonly used schemes for homomorphic encryption, namely LWE encryption (bit-wise HEs) and RLWE encryption (word-wise HEs).

The notation $LWE^{n,q}{}_s(m)$ is employed to represent the LWE encryption of the message $m \in \mathbb{Z}_q$ using the secret key $s \in \mathbb{Z}_q{}^n$, and abbreviated as $[m]_1$. In the same vein, the RLWE encryption of the message $m \in R_{n,q}$ under the key $s \in R_n$ is denoted as $RLWE^{n,q}{}_s(m)$, with a shorthand notation of $[m]_2$. It is important to note that all LWE and RLWE ciphertexts belong to the ring R_n, q. Next we introduce some linear operations for homomorphic encryption.

– Addition (+) and Multiplication (·). In (R)LWE, if we have ciphertexts c_0 and c_1, encrypting ring elements r_0 and r_1, the operation $c_0 + c_1$ (or $c_0 \cdot c_1$) yields a ciphertext encrypting $r_0 + r_1$ (or $r_0 \cdot r_1$).
– PtMult($\diamond$). Subject to the operation $r \diamond c_0$, the ciphertext c_0, encrypting a ring element r, transforms into a ciphertext that encrypts $r \cdot t$, where t is a given plaintext element.

In the case of RLWE encryption schemes, such as CKKS, it is also possible to combine several messages into a singular ciphertext and efficiently perform homomorphic computations using Single Instruction Multiple Data (SIMD) techniques. Unlike other homomorphic encryption schemes where the plaintext domain is integers, CKKS is an RLWE-based homomorphic encryption scheme that allows packed encryption computations on a series of floating-point numbers. This characteristic makes CKKS particularly suitable for privacy-preserving solutions during the computing process.

Leveraging the Chinese Remainder Theorem in the ring $R_{n,q}$, we can represent multiple plaintext data as a vector. This vector is subsequently encoded into a polynomial on the ring $R_{n,q}$, enabling various encryption operations on this polynomial. This methodology enables the completion of the SIMD batch processing described above. Here are some commonly used operations based on SIMD technology:

– SIMD Addition and Multiplication. In the addition $c_0 + c_1$ (or multiplication $c_0 \cdot c_1$) operation, RLWE ciphertexts c_0 and c_1 encrypting vectors **u** and **v** result in a ciphertext c. This ciphertext encrypts the vector **u** + **v** (or **u** ∘ **v**).
– Rotation. In the presence of an RLWE ciphertext c encrypting the vector **v**, an integer $n \in N$, and an evaluation key, the operation $Rot(\mathbf{c}, n)$ generates an RLWE ciphertext. This ciphertext encrypts the vector obtained by left-shifting all components of **v** by n positions concurrently.
– Switch. The RLWE ciphertext c encrypting the vector **v** undergoes the Swt operation, leading to a new RLWE ciphertext. This ciphertext encrypts a ring element v with coefficients $v_i = \mathbf{v}_i$ across all possible positions.
– Transform. The operation $Transf\ (c, i)$, applied to the RLWE ciphertext $c \in RLWE\ s^{n,p}(m)$ and an integer $i \in n$, results in the transformation of c into an LWE-encrypted ciphertext LWE $s^{n,p}\ (m_k)$. This LWE ciphertext corresponds to the i-th coefficient of m under the same key.

2.3 System Model

In the MLaaS (Machine Learning as a Service) system illustrated in Fig. 1, private data is in the possession of the client. The cloud server, featuring a trained deep learning model, provides inference services using data received from the client. For instance, a doctor transmits encrypted patient data to the server. The server runs a neural network model and sends encrypted predictions back to the doctor. After decryption, it can help doctor to analyse the diagnostic process and the creation of medical rehabilitation plans.

We focus lies on neural networks, which have achieved widespread success and demonstrated remarkable performance in image classification and face recognition. A neural network is composed of layers that learn the complex relationships within input data. It operates on a series of linear and non-linear transformations to infer results. For instance, given a patient's medical data as input, it can determine whether the patient has a particular disease. Linear transformations come in two forms: matrix multiplication and convolutions. Non-linear transformations employ activations to approximate complex functions and pooling to reduce dimensions. Neural networks iteratively apply linear and non-linear transformations, reducing the dimension of input data, and ultimately producing classification results.

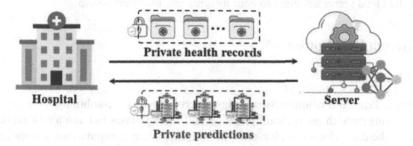

Fig. 1. A schematic diagram of an MLaaS system.

The discussion that follows will specifically target image classification, employing it as an illustration to convey a distinct comprehension of neural network architecture, visually depicted in Fig. 2.

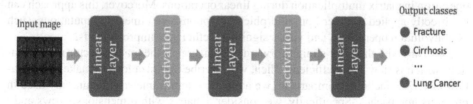

Fig. 2. A schematic diagram of an neural network.

Matrix multiplication is indeed the most common form of linear layer in neural networks. In image classification tasks, the input data is typically represented as a matrix or a tensor, where each element corresponds to a pixel or a feature. The linear layer in the network performs a matrix multiplication operation between the weight matrix and input data, followed by the addition of a bias term. Executing matrix multiplication involves taking the dot product of the weight matrix W with dimensions $s \times l$ and a input vector data of size $l \times 1$. This operation produces a vector with dimensions $s \times 1$.

Non-linear activation functions are commonly applied after the linear layer to introduce non-linearity and enable the network to capture more complex relationships in the data. Activation functions frequently used include ReLu, given by $f(x) = \max 0, x$; sigmoid, denoted as $f(x) = \frac{1}{1+e^{-x}}$; and tanh, expressed as $f(x) = \frac{e^{2x}-1}{e^{2x}+1}$. This combination of the linear and non-linear operations is the fundamental building block in neural network architectures for image classification and other tasks.

2.4 Threat Model

We have outlined the requisite security properties, adopting a semi-honest model akin to previous works [19, 36]. In this model, both parties seek to extract additional information from the received messages, assuming limited computational capabilities. In simpler terms, while following the protocol, the client endeavors to discover model parameters, while the cloud server attempts to gain insights into the client's data.

3 System Description

3.1 Linear Layers

The linear layer in a neural network plays a crucial role by combining the input data with weights through matrix multiplication and adding biases to learn a new representation of the data. Homomorphic encryption-based linear computations, comprising a sequence of Add, Mult, and Perm operations, have consistently emerged as the predominant component in privacy-preserving neural network models, as indicated by research experiments. In this context, encrypted vectors from the client and plaintext weight matrices from the server serve as inputs, resulting in an encrypted dot product as the output. Among these, Perm operations is the most time-consuming part of linear operations, making it essential to reduce permutation operations to improve the efficiency of neural networks. We have designed a non-interactive approach to reduce the transpose operation in matrix multiplication during linear operations. Moreover, this approach can be directly applied to other homomorphic encryption-based linear computations, such as convolution operations, and yields significant efficiency improvements.

We start with the most straightforward explanation of the matrix-vector multiplication, which is slow and inefficient. Then, we describe optimizations to make the operation faster. To facilitate comparison, we adopt a system framework commonly used in previous approaches. Specifically, we consider a matrix with dimensions s rows and l columns, representing a linear layer with s input elements and l output elements. The number of slots for ciphertext is denoted by n. For ease of discussion, we assume that n, s, and l are powers of 2 (otherwise, we can pad them with zeros to the nearest power of 2). Typically, to enhance computational efficiency, we set n to be sufficiently large for batch processing of more data. Thus, without loss of generality, we reasonably assume that both s and l are smaller than n.

The Naive Method: We consider the matrix-vector multiplication process of $\mathbf{Ax} = \mathbf{b}$, as depicted in Fig. 3. Here, $\mathbf{A}$ is an $s \times l$ plaintext matrix, representing the neural network model weights held by the server; the client offers an RLWE-encrypted vector $[\mathbf{x}]_1$ as a representation of the uploaded data. After the matrix multiplication, the result is a homomorphically encrypted vector $[\mathbf{b}]_1$. In the naive model, individual plaintext vectors a_i are created by the server through encoding each row of matrix $\mathbf{A}$ separately. Then the server performs homomorphic multiplication with the encrypted vector $[\mathbf{x}]_1$ for each plaintext vector $\mathbf{a}_i$, yielding intermediate results $[\mathbf{v}_i]_1 = [\mathbf{a}_i \circ \mathbf{x}]_1$. Note that due to the characteristics of homomorphic encryption, the size of all encryption vectors is the number of ciphertext slots n. By summing up each element of $\mathbf{v}_i$, we obtain the j-th element $\mathbf{b}_j$ of the corresponding result vector $\mathbf{b}$.

To derive the final result vector b from matrix multiplication, we must individually sum up the components of each intermediate vector $\mathbf{v}_i$. However, due to the characteristics of SIMD technology, encoding the vectors in a packed manner results in a corresponding ring element. Performing the necessary operations on the ring element to obtain the sum is not straightforward. Therefore, we rely on the permutation operation described earlier. As depicted in Fig. 3, during an operation named Ras, we cyclically rotate the positions of the intermediate vector $\mathbf{v}_i$ and then conduct SIMD addition. By repeating this process multiple times, we eventually obtain a ciphertext. Each component of the encrypted vector corresponds to the j-th component $\mathbf{b}_j$ of the result vector. Thus, a total of s Ras operations are needed, generating s ciphertexts, each corresponding to one of the s components of the encrypted result vector. In the meantime, if we want to consolidate these s ciphertexts into one, we can achieve this by taking the sum of the result obtained from multiplying each of the s ciphertexts with a unit vector (a vector with only one element as 1 and all other elements as 0). The resulting ciphertext $[\mathbf{b}]_1$ will be the final encrypted result.

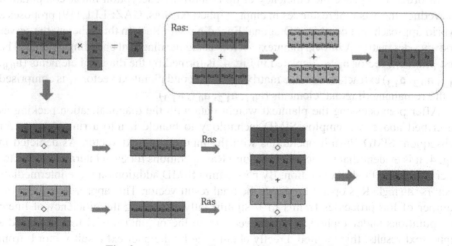

Fig. 3. A schematic diagram of the Naive Method.

162 H. Tao et al.

In this process, the server is able to compute the dot product between the plaintext weight matrix $\mathbf{A}$ and the encrypted input vector $[\mathbf{x}]_1$, and obtain the encrypted dot product $[\mathbf{b}]_1$ without learning the plaintext data $[\mathbf{x}]_1$. This ensures the privacy protection of the input data vector during computation. In the naive model process, without considering the final multiplication with the unit vector, there are a total of s SIMD PtMult operations, $s \log l$ Permutation operations and $s \log l$ SIMD Addition operations.

The Diagonal and Hybrid Method: The Diagonal Model [15] offers another potential solution to the problem of multiple output ciphertexts. The fundamental concept of this method involves representing the elements of the plaintext weight matrix $\mathbf{A}$ as s vectors $(\mathbf{a}_0, \mathbf{a}_1, ..., \mathbf{a}_{s-1})$ in accordance with the diagonal order. Then, each vector $\mathbf{a}_i$ is multiplied with a different transposed ciphertext vector $[\mathbf{x}_i]_1$, and finally, all corresponding intermediate result cipher-text vectors $[\mathbf{v}_i]_1$ are summed to obtain the corresponding final result vector $\mathbf{b}$. This Diagonal Model efficiently consolidates the results from multiple output ciphertexts into a single ciphertext $[\mathbf{b}]_1$. And the Diagonal Method does not require Ras operation, reducing the complexity and providing a possible solution for handling multiple encrypted output results in privacy-preserving computations based on homomorphic encryption.

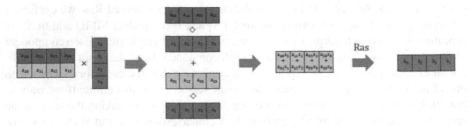

Fig. 4. A schematic diagram of the Hybrid Method.

In order to improve the efficiency of homomorphic encryption linear computation and reduce the waste of resources in empty ciphertext slots, GAZELLE [19] proposes a hybrid approach that combines Diagonal Encoding with RaS. In this scheme, the server first encodes matrix $\mathbf{A}$ into n_0 plaintext vectors using the diagonal encoding method. The first plaintext vector $\mathbf{a}_0$, as depicted in Fig. 4, is formed by the diagonal elements $(\mathbf{a}_{0,0}, \mathbf{a}_{1,1}, \mathbf{a}_{0,2}, \mathbf{a}_{1,3})$ extracted from the matrix $\mathbf{A}$. The second plaintext vector a_1 is comprised of the remaining diagonal elements $(\mathbf{a}_{0,1}, \mathbf{a}_{1,2}, \mathbf{a}_{0,3}, \mathbf{a}_{1,0})$.

After preprocessing the plaintext weight data with the diagonalization packing as described above, we employ SIMD technology to bundle it into a ring element for subsequent SIMD PtMult operations with the input ciphertext vector. As depicted in Fig. 4, it is evident that we no longer require Ras operations for each intermediate vector after the SIMD PtMult operation. By performing SIMD addition on these intermediate vectors, a single Ras operation yields the final result vector. This approach reduces the number of Ras processes from s to 1, significantly enhancing the efficiency of linear computations under ciphertext. Moreover, unlike the original model that produced s ciphertext results, this method directly obtains the final ciphertext result vector b from the matrix multiplication.

As explained in the preceding sections, to boost batch processing efficiency, the number of ciphertext slots n is typically set to a larger value. To make full use of the available ciphertext slots, GAZELLE [19] enhances the efficiency of linear computations by packing multiple input vectors into one. Specifically, n/l input vectors can be packed into one input vector, and correspondingly, n/l weight vectors can be packed into a diagonal encoding matrix for subsequent matrix multiplication operations. This process transforms into a preprocessed matrix with $s \times l/n$ rows and n columns, multiplied by a packed $n \times 1$ input encrypted vector. Similarly, by performing a Ras operation on the vector after SIMD addition, the final ciphertext result vector b can be obtained directly. The hybrid method requires a total of $s \times l/n$ SIMD PtMult operations, $s \times l/n - 1 +$ log n/s Permutation operations, and $s \times l/n - 1 + \log_{n/s}$ SIMD addition operations.

Our Fast Method: In the subsequent GALA [36] model, the authors proposed utilizing a method based on secret sharing to enable the RaS operation to be performed in plaintext, thereby significantly reducing the transposition operations in matrix multiplication. [19] and [36] categorized the permutation in matrix multiplication into HstPerm and Perm. It is generally preferred to have a larger value of n to pack more data efficiently and achieve high-performance SIMD HE. However, in the hybrid method, with the increase in the number of ciphertext slots n, the required number of permutation operations proportionally escalates, significantly augmenting the computational overhead in ciphertext-based calculations. Therefore, GALA introduces a novel row-wise weighted matrix encoding scheme, combined with secret sharing techniques, which dramatically reduces the number of permutation operations in ciphertext-based linear computations, thereby enhancing computational efficiency. In GALA's scheme, the cost of transpositions in matrix multiplication is reduced to only $s \times l/n - 1$ Permutation rotations, significantly decreasing the overhead required for linear computations.

We propose a novel scheme for fast linear computations. Similar to GALA's approach, which leverages secure multi-party computation to eliminate permutations in RaS, we discovered that using lookup tables can achieve the same effect. Additionally, in our scheme, the cost of permutations in matrix multiplication is reduced to only $s \times l/n - 1$ HstPerm rotations rather than $s \times l/n - 1$ Perm rotations, which is lower than the cost required by GALA. Figure 5 demonstrates how our proposed scheme performs matrix-vector computations, emphasizing its efficiency in managing permutations and enhancing linear calculations.

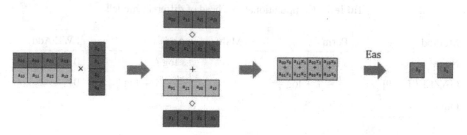

Fig. 5. A schematic diagram of our Fast Method.

Same as GAZELLE, the server first encodes matrix $\mathbf{A}$ into n_0 plaintext vectors using the diagonal encoding method. The first plaintext vector $\mathbf{a}_0$ is formed by the diagonal elements ($\mathbf{a}_{0,0}$, $\mathbf{a}_{1,1}$, $\mathbf{a}_{0,2}$, $\mathbf{a}_{1,3}$) extracted from the matrix A. The second plaintext vector $\mathbf{a}_1$ is comprised of the remaining diagonal elements ($\mathbf{a}_{0,1}$, $\mathbf{a}_{1,2}$, $\mathbf{a}_{0,3}$, $\mathbf{a}_{1,0}$). By performing a series of permutation operations on the encryption vector $[\mathbf{x}]_1$, and uses SIMD PtMult to perform elementwise multiplication with $\mathbf{a}_i$. As a result, the server gets s intermediate ciphertext vector, $[\mathbf{v}_i]_1 = [\mathbf{a}_i \, \mathbf{x}^1]_1$.

Next, what differs is that after performing the SIMD Addition operation on $[\mathbf{v}_0]_1$ and $[\mathbf{v}_1]_1$ to get a new intermediate ciphertext vector $[\mathbf{u}]_1$, we use the Switch operation to transform the encrypted ciphertext of vector $[\mathbf{u}]_1$ into an encrypted ciphertext of a ring element u. In this process, each coefficient u_i of the ring element u is represented by $\mathbf{u}_i$. Then, correspondingly, we perform another Transform operation to obtain n LWE-encrypted ciphertexts, each representing the coefficient u_i of the ring element u. Based on this scenario, we can naturally perform homomorphic addition operations on each component of vector u to obtain the LWE-encrypted results of each component of the final matrix-vector multiplication result vector $\mathbf{b}$, i.e., $\mathbf{b}_0$ and $\mathbf{b}_1$. It is worth nothing that the Switch operation and Transform operation are essential for subsequent lookup table operations. Therefore, our approach only introduces the time required for LWE homomorphic addition operation but offsets the SIMD PtMult operations and SIMD Addition operations required by RaS. Moreover, LWE homomorphic addition operation can be embedded into the lookup table process. As the lookup table undergoes inherent key conversion operations before performing LUT operations, it significantly reduces the dimension of the ciphertext. Our experiments show that the time required for one LWE homomorphic addition operation is only a tiny fraction of the SIMD Addition operations under the original CKKS ciphertext dimension, greatly reducing the overhead of linear computations. Similarly, we enhance the utilization of ciphertext slots by packing multiple input vectors x into a single ciphertext and multiple different rows into a single plaintext vector. Consequently, our approach requires $s \times l/n$ SIMD PtMult operations, $s \times l/(n-1)$ SIMD Addition opeations, $s \times l/(n-1)$ Permutation rotations, and $s(l-1)$ LWE additions (Add). The result is s LWE ciphertexts, which are utilized for the subsequent non-linear layer's lookup table operations. Table 1 compares the computational overhead of different models. We can see that our fast method dramatically reduces the computational complexity.

Table 1. Computational overhead of different models.

Method	Perm	Mult	Add	LWE Add
Naive	$s \log l$	s	$s \log l$	0
GAZELLE [19]	$\frac{sl}{n} - 1 + \log \frac{n}{s}$	$\frac{sl}{n}$	$\frac{sl}{n} - 1 + \log \frac{n}{s}$	0
Our	$\frac{sl}{n} - 1$	$\frac{sl}{n}$	$\frac{sl}{n} - 1$	$s(l-1)$

3.2 Non-linear Layers

The non-linear layers in a neural network introduce non-linear transformations, enabling the network to learn complex non-linear relationships. The incorporation of these non-linear activation functions allows neural networks to express more intricate non-linear relationships, thereby enhancing the network's representational capacity and enabling it to better handle various complex machine learning tasks. In order to avoid the significant communication and computational overhead of interacting non-linear layers in secure multi-party computation schemes, we aim to perform neural network inference using fully homomorphic encryption throughout the process.

Meanwhile, to strike a balance between word-wise HEs that efficiently perform SIMD homomorphic computations by packing multiple plaintexts into one ciphertext and bit-wise HEs that support arbitrary functions represented by boolean circuits, we adopt the approach from [23] to implement the conversion between word-wise HEs ciphertexts and bit-wise HEs ciphertexts. Furthermore, we utilize the lookup table based on LWE ciphertexts to perform arbitrary non-linear computations. We embed the fast matrix addition operation discussed in the previous section before the lookup table operation, as illustrated in Algorithm 1.

Algorithm 1: ReLu activation functions

> **Data:** $RLWE_s^{n,q}(\mathbf{u})$, look-up table function $ReLu(x)$
> **Result:** $RLWE_s^{n,q}(ReLu(\mathbf{b}))$

1 Switch: $ct' = RLWE_s^{n,q}(u)$
2 **for** $i \leftarrow 1$ **to** n
3 $\quad ct_i = Transf^i(RLWE_s^{n,q}(u)) = LWE_s^{n,q}(u_i)$
4 Key-Switch: $ct_i = KS(LWE_s^{n,q}(u_i)) = LWE_{s'}^{n',q}(u_i)$
5 **end for**
6 homomorphic addition: $ct_j = LWE_{s'}^{n',q}(b_i)$ for all $j \in \langle n_0 \rangle$
7 **for** $j \leftarrow 1$ **to** n_0
8 Evaluate the look-up table in parallel:
9 $\quad ct_j' = LUT(LWE_{s'}^{n',q}(b_i)) = LWE_{s'}^{n',q}(ReLu(b_i))$
10 **end for**
11 Repacking: $ct = Repack(LWE_{s'}^{n',q}(ReLu(b_i))) = RLWE_s^{n,q'}(ReLu(\mathbf{b}))$

We use the ReLu activation function as an example to illustrate our non-linear layer process. Firstly, we use the Switch operation to transform the encrypted ciphertext of vector $[\mathbf{u}]_C$ into an encrypted ciphertext of a ring element u. In this process, each coefficient u_i of the ring element u is represented by u_i. Then, correspondingly, we perform another Transform operation to obtain n LWE-encrypted ciphertexts, each representing the coefficient u_i of the ring element u. Simultaneously, we reduce the dimensionality of the ciphertexts through key switching operations to enhance the efficiency of subsequent operations. Based on this scenario, we can naturally perform homomorphic addition operations on each component of vector $\mathbf{u}$ to obtain the LWE-encrypted results of each component of the final matrix-vector multiplication result vector $\mathbf{b}$, i.e., $\mathbf{b_0}, \dots,$ $\mathbf{b_1}$. Next, we perform the lookup table operation with the ReLu activation function on n_0 ciphertexts $\text{LWE}_{s'}^{n',q}$ ($\mathbf{b}_i$), obtaining n_0 corresponding result ciphertexts $\text{LWE}_{s'}^{n',q}$ (ReLu($\mathbf{b}_i$)). Finally, we utilize a repackaging function to bundle the n_0 result ciphertexts into a single RLWE ciphertext $\text{RLWE}_{s'}^{n,q}$ (ReLu($\mathbf{b}$)) representing an encrypted vector $\mathbf{b}$.

3.3 Noise Management

Homomorphic encryption ensures the security of plaintext messages by introducing noise. Performing a series of homomorphic operations on ciphertexts will lead to an increase in noise. In the event that the noise goes above a designated threshold, there is a risk of decryption failure or errors. Therefore, managing the noise of ciphertexts during computations becomes particularly crucial.

We assume that the initial noise of two ciphertexts are e_0 and e_1, and the noise increases to $e_0 + e_1$ after a SIMD Addition operation. After a single SIMD PtMult operation, the noise increases by a constant factor to $e_{mult}\eta_0$. Similarly, following a permutation rotation operation, the noise rises to ee_0. Typically, we assume $e > e_{mult} \gg e_0$. Table 2 describes the growth of noise for the three schemes presented in Sect. 3.1. In our work, we utilize the hierarchical HE scheme CKKS, ensuring the correctness of ciphertexts after respective computation operations by predefining the required multiplication depth.

Table 2. Noise growth for different models.

Method	Noise growth
Naïve	$le_0e_{mult} + (l-1)e$
GAZELLE [19]	$le_0e_{mult} + (l - \frac{n}{s})e_{mult}e + (\frac{n}{s} - 1)e$
Our	$le_0e_{mult} + (l - \frac{n}{s})e_{mult}e$

3.4 Security Analysis

In our scheme, the cloud server can only has the encrypted input data, which prevents data leakage from reconstruction attacks or membership inference attacks, ensuring the protection of client privacy. In the meantime, the client can only obtain the results after homomorphic computations, having no knowledge of the server's computation process. It prevents the exploitation of the server's prediction service as a black-box oracle for extracting model parameters and deducing the training dataset. The security of both the input data and the model parameters relies entirely on the security of HE schemes like CKKS.

Li et al. [21] emphasized that the approximate decryption outcome in CKKS might reveal supplementary details about the decryption key. They effectively devised a passive attack capable of retrieving the decryption key when provided access to the decryption outcomes. Consequently, the client must refrain from divulging the decryption results or distributing them to individuals who aren't entirely trustworthy.

4 Experiments

Table 3. Computational overhead of different operations.

Operation	Perm	Mult	Add	LWE Add
Time(ms)	335.31	5.45	5.05	0.0025

Table 4. Computational overhead of different models.

Method	Perm	Mult	Add	LWE Add	Time (ms)
		Dimension:1 × 1024			
Naive	10	1	10	0	3352.62
[19]	10	1	10	0	3356.32
Our	0	1	0	1023	6.67
		Dimension:8 × 256			
Naive	64	8	64	0	21630.6
[19]	8	2	8	0	2708.51
Our	1	2	1	2040	346.99
		Dimension:16 × 128			
Naive	112	16	112	0	37864.2
[19]	7	2	7	0	2370.61
Our	1	2	1	2032	346.24
		Dimension:16 × 64			
Naive	64	16	64	0	32460.1
[19]	6	1	6	0	2026.82
Our	0	1	0	1008	6.67

We conducted our experiments on Ubuntu 18.04, and have an Intel i7-10700F CPU, running at 2.90 GHz with 16 GB of system memory. The dimension n of the RLWE is 2^{16}, while the dimension n' of the LWE ciphertext after key switching is 2^{10}. The dimension $\underline{n}$ of the ciphertext in the LUT function is also 2^{10}. According to [23] and [1], all selected parameters satisfy at least 119 bits of security. Based on the aforementioned parameter settings, we tested the running time of our scheme and the previous scheme for matrix multiplication under CKKS encryption. Table 3 compares the computational overhead of different operations. We can observe that the time taken for the Perm operation is 61 times that of the Mult operation and 66 times that of the Add operation. Furthermore, the time for Slot-wise Add operation is 2000 times greater than that of LWE Add operation. As shown in Table 4, our approach requires lower computational complexity compared to other methods, significantly reducing the time required for linear operations. Across various matrix dimensions, the acceleration achieved can reach up to 500×.

Table 5. Model accuracy in different dimensions.

Dimension (n)	10	11	12	Plaintext
Accuracy	97.85%	98.25%	98.25%	98.25%

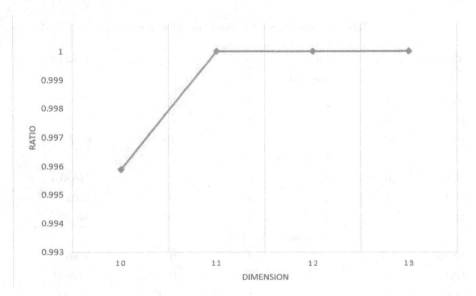

Fig. 6. The ratio of accuracy between inference under ciphertext and plaintext for various dimensions.

We employed PyTorch to pretrain a neural network consisting of three hidden layers on the minst dataset and utilized the model's parameters for making predictions on encrypted data. Table 5 and Fig. 6 illustrate the precision of our proposed model. As the dimension of the LUT increases, the accuracy of our approach improves progressively, achieving results comparable to inference predictions made under plaintext conditions. For other complex models and datasets, increasing the dimension of the LUT can achieve high-precision prediction of the model, at the expense of increased LUT time.

As illustrated in Fig. 7, although the proportion of time taken by the non-linear layer in the model increases with the augmentation of LUT dimension, we can effectively accelerate LUT calculations through parallel computing. This approach significantly reduces the time portion occupied by the non-linear layer in the model. Figure 8 showcases the time distribution of the non-linear layer in the model across different threads in a higher-dimensional ($n = 12$) LUT model. It can be observed that with the increase in threads, the time portion of the non-linear layer in the model decreases from 50.57% to 29.81%, resulting in substantial reduction.

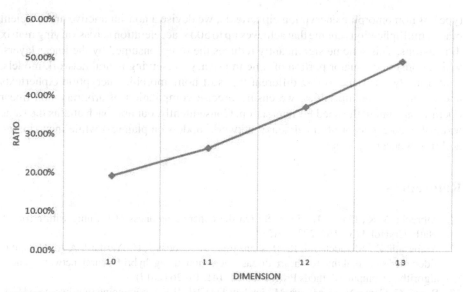

Fig. 7. The proportion of time taken by the non-linear layers across different dimensions.

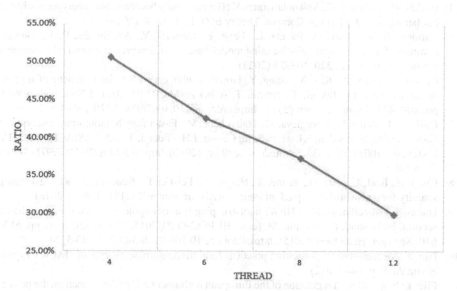

Fig. 8. The proportion of time taken by the non-linear layers under different threads.

5 Conclusion

In this paper, we introduce a non-interactive privacy-preserving neural network framework based on homomorphic encryption. This framework safeguards the security of training data and model parameters for MLaaS in cloud environments, enabling computation and inference over floating-point numbers. Leveraging the characteristics of two types of homomorphic encryption ciphertexts, we devise a non-interactive and efficient matrix multiplication scheme that achieves up to $500\times$ acceleration across varying matrix dimensions. This scheme significantly reduces the time consumed by the linear layers, which constitute a major portion of time in privacy-preserving neural network models. Additionally, by transforming different types of homomorphic encryption ciphertexts and employing lookup tables, we ensure precise computation of arbitrary non-linear operations without the need for interaction. Consequently, our approach attains the same level of accuracy as pre-trained neural network models on plaintext while incurring no additional accuracy loss.

References

1. Albrecht, M.R., Player, R., Scott, S.: On the concrete hardness of learning with errors. J. Math. Cryptol. **9**(3), 169–203 (2015)
2. Arabasadi, Z., Alizadehsani, R., Roshanzamir, M., Moosaei, H., Yarifard, A.A.: Computer aided decision making for heart disease detection using hybrid neural network-genetic algorithm. Comput. Methods Prog. Biomed. **141**, 19–26 (2017)
3. Boura, C., Gama, N., Georgieva, M., Jetchev, D.: CHIMERA: combining ring-lwe-based fully homomorphic encryption schemes. J. Math. Cryptol. **14**(1), 316–338 (2020)
4. Brakerski, Z., Gentry, C., Vaikuntanathan, V.: (leveled) fully homomorphic encryption without bootstrapping. ACM Trans. Comput. Theory **6**(3), 13:1–13:36 (2014)
5. Candela, E., Doustaly, O., Parada, L., Feng, F., Demiris, Y., Angeloudis, P.: Risk-aware controller for autonomous vehicles using model-based collision prediction and reinforcement learning. Artif. Intell. **320**, 103923 (2023)
6. Cheon, J.H., Kim, A., Kim, M., Song, Y.: Homomorphic encryption for arithmetic of approximate numbers. In: Takagi, T., Peyrin, T. (eds.) ASIACRYPT 2017. LNCS, vol. 10624, pp. 409–437. Springer, Cham (2017). https://doi.org/10.1007/978-3-319-70694-8_15
7. Chillotti, I., Gama, N., Georgieva, M., Izabachène, M.: Faster fully homomorphic encryption: bootstrapping in less than 0.1 seconds. In: Cheon, J.H., Takagi, T. (eds.) ASIACRYPT 2016. LNCS, vol. 10031, pp. 3–33. Springer, Heidelberg (2016). https://doi.org/10.1007/978-3-662-53887-6_1
8. Chou, E., Beal, J., Levy, D., Yeung, S., Haque, A., Fei-Fei, L.: Faster cryptonets: leveraging sparsity for real-world encrypted inference. arXiv preprint arXiv:1811.09953 (2018)
9. Ducas, L., Micciancio, D.: FHEW: bootstrapping homomorphic encryption in less than a second. In: Oswald, E., Fischlin, M. (eds.) EUROCRYPT 2015. LNCS, vol. 9056, pp. 617–640. Springer, Heidelberg (2015). https://doi.org/10.1007/978-3-662-46800-5_24
10. Fan, J., Vercauteren, F.: Somewhat practical fully homomorphic encryption. IACR Cryptol. ePrint Arch, p. 144 (2012)
11. File, I.: Proposal for a regulation of the European parliament and of the council on the protection of individuals with regard to the processing of personal data and on the free movement of such data (general data protection regulation). General Data Protection Regulation (2012)
12. Gentry, C.: Fully homomorphic encryption using ideal lattices. In: STOC, pp. 169–178. ACM (2009)
13. Gentry, C., Sahai, A., Waters, B.: Homomorphic encryption from learning with errors: conceptually-simpler, asymptotically-faster, attribute-based. In: Canetti, R., Garay, J.A. (eds.) CRYPTO 2013. LNCS, vol. 8042, pp. 75–92. Springer, Heidelberg (2013). https://doi.org/10.1007/978-3-642-40041-4_5

14. Gilad-Bachrach, R., Dowlin, N., Laine, K., Lauter, K.E., Naehrig, M., Wernsing, J.: Cryptonets: applying neural networks to encrypted data with high throughput and accuracy. In: ICML. JMLR Workshop and Conference Proceedings, vol. 48, pp. 201–210. JMLR.org (2016)
15. Halevi, S., Shoup, V.: Algorithms in helib. In: Garay, J.A., Gennaro, R. (eds.) CRYPTO 2014. LNCS, vol. 8616, pp. 554–571. Springer, Heidelberg (2014). https://doi.org/10.1007/978-3-662-44371-2_31
16. Han, M., Xu, P., Xu, L., Xu, C.: TCA-PEKS: trusted certificateless authentication public-key encryption with keyword search scheme in cloud storage. Peer Peer Netw. Appl. **16**(1), 156–169 (2023)
17. Hesamifard, E., Takabi, H., Ghasemi, M.: Deep neural networks classification over encrypted data. In: CODASPY, pp. 97–108. ACM (2019)
18. Jiang, X., Kim, M., Lauter, K.E., Song, Y.: Secure outsourced matrix computation and application to neural networks. In: CCS, pp. 1209–1222. ACM (2018)
19. Juvekar, C., Vaikuntanathan, V., Chandrakasan, A.P.: GAZELLE: a low latency framework for secure neural network inference. In: USENIX Security Symposium, pp. 1651–1669. USENIX Association (2018)
20. Kim, M., Song, Y., Wang, S., Xia, Y., Jiang, X., et al.: Secure logistic regression based on homomorphic encryption: design and evaluation. JMIR Med. Inform. **6**(2), e8805 (2018)
21. Li, B., Micciancio, D.: On the security of homomorphic encryption on approximate numbers. In: Canteaut, A., Standaert, F.-X. (eds.) EUROCRYPT 2021. LNCS, vol. 12696, pp. 648–677. Springer, Cham (2021). https://doi.org/10.1007/978-3-030-77870-5_23
22. Liu, B., Jing, L., Li, J., Yu, J., Gittens, A., Mahoney, M.W.: Group collaborative representation for image set classification. Int. J. Comput. Vis. **127**(2), 181–206 (2019)
23. Lu, W., Huang, Z., Hong, C., Ma, Y., Qu, H.: PEGASUS: bridging polynomial and non-polynomial evaluations in homomorphic encryption. In: IEEE Symposium on Security and Privacy, pp. 1057–1073. IEEE (2021)
24. May, A., et al.: Kernel approximation methods for speech recognition. J. Mach. Learn. Res. **20**, 59:1–59:36 (2019)
25. Mei, L., Xu, C., Xu, L., Yu, X., Zuo, C.: Verifiable identity-based encryption with keyword search for iot from lattice. Comput. Mater. Contin **68**, 2299–2314 (2021)
26. Nasr, M., Shokri, R., Houmansadr, A.: Comprehensive privacy analysis of deep learning: Passive and active white-box inference attacks against centralized and federated learning. In: IEEE Symposium on Security and Privacy, pp. 739–753. IEEE (2019)
27. Riazi, M.S., Samragh, M., Chen, H., Laine, K., Lauter, K.E., Koushanfar, F.: XONN: xnor-based oblivious deep neural network inference. In: USENIX Security Symposium, pp. 1501–1518. USENIX Association (2019)
28. Rouhani, B.D., Riazi, M.S., Koushanfar, F.: Deepsecure: scalable provably-secure deep learning. In: DAC, pp. 2:1–2:6. ACM (2018)
29. Smart, N.P., Vercauteren, F.: Fully homomorphic SIMD operations. Des. Codes Cryptogr. **71**(1), 57–81 (2014)
30. Tramer, F., Zhang, F., Juels, A., Reiter, M.K., Ristenpart, T.: Stealing machine learning models via prediction apis. In: USENIX Security Symposium, pp. 601–618. USENIX Association (2016)
31. Wagh, S., Gupta, D., Chandran, N.: Securenn: 3-party secure computation for neural network training. Proc. Priv. Enhancing Technol. **2019**(3), 26–49 (2019)
32. Wang, B., Gong, N.Z.: Stealing hyperparameters in machine learning. In: IEEE Symposium on Security and Privacy, pp. 36–52. IEEE Computer Society (2018)
33. Wang, W., et al.: Rafiki: machine learning as an analytics service system. Proc. VLDB Endow. **12**(2), 128–140 (2018)
34. Xu, C., et al.: Correction to: lie-x: depth image based articulated object pose estimation, tracking, and action recognition on lie groups. Int. J. Comput. Vis. **126**(8), 897 (2018)

35. Yu, X., Xu, C., Xu, L., Mei, L.: Hardening secure search in encrypted database: a kga-resistance conjunctive searchable encryption scheme from lattice. Soft. Comput. **26**(21), 11139–11151 (2022)
36. Zhang, Q., Xin, C., Wu, H.: GALA: greedy computation for linear algebra in privacy-preserved neural networks. In: NDSS. The Internet Society (2021)
37. Zhang, Q., Yang, L.T., Chen, Z.: Privacy preserving deep computation model on cloud for big data feature learning. IEEE Trans. Comput. **65**(5), 1351–1362 (2016)

Author Index

© ICST Institute for Computer Sciences, Social Informatics and Telecommunications Engineering 2024
Published by Springer Nature Switzerland AG 2024. All Rights Reserved
J. Liu et al. (Eds.): TridentCom 2023, LNICST 523, p. 173, 2024.
https://doi.org/10.1007/978-3-031-51399-2

Printed in the United States
by Baker & Taylor Publisher Services

Printed in the United States
by Baker & Taylor Publisher Services